BEATRIX VON RAGUÉ

A History of Japanese Lacquerwork

TRANSLATED

FROM THE GERMAN BY

ANNIE R. DE WASSERMANN

UNIVERSITY OF TORONTO PRESS

TORONTO AND BUFFALO

English edition
©University of Toronto Press 1976
Toronto and Buffalo

Printed in Canada

First published as
Geschichte der Japanischen Lackkunst
(Stiftung Preussischer Kulturbesitz
Handbücher der Staatlichen Museen)
©1967 by Walter de Gruyter & Co. Berlin

Library of Congress Cataloging in Publication Data

von Ragué, Beatrix
    A history of Japanese lacquerwork.

    Translation of Geschichte der japanischen Lackkunst.
    Bibliography: p.
    Includes index.
    1. Lacquer and lacquering–Japan.   1. Title.
    NK9900.7.J3R3313   745.7'2'0952   73-92299
    ISBN 0-8020-2135-2

The illustration on the jacket shows a box and cover of about 1760 (see Pl 171 between pp. 212 and 213). The illustration on the title page shows the lid of a toilet box of about 1400 (see Pls 81 and 82, pp. 102-3).

In memory of my teacher
Professor Werner Speiser

Preface

For some considerable time Japanese lacquerwork has had its share of devotees and collectors in the West. But until now there has been very little to help them take the step from admiration to more exact knowledge, since only a handful of experts have access to the comprehensive, though not always systematic, Japanese literature on the subject, and relatively little has yet been written in any western language about the history of this craft.

Anyone interested in lacquerwork is, of course, grateful for the books by Otto Kümmel (*Das Kunstgewerbe in Japan*) and Martin Feddersen (*Japanisches Kunstgewerbe*) which both include a chapter on lacquerwork. But naturally these chapters are too short to trace a development that spanned more than a thousand years. Also, they are written with a heavy bias toward those items that are most accessible to the collector in the West, that is, relatively late pieces. Nor could earlier writers possibly have foreseen the many new and important facts that recent research, mainly by the Japanese, has brought to light.

This book, therefore, is designed to fill a gap. Whenever possible I have tried to link the development of Japanese lacquerwork to dated pieces. These give a sequence of fixed points of reference which simplify the task of fitting in the numerous other items which, though undated, are significant from an artistic point of view. With this aim in mind I have referred to as many dated objects as possible both in the text and in the illustrations. (Naturally, in the case of the vast number of small dated medicine boxes and sake bowls of the late period, no attempt has been made to be comprehensive.) Because I wanted to fit undated works as precisely as possible into my time scale, I have preferred an attribution like 'c. 1400,' for example, to the less specific 'first half of the Muromachi period.' It is quite likely that not everyone will agree with all the dates I give, but the fact remains that at some stage an attempt at a more accurate system of dating has to be made.

I considered it important to refer occasionally to examples from related arts such as ceramics, metalwork, and textiles. The relationships between the various branches of Japanese applied art have so far been insufficiently explored. However, the examples I have chosen might give some indication of how closely the stylistic phenomena of lacquerwork are connected with the overall development of Japanese art and handicrafts. If these links were to be explored yet further, a clearer light might be thrown on the whole field of applied art.

The numerous and often complicated techniques of lacquerwork have been dealt with as briefly as possible in this book, so as not to interrupt the analysis of stylistic development more than is necessary. This is all the more justified in view of the fact that a book by Kurt Herberts (*Das Buch der*

Preface *ostasiatischen Lackkunst*) gives extensive information about the technical aspects of the craft.

One word more about the choice of illustrations. However tempting it may be in other contexts to show as many unknown works as possible, in a historical analysis, it is essential to give prominence, after the pieces with known dates, to works of artistic merit. The fact that several of these can already be seen in other, usually Japanese, publications should be no reason to preclude their being illustrated here.

I would also like to take this opportunity to express my warm thanks to a number of people.

Without the invaluable aid of the Japanese research referred to in the bibliography, and that I have most extensively evaluated and used, it would have been impossible for me to write this book. But often more illuminating than either books or articles were the discussions I was able to have with Japanese experts and colleagues. Above all my thanks go to Professor Saburō Mizoguchi for the tireless way in which he has helped me ever since my first visit to the National Museum in Tōkyō. Time and again he has come to my assistance with word and deed, answered countless questions, and generally smoothed my path. I would also like to thank Professor Yasuji Maeda for turning my attention to other areas of Japanese applied art, apart from lacquerwork, and Professor Jō Okada who gave me much important information and advice. When it came to the laborious task of assembling the illustrations the help of Mr Hirokazu Arakawa of the National Museum in Tōkyō and Mr Motoo Yoshimura of the National Museum in Kyōto proved invaluable.

My special thanks go to the lacquermakers in whose workshops I was able to gain invaluable knowledge, and to all the collectors and museum officials who allowed me both to look at their precious specimens in peace and at such proximity and, where necessary, to reproduce them as illustrations for this book. If there are any mistakes in the book, they should certainly not be attributed to any lack of co-operation on the part of those whom I consulted.

Then I would like to thank both the Stiftung Preussischer Kulturbesitz, whose financial assistance made it possible for the book to appear in its present form, and also the publisher Walter de Gruyter & Co. of Berlin. Last, but not least, my thanks to Mrs Charlotte Hasse for the long-suffering and reliable way in which she copied one 'final' draft of the manuscript after another.

Beatrix von Ragué
Berlin
October 1965

Preface to the English edition

After the original German edition of this book was published in 1967, a number of articles were published on the subject of Japanese lacquerware – mostly in Japanese. Since none of those available to the author contained any new material that would have materially changed the contents of this book, they were not included here. For this reason the English edition of the book is an exact translation of the original German text. The sole exception, apart from the correction of the very few errata and misprints, is on p. 151: according to Motoo Yoshimura, the name Kōami Kyū should be amended to read Kōami Matazaemon.

For the present English edition, a translation by J. Gabriel served in parts as a working paper. My warm appreciation and thanks go to Annie R. de Wasserman who carefully and meticulously adhered to the letter and the spirit of the German in translating it into this English edition.

Beatrix von Ragué

Contents

Preface vii

Preface to the English edition ix

1
Origins and apprentice years 3

2
Early Heian period: the rise of an indigenous style 21

3
Eleventh and twelfth centuries: the golden age of Heian lacquerwork 37

4
Kamakura period 61

5
Muromachi period I: Nambokuchō period to the Higashiyama period 89

6
Muromachi period II: from the end of the Higashiyama period to 1567 123

7
Momoyama period 141

8
Early Edo period 169

9
Mid- and late Edo period 201

10
From the Meiji period to the present day 225

Notes 247

Bibliography 267

List of dated lacquer objects 273

Glossary of more common Japanese descriptive terms 277

Japanese names and technical terms with their corresponding
written characters 279

Period table 287

Japanese provinces 289

Index 290

Origins and apprentice years 1

A history of Japanese lacquerwork

THE SAP OF THE LACQUER TREE, *RHUS VERNICIFERA*, WAS FIRST USED IN JAPAN centuries before the history of Japanese art lacquerwork as such can ever be said to have started. The earliest known lacquered objects on Japanese soil were discovered in the course of excavations carried out in a number of different provinces; their dating is still uncertain and varies between the third century BC and the fourth century AD. [1]

Probably the most important finds were made after the end of the Meiji period in the village of Korekawa near Hachinohe in the northern Japanese province of Aomori. Numerous lacquered artifacts were discovered, made of materials ranging from wood, pottery, and basket-work to an asphalt-like composition. There were, though often only in a fragmentary state, bottles, bowls, arm and ear ornaments, bows, and even a wooden sword – all covered with a layer of red (less often black) lacquer. It is virtually the lacquer skin alone of some of the wooden fragments that has withstood natural decay. [2]

Even in these early artifacts lacquer was used not only as a protective layer but also to fulfil a decorative function. For example, a bowl with relief carving is lacquered black inside and red outside; a ring-shaped object (Pl. 1), perhaps a bracelet, has a design in red lacquer on a dark ground; there is a red lacquered bow with a motif of two narrow parallel black lines. On the basis of the shape and decoration of ceramic objects, the Korekawa finds have been attributed, so far, to the late Jōmon period, but research still being carried out may come to the conclusion that they belong to the Kofun period. [3]

Finds dating from prehistoric times (prior to the third century AD) were also made in other localities: lacquered combs were dug up both in Namioka (Aomori province) and in the district of Semboku (Akita province); a lacquered basket was discovered in Matsumine (Yamagata province), another near the temple of Shimpuku-ji (Saitama province), and a comb and a basket in Numazu (Miyagi province). Apart from these objects there are numerous ceramic wares covered with a layer of a glossy red or

Plate 1 Bracelet decorated with lacquer. ca 4th c. Ht. 1cm, width 0.88cm, diam. 7.5cm. Tōkyō, Bunkazai Hogo Iinkai

black substance, but whether it is lacquer in every case is not known for certain.[4]

Because lacquered objects appear so early, it has been suggested that the lacquer tree was, in fact, indigenous to Japan and was not introduced from China and Korea as – at a later date – was the highly developed true art of lacquerwork.[5] At any rate there is no doubt that one should regard these early examples of lacquerwork in Japan as an integral part of Japanese culture; they are in no way related to Chinese lacquerwork which at that time had already achieved a remarkably high standard.

A few lacquered bows, combs, and bracelets, dating from the Yayoi period, which followed the Jōmon period, have been excavated, but they are inferior in technique. All of that changed in the Kofun period (c. third to sixth century) when the ruling Yamato clan found employment at its court for a number of specialist craftsmen in various fields. These craftsmen were assigned to definite guilds, and the term 'urushibe', which was used to describe the lacquerworkers, occurs frequently in later references to this period – for example in the 'Kyūji hongi', the original manuscript of which has been lost, but extracts from which have survived in later historical works. It also mentions the name of the legendary Mimi no Sukune who is said to have been the first leader of the urushibe and to have lived at the time of the Emperor Kōan.[6]

Excavations indicate that in this Kofun period lacquer was used more frequently and that it was technically improved. Lacquer was used on the hand-grips of bows, wooden ceremonial swords, leather shields and even iron helmets. Since the number of craftsmen working for the Yamato court was large enough to include a separate guild for workers in wood, one may conjecture that the work of the urushibe consisted, for the most part, of lacquering objects made by the workers in wood. Historical sources from the time of the Emperor Yōmei (586-587) onwards bear witness to increasingly frequent decrees requiring the planting of lacquer trees and the levying of taxes in the form of specific amounts of raw lacquer; but they give no further indication of how the lacquer was employed or of what the lacquered objects looked like.

Thus, even though lacquer had certainly been known and used in Japan since prehistoric times, it was only after the introduction of Buddhism in the middle of the sixth century AD[7] that it became a medium for major works of art. In the early days of establishing Buddhist culture and Buddhist art in Japan, the Chinese and Koreans acted both as disseminators of the faith and as teachers. The earliest examples in Japan of lacquerwork as a highly developed art form were certainly either made by Korean or Chinese craftsmen or at least were directly influenced by them.

The oldest surviving example is the famous Tamamushi shrine (*Tamamushi-zushi*) in the Hōryū-ji, probably made around the middle of the seventh century (Pl. 2). This 2.33m high shrine takes its name from the tamamushi beetle (*chrysochroa elegans*), whose blue-green iridescent wing cases are underlaid beneath the openwork metal fittings. The shrine consists of a high base surmounted by a somewhat lower and smaller palace-like building which enshrines a Buddha sculpture. The side walls of both the base and the main part of the shrine are painted with red, yellow, and green lacquer on a black lacquer ground. Plate 2 shows the back of the shrine with the side doors open.[8]

Beautiful and important though this shrine is, one can hardly describe it as typically Japanese; in fact one cannot even be certain that the workmanship is Japanese at all. The landscape forms and the style in which the figures are painted are reminiscent of Chinese paintings of the Eastern Wei and Northern Ch'i periods (534-550 and 550-577 respectively); the links with Korea are even closer.[9] Numerous metal objects underlaid with tamamushi wings have come to light in the course of excavations in Korea, particularly in the so-called Grave of the Gold Crowns in Kyôngju (southeast Korea), which dates from the fifth to sixth centuries. In these finds the choice of certain specific parts of the wings and the way they are used under metal openwork exactly matches the technique employed in the Tamamushi shrine. Metal plaques similarly adorned were also discovered in Korean graves of the Koguryō kingdom (37 BC-668 AD), so the technique of tamamushi inlay is evidently native to Korea. The Tamamushi shrine is

Plate 2 Tamamushi shrine; rear view. Mid 7th c. Total ht. 2.33m. Nara, Hōryū-ji

the only example of this type of decoration in Japan. Some decorative motifs in the painting of the shrine also point to Korea.[10]

Despite all this evidence, the Tamamushi shrine need not necessarily have originated in Korea – for instance, hinoki wood, the material it is made of, argues in favour of Japan. But the links between the two countries were close at that time. Already, long before the shrine was built, many Koreans had come to Japan, and certainly one can hardly overestimate the role which, from the fifth to the seventh centuries, Korean artists and craftsmen played in the early art, particularly the Buddhist art, of Japan.[11] It is probably correct to place the Tamamushi shrine within the overall context of Korean art in Japan, whether it was made by Koreans in Japan or whether Japanese craftsmen created it, referring back to Korean models. It is the oldest example of the true art of lacquerwork to have survived in Japan and probably to have been made there as well.

In 701, some fifty years after the Tamamushi shrine was made, a codex of Japanese laws, known as Taihō-ritsuryō, was promulgated. Among other things, it ordered the establishment of a department of lacquer within the finance ministry. This department was to consist of a department head, an assistant, a deputy, twenty lacquerers, six assistants, and one servant. The codex also decreed that lacquered utensils, as well as lances and saddles, were to be signed with the full name of the maker and granted permission for the sale, on the open market, of any not needed by the imperial court. Lacquer trees were to be planted around every house: according to the size of the property, no less than forty, seventy, or one hundred trees. A fixed amount of lacquer, depending on the number of trees, was levied as a tax.[12]

A brief glance at Japanese history will explain why such stipulations were necessary. Ever since Shōtoku Taishi (573-621) became regent in 593, a series of political and cultural changes had been taking place. The effect of these changes was to strengthen the position of the imperial court, restrict the power of the nobility, encourage the development of a new civil servant class, and incorporate into the spiritual and material life of Japan not only the Buddhist doctrine, but also the highly developed culture of China linked with it.[13] In the seventh and eighth centuries Japan abandoned its hitherto simple and modest way of life and, at surprising speed, achieved the status of an important civilized nation.

Through Buddhism the Japanese learnt innumerable skills, both practical and theoretical. At the same time, Buddhism provided craftsmen and artists with work, for in its service, temples were built throughout the country and had to be fitted out with sculptures and all the appurtenances of religious worship. Langdon Warner in his book, *The Enduring Art of Japan*, describes how in the eighth century all the craftsmen working on the new temples must have made Nara, the capital, look rather like a vast army encampment. The lacquerworkers must have played a by no means insignificant part in all this, and the laws about the planting of lacquer trees and the levying of taxes in the form of raw lacquer are doubtless a direct consequence of the sudden leap in demand for lacquer articles.

Most buildings of this period, together with their furnishings, have fallen victim to either war or fire, but some eighth-century dry-lacquer sculptures have survived,[14] above all in the Tōdai-ji, Kōfuku-ji (Pl. 3), Akishino-dera and Tōshōdai-ji temples.[15] The technique applied in these works is the so-called dry-lacquer technique (known in Japanese formerly as 'soku' and now as 'kanshitsu'). It originated in China and was already in use there in the Han period (206 BC-220 AD). It involves moulding statues and other objects out of hempen cloth saturated with raw lacquer. A clay shape or a simple wooden framework serves as a temporary core. As soon as the lacquer has dried and the cloth is stiff, the core can be removed, and the surface of the kanshitsu article, which is very light, can be further decorated with lacquer or painting. Since the moist fabric is so easy to mould, a degree of grace and delicacy of modelling scarcely possible in wood carving can be achieved in dry lacquer. In the Nara period, particularly difficult sections, those involving decorative ornaments for instance, were sometimes modelled and superimposed in a mixture of sawdust and lacquer (Pl. 4) which when dry was sometimes carved, lacquered over in several layers and in a

Plate 3   Head of Ashura. ca 735. Dry lacquer. Nara, Kōfuku-ji

few cases finally covered with gold leaf before being superimposed on the article. [16]

An incomparable wealth of eighth-century temple vessels, works of art and more utilitarian objects has survived in the Shōsōin. This 'main treasury' of the Tōdai-ji temple was built in connection with the dedication ceremony in 752 of the large Bronze Buddha in Nara. The difficult and expensive casting of this colossal statue – it was more than 16m high – was an event of national importance for Japan, and the solemn 'eye-opening ceremony' took place in the presence of the whole imperial court and hundreds of priests and monks. Implements used in the ceremony are stored in the southern part of the Shōsōin.

In 756, a few years after the completion of the Bronze Buddha, the pious Emperor Shōmu died. The great cult image had been cast on his orders and

Plate 4 Nimbus decorated with dry-lacquer modelled in relief. 8th c. Ht 72cm. Nara, Hōryū-ji

he had founded the Tōdai-ji temple to contain it. The Emperor's links with the Tōdai-ji having been particularly close, forty-nine days after his death the dowager Empress Kōmyō donated all his personal effects to the temple. These articles recorded in deeds of gift still extant, [17] are kept in the northern part of the Shōsōin. The rest of the collection in the 1200-year-old treasure-house consists of medicines and weapons, implements used on the first anniversary of Emperor Shōmu's death and other gifts, some later in date, from the imperial court and the nobility.

The Shōsōin is thus the oldest museum in the world, and its contents, reflecting as they do the richness of T'ang culture, which was a model for its time, are of the greatest significance for the history of art and culture. Many of the items there originated in China; others, such as the Sassanian glass, came all the way from Persia. Although some of the objects were certainly made in Japan itself, one cannot tell whether by Japanese, Chinese or Korean craftsmen.

Some 150 of the articles in the Shōsōin come under the general heading of lacquerwork. As varied as their functions – furniture, musical instruments, boxes, weapons etc. – are the materials of which they are made and the techniques employed in their decoration. A quiver, dated 764 in an accompanying description, is therefore one of the earliest examples of lacquerwork in Japan to have an exact date; it is made of woven plant tendrils which are lacquered over. [18] Other materials used for the substructure are wood, woven bamboo, cloth (dry-lacquer, see pp. 7-9) and 'shippi.'

The latter is a form of dry-lacquer in which a piece of leather is used instead of hempen cloth. Cow, deer, or sometimes even wild boar hide was soaked in water and then pressed into a wooden mould where it dried to the desired shape. For additional strength, before lacquering hempen cloth was glued either over the whole box – the shippi technique was mainly confined to boxes – or at least over the corners. The edges of the boxes and the covers were often further reinforced by winding a string horizontally around them four or five times. The application of the lacquer followed. Several shippi boxes of the Nara period have survived, in the Shōsōin as well as in the Hōryū-ji and Shitennō-ji temples. This easily mouldable material continued in regular use up to the subsequent Heian period. From the point of view of appearance and weight, kanshitsu (hempen cloth) and shippi (leather) pieces are easily confused. But, in shippi work, shrinkage of the leather causes characteristic radial cracking which allegedly does not occur in kanshitsu lacquer. [19]

Some items in the Shōsōin have no decoration on the smooth black surface of the lacquer. Study of such pieces has shown that generally a fairly thin priming was first applied to the substructure (wood, leather, basketwork). In the case of works of the Nara period this was usually followed by two to three layers of black lacquer (coloured with lamp black) and two coats of a shinier, brownish lacquer, called 'kurome,' which gave the black lacquer a beautiful amber-like lustre.

There are no examples of genuine red lacquer among the items in the Shōsōin. Instead, the surface of the wood was sometimes painted red and then coated with transparent lacquer. The best known example of this is a simply shaped cabinet, 1m high, in which the grain of the wood is visible under the lacquer, thereby giving the large flat surfaces added vitality (see Pl. 5: *Seki-shitsu bunkanboku no zushi*). The process can be regarded as an early

forerunner of the Shunkei-nuri technique[20] which was developed some
centuries later. Incidentally, this cabinet is definitely the work of a Japanese
as opposed to a Chinese or Korean craftsman.

Besides undecorated lacquered articles of this kind there is an abundance
of beautifully ornamented pieces. Judging from the works that have survived in the Shōsōin, the favourite method of decoration in the eighth
century was the so-called 'heidatsu' technique, involving the inlay of thin
pieces of sheet gold and silver cut to shape.[21] (In Japan it was later known as
'hyōmon.') Just like kanshitsu and shippi, this technique also originated in
China where it had been known as far back as the late Chou period. But
whereas in China hardly anything has survived,[22] the heidatsu lacquers in
the Shōsōin, which were definitely made by Chinese masters, show this art
at its very best.

Plate 6 illustrates what is probably the most beautiful of these heidatsu
lacquers, the case for an eight-lobed mirror (*Gin-heidatsu hakkaku kagami-*

Plate 5 Cabinet. 8th c. Ht 1m. Nara, Shōsōin

bako). It is made in the shippi technique and its decoration of cut silver inlay, both on the lid and on the curved sides, shows superb craftsmanship. The sheet silver, which is considerably thicker than silver foil, is slightly raised above the dark lacquer and is finely engraved.

The elegant shape of the box, the complex detail and carefully calculated balance of the composition, based on a central blossom-like star motif, together with the perfection of the craftsmanship, represent such a high standard of artistic achievement that there can be no doubt that the case originated in China. Also the actual design itself, which is closely related to contemporary Chinese textile patterns derived from Persia, indicates Chinese workmanship.[23] Time and again works of this period show a preference for large circular patterns. Although the individual elements are often based on natural forms, the overall design is not naturalistic; its purpose is solely decorative. Strength and richness are characteristics common to all such patterns.

In spite of its Chinese provenance, it is right to include this mirror case in a history of Japanese lacquerwork since masterpieces of this kind represented a criterion for Japanese lacquer artists, In their attempt to come to terms with the problem, naturally they first tried imitating the Chinese models and did not, therefore, immediately develop their own individual style. For this very reason it is almost impossible in the case of the Shōsōin lacquers to distinguish between Chinese examples and those which are

Plate 6 Mirror box with heidatsu decoration. Detail of lid from above. 8th c. Ht 10.5cm, max. diam. 36.5cm. Reproduced from *Treasures of the Shōsōin*

definitely of Japanese origin. Even Japanese experts are unable to do so; generally they regard a certain delicacy and 'softness' as indicative of Japanese work (see p. 18).

Heidatsu lacquers were sometimes made even more colourful by alternating gold and silver metal inlays, as we can see in another eighth-century shippi box from the Shōsōin (Pl. 7: *Kingin-heidatsu shippibako*). Its precise, rectilinear shape and sharp edges still further emphasized by the beaded border line, are characteristic of boxes of the Nara period and represent a strong contrast to the softer, slightly convex shapes of the following Heian period. The superbly designed decoration of the box clearly illustrates the receptive nature of T'ang art, for the motif of the bird in the beaded border line medallion, that of the birds with twigs in their beaks and, for that matter, the beaded border itself all derive from Persia. The strutting phoenix in the centre is closely related to the one modelled in dry-lacquer on the nimbus in Plate 4; the vital intensity of its movement, the sparse, brilliant way in which it is drawn, are quite typical of T'ang art at its best. Similar birds can also be seen in contemporary textiles.[24] Equally magnificent are the representations of long-tailed birds on leafy tendrils on

Plate 7 Dry-lacquer box with gold and silver heidatsu. 8th c. Lid: 6.3:33:27cm. Reproduced from *Treasures of the Shōsōin*

the sides of the lid. This box is one of a matching pair. In the other, the decoration is identical except that the use of the gold and the silver has been reversed.

The Shōsōin contains samples of yet another type of inlay: cut mother-of-pearl. Once again the technique originated in China, where, in the eighth century (that is, at the time the Shōsōin treasures were being collected in Japan), it must have been employed in the most extravagant manner, because the Emperor Su-tsung (756-762) finally banned, on the grounds of excessive luxury, the making of objects which involved the use not only of mother-of-pearl but also of amber and rock crystal. [25]

There are quite a number of items (mirrors, boxes, lutes, etc.) in the Shōsōin, in which mother-of-pearl, amber, and sometimes tortoiseshell inlay as well, are used in combination; but inlays in mother-of-pearl alone are also common. (For instance, the backs of no less than nine mirrors are exquisitely decorated with mother-of-pearl.) But, with one exception, in none of these works is any use made of lacquer. In the mirrors, the iridescent pieces of shell are inlaid in a resinous ground; in the other objects, in the exposed unlacquered wood. Since the wood came from countries to the south, and since the shells from which the mother-of-pearl is cut were often used as money in the Indian Ocean and the South Seas, and since, finally, even today, the art of mother-of-pearl inlay in wood still flourishes in Vietnam and Thailand, it is assumed that the technique came to China from the south at some undetermined stage, reached its first apex there in the T'ang period, and was thence introduced into Japan. [26]

But only the method of inlaying mother-of-pearl in a lacquered ground was adopted by the Japanese; this process is called 'raden'. A round girdle box (Pl. 8: *Raden-gyoku no obi-bako*) in the Shōsōin is the oldest example extant showing mother-of-pearl inlaid in lacquer. In addition to the lightly engraved mother-of-pearl, the lacquerer has used rock crystal underpainted in colours.

It is remarkable that, of the large number of works with mother-of-pearl inlay which have survived in the Shōsōin, there is only this one box with mother-of-pearl inlay in a lacquer ground. But this fact does not necessarily lead to the conclusion that in China in the eighth century inlays in wooden grounds generally prevailed and that mother-of-pearl inlays in lacquer grounds became more frequent later.

Although this girdle box was probably made by a Chinese craftsman, it marks the beginning of a centuries-long Japanese tradition of raden art. While in Japan this art went from strength to strength to reach its full flowering in the Kamakura period, in China mother-of-pearl inlay appears to have gone out of fashion temporarily after the T'ang period. At any rate, the 'Po-chê-pien', a Chinese manuscript of the beginning of the twelfth century, [27] describes the Japanese as the originators of mother-of-pearl lacquerwork – which would indicate that earlier Chinese examples of the technique had been forgotten in China while Japanese raden lacquer was familiar and prized. [28] Not until the fifteenth century would Japanese mother-of-pearl lacquerwork again be influenced by China.

In addition to the inlay techniques (heidatsu and raden), other methods of decorating the lacquer ground were also used on the objects in the Shōsōin collection, three different painting techniques: 'mitsuda-e,' 'yushoku' and 'kingin-e' (also known as 'kingindei-e').

For mitsuda-e a vegetable oil was boiled with lead oxide (mitsudasō), to dry the oil more quickly; colouring matter was then mixed into that binding agent. It was not really a lacquer technique as much as a kind of oil painting on a lacquer base. Yushoku, a type of gouache painting with a protective coating of oil, is more common. This oily coating served also to imitate the effect of tortoiseshell over a coloured ground popular in the Nara period, and that is probably one reason for yushoku painting occurring as frequently as it does. Quite a number of the articles in the Shōsōin, generally described as mitsuda-e, are really examples of yushoku. [29]

No doubt influenced by the love of colour apparent in T'ang art, both techniques were employed to add colour and life to the black-lacquer ground, but neither had any lasting effect on the future development of the art of Japanese lacquerware. Indeed, for centuries after the Nara period, right up to the Momoyama and Edo periods, there was no more colour decoration on lacquer grounds in Japan. But the third painting technique, kingin-e, which also originated in China, comes much closer to the typically Japanese quality of later lacquer works, for kingin-e did not aim at bright effects but was, as the literal translation indicates, a 'gold-and-silver-paste-picture.' Gold and silver dust were bound with glue and painted onto a

Plate 8 Girdle box with mother-of-pearl and rock crystal inlay. 8th c. Lid: ht 4.5cm, diam. 25.6cm. Reproduced from *Treasures of the Shōsōin*

black lacquer ground. (Sometimes also onto plain wooden grounds.) The advantage of kingin-e, in contrast to the later Japanese sprinkling techniques, was that the artists' skill in applying the brush could come into full play; the disadvantage was that the coat of paint quickly flaked off. Kingin-e was not suitable, therefore, for objects that were used frequently. The lack of solidity in the overall construction of some of the kingin-e boxes in the Shōsōin, therefore, permits the conclusion that they were intended not for actual use but rather as votive gifts in Buddhist commemorative ceremonies.[30] The mirror case in Plate 9, the body of which is shippi (*Shippi-kingin-e hakkaku no kagamibako*), is a particularly beautiful and well preserved example of kingin-e painting. The amazingly good state of preservation is attributed to the fact that, in this instance, proportionally more glue was added and, as a result, the adhesive power of the paint was greater than in other pieces.

Kingin-e is important from the historical point of view in that it marks a step towards the black, gold, and silver effect which was to play such a decisive role in Japanese lacquerwork. When it was discovered, later in the Heian period, that the same result could be achieved with more permanent techniques, kingin-e was dropped.

The objects in the Shōsōin, therefore, show that in the mid-eighth

Plate 9 Mirror case with gold and silver painted decoration. 8th c. Ht 3cm, max. diam. 21cm. Reproduced from *Treasures of the Shōsōin*

century two types of inlay (heidatsu and raden) and three painting techniques (mitsuda-e, yushoku, kingin-e) were being used in conjunction with a lacquer ground. Yet, as if by some historical irony, only one single item has survived which anticipates the most important of the later Japanese lacquer techniques, that is, those in which the design is first drawn with lacquer and then sprinkled with gold dust. The sole example of this technique in the Shōsōin collection is a sword scabbard decorated with floral scrolls and mythical animals in coarse-grained gold dust on a black lacquer ground (Pl. 10).

The sword and its scabbard are recorded in the old Tōdai-ji inventory of 756, and the text states that on the scabbard (*Kingin densō karatachi no saya*) 'makkinru' was used. This word, which is neither current nor even understood today, occurs only in the Shōsōin inventory in this one place. Two arrows, now in the National Museum in Tokyo, have survived from about the same period. They are decorated with black lacquer and coarse gold filings behind the head and near the notch. At that, the gold dust has not been sprinkled in any definite pattern, but merely serves to enliven the lacquer ground.[31] Yet indubitably a sprinkling technique was used for the arrows just as it was for the scabbard. There is still some controversy in Japan about these pieces, but seeing that in the case of the scabbard the sprinkled gold dust was lacquered over and the surface was then polished and repolished until the decoration reappeared, makkinru and the later 'togidashi' (cf. p.25) are now regarded as one and the same technique.

The technique of scattering gold dust onto the still damp lacquer ground, or the still damp lacquer design, was previously thought to have been a Japanese discovery, for there were no references in China either to the written character for the word 'makkinru' or to objects decorated in this manner. Yet the Chinese lacquer articles of the Han period excavated in Lolang in Korea are said to include an example of scattered gold dust. In this instance, however, the gold dust was scattered not onto lacquer but onto glue.[32] Even if Chinese craftsmen of the Han period had been familiar with the technique of scattering metal dust onto a lacquer ground – and there is

Plate 10 Sword scabbard showing makkinru technique. Detail. 8th c. Reproduced from *Treasures of the Shōsōin*

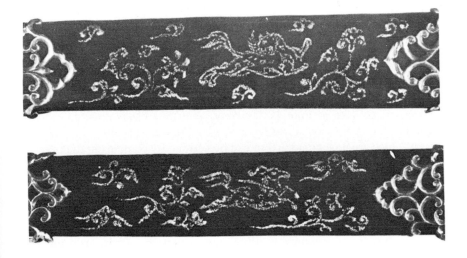

no proof that they were – the process must have been completely forgotten since. In Japan, however, it evolved and reached its apex in the form of 'makie,' or 'sprinkled picture', from the Heian period onwards. [33] Indeed, it became the 'most Japanese' of all the lacquer techniques, perhaps the most Japanese craft of all.

In shapes, colours and technical processes, therefore, the lacquer objects of the Nara period in Japan that have survived present a rich and varied sight. Grounds of the most varied kinds are decorated in manifold inlay and painting techniques, and the decoration itself offers a multiplicity of patterns, of which the large, complex circular designs and other western elements, like the beaded border line are particularly striking. (These motifs recur repeatedly not only in lacquer objects but also in contemporary textiles, ivories, and mother-of-pearl articles.) [34] The fully developed art of the T'ang period in China, particularly the lacquerwork, provided a large reservoir of potentialities. Yet by no means all of these potentialities survived or were further developed in Japan.

For the very reason that the T'ang style so evidently predominates, the lacquer objects in the Shōsōin and (though there are fewer of them) those in other collections, raise the question of whether one can really speak of lacquerwork of the Nara period rather than simply of lacquerwork of the Chinese T'ang period. Or, putting it another way, must the examples of lacquerwork of this period that have survived in Japan necessarily have been imports, or could they also be Japanese copies? This question cannot be answered with absolute certainty from a study of the objects alone. In the case of the three-colour glazed ceramic wares in the Shōsōin, all at one time considered to be of Chinese origin, it has become possible, of late to distinguish between imported originals and Japanese copies. [35] The quality of these Japanese ceramics gives one grounds for suspecting that among all those lacquer articles there must also be at least one or two items made by Japanse craftsmen, in spite of the fact that – as yet – there are no signs of an independent style. It is quite inconceivable that the numerous unquestionably Japanese lacquer objects of the subsequent Heian period should have had absolutely no antecedents.

Furthermore, written sources of the Nara period indicate that the art of lacquering was at that time not only flourishing, but rapidly evolving in Japan. There are numerous references to technical terms and descriptions which would not have been necessary if Japan had not been busy producing lacquerware. We find words such as 'do-shitsu' (ceramic lacquering), 'soku-nuri' (dry-lacquer lacquering), 'boku-shitsu' (black lacquer) etc., as well as others the meanings of which are lost to us today. [36] The meanings of technical terms have undergone considerable changes over the centuries, but here the old inventory of the Tōdai-ji, which dates from 756, is most illuminating. Since it contains descriptions of the objects donated at that time and the items themselves have survived in the Shōsōin, many of the terms which are no longer current can be verified by comparing the two.

Thus, it is evident that there very definitely was a Japanese lacquer art in the Nara period, even though it does not reveal any individual characteristics. Finally, in summarizing the evolution up to the end of this period the following may be said: lacquer was used in Japan from prehistoric times as a means of protection and decoration, albeit to begin with in a very simple manner. Important encounters with Korean art (cf. the Tamamushi shrine) were followed by Japan's great period of apprenticeship in the school of T'ang art. There, Japanese craftsmen familiarized themselves with a highly developed lacquer art and numerous techniques which, initially, they assimilated and copied. Thus the foundations were laid on which Japan was later to build and develop its own unmistakable art of lacquerwork .

Origins and apprentice years

Early Heian period:
the rise of an indigenous style

THE YEAR 794, WITH THE TRANSFER OF THE CAPITAL FROM NARA TO Kyōto – then known as Heian-kyō – was the beginning of the Heian period. This period lasted almost four hundred years and is divided, from the point of view of the history of lacquerwork, into two separate and distinct parts.

The first, which extends to about the end of the tenth century, is by its very nature a period of transition from the Chinese-influenced art of the Nara period to an independent Japanese style. This change, which is also apparent in other branches of Japanese art, in the case of lacquer objects visibly affected both their shape and their decoration.

In lacquerwork, the dozen or so items which illustrate this stylistic development are not distributed evenly over the approximately two-hundred-year period, and only one single article has a definite date. Nevertheless, a careful analysis of the lacquer pieces reveals how the shapes and techniques altered, and this, in turn, makes it possible to put a tentative date on the whole group.

At the beginning of the period we have some examples of decorative painting which, hidden under layers of lacquer applied at a later date, were only discovered very recently in the course of restoration work. They are to be found in a large, rather shallow, 5m-high shrine which stands in the so-called Mandara Hall of the Taima-dera temple and serves to house a famous woven cult image. This woven image, the 'Taima-mandara,' is a work of the eighth century and the shrine and hall were erected for it. They date from the very beginning of the Heian period, but still show close links with the art of the Nara period. [1]

In the course of reconstruction work and repairs carried out in the middle of the thirteenth century, the shrine was given its present doors (dated 1242; see p.65) and base (dated 1243; see p.68). Presumably at the same time the old painted decorations, dating from the beginning of the Heian period, were lacquered over, to remain undiscovered until the recent thorough restoration.

The decoration consists of hōsōge blossoms, birds and butterflies painted in the kingin-e technique on the ceiling of the shrine and on the inner faces of its supporting columns (Pl. 11). There are also traces of birds and genies in hyōmon inlay on the ceiling. The kingin-e painting *Man-dara-dō-zushi kingin-dei-e hashira*) must have been radiantly beautiful when new, for even today, what remains – the dark hall unfortunately makes it difficult to see – still bears eloquent witness of its former glory.

The very techniques indicate how closely this decoration is linked to the Nara period (and consequently point to its early date of origin). Both gold and silver painting on a lacquer ground and cut-silver decorative inlay were familiar processes in Japan, at least since the date of the construction of the Shōsōin, yet both gradually fell into disuse in the course of the Heian period. Also, the decoration is still rich in foreign adaptations. The cloud forms stem from China, as do the birds with twigs in their beaks and the way of representing the butterflies 'in plan.'

The large hōsōge blossom on the ceiling of the shrine (Pl. 12) provides the clearest evidence of the links with the art of the Nara era. As in the complex circular patterns of the Nara period, the central blossom is developed into a large, decorative, flat design. To match the construction of the Mandara shrine, instead of being round, the design in this instance is rhomboid. But like the Nara designs it is based on the principle of joining together, to the requisite degree, any number of individual parts which might also be regarded as independent decorative elements.

Written sources of the Heian period prove that hyōmon – a favourite technique of the Nara period – was used only until the middle of the tenth century.[2] In the later Heian period it appears that hardly any hyōmon work was produced at all.[3] (On the other hand, this inlay technique – then known as 'kanagai' – was taken up again from the Kamakura period onwards and was used in conjunction with makie – a combination which occurs particularly frequently in the Muromachi period.) Of hyōmon works of the early Heian period, however, very little has survived. Apart from the few remains discovered on the Taima shrine, there is only one box for priests' stoles (Pl. 13) to give us some idea of how the Japanese lacquermasters employed the technique after the Nara period.

What is interesting is how the stole box (*Hōsōge-gin-hyōmon kesabako*) combines old-fashioned elements from the Nara period with new ones characteristic of the developing Heian style. Apart from the hyōmon technique, two other decorative devices are old-fashioned: the beaded border line motif (on the sides) and the border of palmetto-like leaves. What is new in the Heian style is the shape of the box: low, rectangular and with gently rounded corners, which clearly distinguish it from the generally sharp-cornered, rectilinear examples of the Nara period. The most important

Plate 11 Pillar with decoration painted in gold on a lacquer ground. Detail. ca 800. Taima-dera, Nara province.

characteristic, however, is the completely new formal element of the so-called 'chiri-i.' This 'dust ledge' – 'dust place' being the verbatim translation of the word – is a recessed rim of the box top, here decorated with the palmetto-like leaves, from which the flat top of the lid rises in a gentle S curve.

Thus, the shape of the box is softened and made more fluid in two ways: looked at in plan, the sides no longer meet each other at right angles, but are linked by softly rounded corners: and in elevation, the sharp right angle between the sides of the box and the top of the lid has been replaced by a curve. The 'dust ledge' interrupts the slight curve and, since in this box it is quite wide, it echoes the horizontal of the top of the lid: that is, the width of the chiri-i emphasizes the flat proportions of this kesabako.

The legacy of Nara lacquerwork is still clearly present in the decoration

Plate 12 Painted ceiling in the Mandara shrine. Detail. ca 800. Taima-dera, Nara province.

and technique of both the Taima-dera paintings and the kesabako in the
Nezu Museum. In addition to these surviving works, written sources up to
about the middle of the tenth century refer to techniques which evidently
continued in the tradition of Nara art.(The sources say nothing about the
style of the objects produced.) Mention is made, for instance, of red lacquer
boxes, black lacquer shrines with hyōmon decoration, lacquer boxes with
ivory inlay, and mirrors and boxes adorned with mother-of-pearl.

From the Engi era (901-923) on, there are a great many references to
'makie.'⁴ This word, which has such significance for the art of Japanese
lacquerwork and which, literally translated, means 'sprinkled picture,' occurs for the first time in the 'Taketori-monogatari,' a tale dating from the
middle of the ninth century. What exactly is meant by makie? Briefly, the
process involves drawing a design in lacquer on a lacquer ground, and then,
before it dries, sprinkling this preliminary design with gold or silver dust.
(Sometimes coloured dust is also used.) The point is that the lacquer design
is not painted with a brush but is sprinkled onto the still damp preliminary
drawing.

The most important types of makie are, in order of historical development, 'togidashi,' 'hiramakie' and 'takamakie.' In togidashi the sprinkled
decoration, when dry, is completely covered with several layers of lacquer,
generally black. Then, by means of very careful polishing down with charcoal, the top layers are gradually worn away until the sprinkled motifs
reappear. As a result of this overlacquering and gradual grinding down of
the top layers, the design now reappears in exactly the same plane as the
surrounding lacquer ground. Finally, the whole surface is generally coated
with transparent lacquer. So, in togidashi, the gold or silver decoration has
a protective skin of polished transparent lacquer and is quite flat.

Hiramakie is much simpler to produce because the sprinkled parts are
simply covered with transparent lacquer thinned with camphor, which is
then polished to a fine gloss. Hiramakie, literally 'flat sprinkled picture,' is,

Plate 13 Box for priests' stoles. Detail. Tōkyō, Nezu Museum (reproduced from
Sekai Bijutsu Zenshū, vol.4, pl.89)

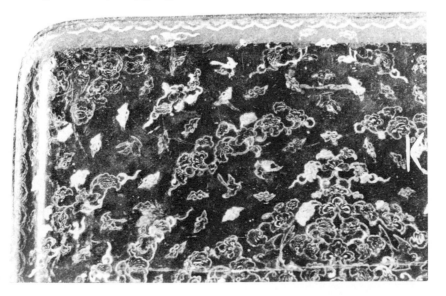

in fact, fractionally raised above the lacquer ground because the sprinkled dust is not polished down.

In takamakie, 'raised sprinkled picture', the decoration is first applied in relief, using a mixture of lacquer and powdered charcoal, tin or emery, and only then is a sprinkling applied as in hiramakie.

There are numerous different kinds of makie, depending on the type and fineness of the metal dust and the overlacquering and final polishing – the latter sometimes being omitted. Where their historical significance for the development of lacquerwork warrants it, these variants will be described in due course.

In the Heian period, up to the end of the twelfth century, only the togidashi technique was used. Its precursor – nowadays generally regarded as identical to togidashi – was the so-called 'makkinru' on the sword scabbard in the Shōsōin (cf. Pl. 10). The sprinkling process seems to have developed gradually from the middle of the ninth century onwards, while the techniques of the Nara period also continued in use for the time being. Within a century more or less, by about 950, makie work apparently surpassed all other types of lacquer both in popularity and in sheer volume of output. Several sources refer to it: the *Utsubo-monogatari*,[6] the famous 'Pillow book' of Sei Shonagon (*Makura no sōshi*),[7] the *Genji-monogatari*,[8] etc., all contain numerous descriptions of beautiful lacquer utensils, which indicate how popular and fashionable the sprinkling technique was at that time. A small number of ninth- to eleventh-century makie objects have survived. They comprise the following:

Arm-rest decorated with flowers and butterflies (*Kachō makie kyōshoku*) in the Fujita Museum, Osaka;[9]
Manuscript box with hōsōge scrolls and winged genies (*Hōsōge karyobinga makie-soku sasshibako*) in the Ninna-ji, Kyōto, dated 919;
Box for priests' stoles with waves and marine animals (*Kaibu makie kesabako*) in the Tō-ji,[10] Kyōto;
Jewel case with hōsōge (*Hōsōge makie hōjubako*) in the Ninna-ji, Kyōto;
Sutra box with hōsōge (*Hōsōge makie kyōbako*), in the Enryaku-ji, Shiga-ken;
Sutra box with lotus scrolls (*Hasu-karakusa makie kyōbako*) in the National Museum, Nara;
Sutra box depicting the acts of piety performed by Buddha (*Butsu-kudoku makie kyōbako*) in the Fujita Museum, Osaka.

These important early examples of makie, which have all been declared National Treasures, deserve and require examination in greater detail.[11] The first object to be considered should certainly be the manuscript box in the Ninna-ji, since an entry in the *Engi-gyoki* (diary of Emperor Daigo, 897-930)[12] fixes its date at 919, which makes it the oldest surviving example of makie work with an exact known date of origin.

The 'sasshibako' (manuscript box, Pl. 14) is rectangular with rounded corners and has a deep overlapping lid with a chiri-i (dust ledge); the top of the lid is flat. The substructure is of lacquered hempen cloth, that is, dry-lacquer; for additional strength, string has been wound four times horizontally round the upper rim of the box proper and then lacquered over. The rounded corners and the dust ledge lend the overall shape an air of gentle elegance that is very appealing.

On the crown of the lid is an inscription in gold togidashi, which indicates the function of the box: namely, to contain the manuscripts which Kōbō Daishi,[13] the founder of the Shingon sect, brought with him on his return from China.[14] The inscription is surrounded by hōsōge scrolls, 'karyobinga' (Sanskrit: kalavinka; winged genies with human torsos, bird's legs and long tail feathers), butterflies, birds and clouds. The decoration, which covers almost the whole surface of the lid, gives the effect of careful balance, but – contrary to one's intitial impression – it is not symmetrical. To the right and left, above and below the space occupied by the inscription, one can make out slight deviations from a pure mirror image. None of the patterns is repeated exactly, all the karyobinga are different and there is a slight clockwise shift in the rich, well-balanced decoration. The sides of the box, each showing a different pattern, bring out the underlying compositional idea with particular clarity. It reveals the legacy of the large, complex patterns of the Nara period. (In the latter, too, there are forms which at first sight appear symmetrical, yet relatively small parts of them are not.)

The decoration has been carried out in gold and silver togidashi, thus producing a colour effect germane to the gold and silver painting of the Nara period.[15] The ground, incidentally, is not pure black lacquer but contains a very thin sprinkling of gold filings ('yasuri-fun'; see p.62). This type of ground, which first occurs in this period and can be found in nearly all Heian makie work, is called 'heijin' (literally: flat dust). The very restrained manner in which the filings have been sprinkled means that, despite occasional flashes of gold, the black lacquer remains the predominant background colour. The sprinkling of the decoration is relatively sparse and coarse-grained.[16] The faces and bodies of the karyobinga, as well as parts of their wings and feathered tails, are outlined in gold, as are the birds, petals, fruits and some portions of the butterflies; the scrolls, leaves and most of the

Early
Heian period

Plate 14 Manuscript box. 919. 8.3:24.4:37cm. Kyōto, Ninna-ji

clouds, on the other hand, are in silver. The distribution of colour does not follow a pattern, but simply fulfils the requirements of decorative effect.

When we compare other early makie articles listed above with this box (dated 919), the shape, technique and decoration provide important points of reference on estimating their dates of origin.

Ignoring the arm-rest for the moment, let us first consider the question of shape. Apart from the Enryaku-ji sutra box, which is an exception, all the boxes have dust ledges (chiri-i) and rounded or inverted corners. In other words, at this stage of stylistic development the severe rectangular or square shape of the box is made noticeably softer and more opulent, in a way that appeals to both the eye and the sense of touch. Even with these early pieces, as happens so often in the art of lacquerwork, the hand quite instinctively 'grasps' their shape – one 'feels' the shape in one's fingers, even without actually touching the object.

This softer box shape, imbued as it is with a charm peculiar to itself, must surely reflect early Heian taste. Certainly three of the boxes are in dry-lacquer (kanshitsu for both boxes in the Ninna-ji and shippi for the sutra box with lotus scrolls), that is, they are made of a material which is in itself soft, pliant and easy to mould. But the shape of both pieces with wooden substructures (the sutra box in the Fujita Museum and the sutra box in the Tō-ji) show the same tendency; what is more, as the walls of the sutra box are of a thinness quite remarkable for wood, the overall effect is quite similar to dry lacquer. The early Heian period appears, therefore, to have recognized and valued the potential of soft, rounded forms inherent in dry-lacquer, a material with which the Nara period had also been familiar, but which it used in a different way. Boxes in the Nara period – except mirror cases, because of their very purpose – had sharp edges and corners and flat lids. These precise, sharp shapes become softer and gentler in the Heian period; one might say that the powerful, masculine character is replaced by a warmer, feminine quality. The great importance of women and their influence during the Heian period thus seems to document itself in the shapes of utensils of Heian culture.

The boxes of the late Heian period and of the Kamakura period have not only rounded-off corners but also curved sides and lids, so that a ground plan shows not a single straight line, and the curving of the lid starts at the dust ledge and extends to the centre of the lid. The boxes of the first half of the Heian period do not yet show such variety but they do display a certain characteristic softness of form.

What now do the decoration and manner of sprinkling convey? All the boxes have a heijin ground. (Only the arm-rest has a pure black-lacquer ground.) But the sprinkling is not identical in every case: in the manuscript box and the stole box (Pl. 15) it is thin and retains the character of the black-lacquer ground; in the jewel case (Pl. 16) it is so dense that it almost gives the impression of a gold-lacquer ground; and the sutra box with lotus scrolls (Pl. 18) comes somewhere in between. The heijin on the sutra box in the Fujita Museum (Pl. 19) is also very thin, but, because of the different, narrative character of its decoration, it should not really be compared with the other boxes in which the decoration is purely ornamental (see p. 33). Finally, the box in the Enryaku-ji (Pl. 17) shows two different kinds of heijin: a fairly thin sprinkling for the ground in general, and a much more generous one for the circles around the scroll patterns.

The stole box (Pl. 15) resembles the manuscript box of 919 in the way the sprinkling not only of the ground but also of the decoration has been carried out; in both boxes the heijin is rather coarse-grained and not very dense. [17] In the arm-rest the sprinkling is cruder still, with the result that the outline of the design lacks definition and, in places, has clearly been exceeded. In the jewel case, however, and in the sutra boxes in the Fujita Museum, the Enryaku-ji, and particularly in the one with lotus scrolls (National Museum in Nara) the sprinkling is very careful and precise.

These findings based on technique alone indicate a chronological sequence in which the arm-rest, the manuscript box and the stole box must antedate the remaining works. This is evidently true of the arm-rest, since it has features similar to those of an arm-rest in the Shōsōin, said to have belonged to the Emperor Shōmu; its decoration, above all its use of the beaded border line, is closely linked to Nara art. Okada considers it to be a work of the Jōgan era (859-876) and therefore the oldest surviving makie work of the Heian period. [18]

The date of origin of the stole box (Pl. 15) cannot be precisely determined, though the manner in which the birds and fish are depicted still shows considerable Chinese influence; the technical execution also argues for a relatively early dating. The box might well belong to much the same period as the manuscript box in the Ninna-ji which dates from 919. Both works may be considered representative of the Engi era (901-923).

Temple legend has it that the jewel case (Pl. 16) once belonged to the Emperor Uda, but on stylistic grounds, it cannot be given a date much before his death in 937. Its inverted corners make it more intricate in shape than the other boxes. It is very carefully worked, with an even, meticulously arranged decoration in gold and silver togidashi on dense gold heijin.

Plate 15   Box for priests' stoles. 1st quarter of 10th c. 12:47,8:39cm. Kyōto, Tō-ji

All the sides show identical motifs, but in such a way that the box and the deeply overlapping lid contrast with one another. For while all the outer sides of the lid depict a short-tailed bird in the centre and a long-tailed one in each corner, on the sides of the box itself a long-tailed bird is shown in the centre and a short-tailed one in each corner. This arrangement indicates a degree of careful planning far removed from any improvisation. Also, the top of the lid, which is decorated with plants and scrolls, has none of the little irregularities and small variations that lent added liveliness to the manuscript box.

Instead, the scrolls are much more distinct and simpler than those on the manuscript box, which – compared with the jewel case – promptly and unmistakably reveals its own much closer relation to Nara art. In the manuscript box the hōsōge scrolls are creations of pure fantasy; their shape and the way they branch are determined solely from the point of view of decorative effect. They constitute a continuous interplay with rich and varied shapes filling the whole surface of the box with exuberant movement, but these scrolls bear no relation to real plants. The jewel box is different. Here the large surface pattern resolves itself into separate motifs – though the whole ground continues to be covered with them – and the individual forms become more distinguishable, simpler and neater. Also, the leaves and flowers are more realistic: even though they cannot be identified with any actual plant, one could imagine such vegetation growing somewhere.

There is a tendency here to simplification and strict order, of which the

Plate 16 Jewel box. 1st half of 10th c. 15.4:20.6:20.6cm. Kyōto, Ninna-ji

manuscript box of 919 as yet shows no sign; but this tendency seems to have set a trend in the second half of the tenth and throughout the eleventh century.

The sutra box in the Enryaku-ji (Pl. 17) also illustrates this tendency in its use of strict symmetry to counteract the legacy of the rich, fluid designs of the Nara period. The box displays many conservative characteristics, both in the lack of naturalism in the decoration and in the shape of the box itself with its sharp corners, but the scrolls are stiffer and considerably more distinct, and the regular way in which they are arranged goes far beyond the 'rational' principle on which the composition of the jewel case is based. Because of severe systematization and stylization of its decoration, Okada already attributes this box to the eleventh century.[19]

The quest for simplicity and conscious order takes another form in the sutra box with lotus scrolls (Pl. 18), which is certainly the latest of these makie works. The arrangement of the decorative elements is very regular and consciously conceived; the long side of the lid – which only comes down over half the box – depicts, for instance, a small butterfly on the left and on the right and a large scroll in the centre, while the section of the box visible below the lid has a large scroll at either end and the small metal plaque for the tying cord in the centre. This type of composition implies a carefully planned harmonious interaction. Here the scrolls can really be identified: they are unmistakably lotus. Strictly speaking, one cannot talk

Plate 17 Sutra box with hōsōge decoration. 11th c. 17:33:20.3cm. Enryaku-ji, Shiga province

of naturalism, since the lotus does not grow scrolls and the representation is therefore necessarily unrealistic; nevertheless, the decoration is no doubt closer to nature in this example than in any of the other makie works. [20]

The trend towards greater simplification, formalization and naturalism in the decoration is accompanied by a new approach to colouring. True, all these makie works are decorated with gold and silver dust, but in very different ways. In the manuscript box of the year 919 the distribution of the gold and the silver is very free. Certainly, gold is generally used for the main elements, silver for the less important ones, but the overall decorative effect alone is what counts; with that in mind even 'unimportant' shreds of clouds are accented with gold. In later works this freedom is replaced by a more logical allocation of colours and colour values.

In the lotus scroll box, the latest of these works, a new colour gradation is introduced: 'aokin' (green gold), a pale light gold dust made from an alloy of gold and silver. The use of this material also substantiates the relatively late dating (mid-eleventh century?) of the box, since in the late Heian period the combination of gold and aokin is much preferred to the stronger contrast of gold and silver dust (see chapter 3), and is frequently used in conjunction with mother-of-pearl inlay. Finally, it is worth noting yet another nuance of colour in the box, resulting from the use of heijin not only for the ground but also within the decoration proper: for the large lotus leaves and the pistils of the blossoms. [21] This form of colour gradation does, in fact, already occur to a small degree, in the manuscript box of the year 919 (in the faces of the karyobinga) and in the sutra box in the Fujita Museum (in the clouds), but the lotus scroll box is the first example on which it is used expressly for the purpose of colour differentiation and as a means of enriching the decorative effect.

Shape, manner of sprinkling, colour and style of decoration therefore combine to present a logical chronology of makie works: beginning with the arm-rest, followed by the Engi group (with the manuscript box of the year 919 as its fixed point) and the jewel case, then on into the eleventh century with the sutra box in the Enryaku-ji, and lastly, the lotus scroll box. In decoration the development is from rich, only apparently symmetrical, Chinese-influenced patterns towards greater simplification, stylization and

Plate 18 Sutra box with lotus scrolls. Mid (?) 11th c. 12.2:31.8:17.5cm. Nara, National Museum

austerity; and, in technique, from a spontaneous manner of sprinkling with arbitrary, freely contrasting colour accents towards a careful, precise sprinkling technique with much richer colour differentiation.

The sutra box in the Fujita Museum (Pl.19) cannot be fitted into the category of the various lacquer boxes so far discussed, because its decoration, which depicts episodes from the Lotus Sutra, is different. The shape of the box (it has rounded corners and the lid rises in a gentle curve from the chiri-i but is in itself almost flat) is conservative and follows on from the early makie boxes of the Engi era; but its pictorial decoration argues for a dating

Plate 19 Sutra box showing the good deeds of Buddha. Detail. 11th c. Overall dimensions 16.7:32.7:23.3cm. Osaka, Fujita Museum

in the late (?) eleventh century.[22] It shows unmistakable evidence of the process of Japanization: while the way in which the rocks, figures, and some of the clouds are done leaves no doubt about the continuing tradition of Chinese painting, 'Yamato-e' – the Japanese pictorial style which was developing at this time – is equally apparent in other parts of the decoration. The excellent technique (gold and silver togidashi) and pictorial representation make this sutra box a true masterpiece.

Some examples of metalwork with known dates provide an interesting frame of reference. Tenth-century mirrors show that in the art of metalwork the transitional style of the early Heian period also still prevailed at this time,[23] while mirrors of the late Heian period are decorated in a purely Japanese style. A bronze sutra box,[24] made around 1007, can be related to the certainly earlier jewel case in the Ninna-ji because of its inverted corners, chiri-i, and flat lid. An additional bronze sutra box (Pl. 20),[25] made shortly before 1031, shows symmetrical scrolls on its top. Although these are not as strongly formalized as those in the lacquer box in the Enryaku-ji are, yet how much more stylized and simpler they are than comparable scrolls in the Nara period or those on the manuscript box of the year 919.

To know the dates of these specimens of metalwork does not, however, make exact dating of lacquer objects any easier, since the stylistic development need not necessarily have been simultaneous in both arts. For example, it is quite conceivable that the shapes of the boxes were first developed in lacquerwork and then applied to the bronze sutra boxes.[26] But, in any

Plate 20 Sutra box (bronze) with hōsōge decoration. ca 1031. 8.3 : 12.1 : 27.1cm.
Enryaku-ji, Shiga province

event, the trend established through the study of lacquerwork articles is confirmed by works in metal.

Textile patterns show familiar tendencies: in the Heian period the striking multicoloured patterns of the Nara period disappear in favour of smaller, individually simpler forms; the 'sumptuous' animals like lions, dragons and phoenixes are replaced by smaller, more realistic representations of insects, butterflies and cranes.

Among the lacquer objects that have survived from the ninth and tenth centuries there is none with raden decoration. It is only from written sources that we know that mother-of-pearl lacquerwork was also produced in the first half of the Heian period. Indeed, this technique must have been at a peak, because records show that among the gifts which the Japanese priest Ka-in presented to the imperial court of China in 988, besides painted screens, hinoki-wood fans, makie writing-boxes etc., there were toilet cases and comb boxes, reading-desks, writing-tables and saddles, all embellished with mother-of-pearl inlay. [27]

Taking the lacquerwork of the first half of the Heian period as a whole, the essential characteristics show themselves to be: on the one hand the residual influence of Nara art, as evidenced by the shape, technique and decoration of the objects; on the other, the gradual inching towards independence, the evolving and the unfolding of an indigenous Japanese style. Written sources confirm the continued use of the 'Chinese' lacquer techniques right up to about the middle of the tenth century, but the new, the Japanese element–as is apparent in makie work–was gaining an ever stronger hold. This process of Japanization is proved in style and technique alike, and the very transitoriness, the combination of 'still is' and 'already is', is characteristic of the lacquerware of the first half of the Heian period.

A glance at the political, sociological and cultural events of the period reveals the extent to which the development of lacquerwork, and the way it was gradually freeing itself from Chinese tutelage, echoed the tendencies of the times, and how, likewise, the growing Japanese potential was very much a sign of the times. In 794, Kyōto, then known as Heian-kyō, replaced Nara as the capital of Japan. This new capital city was still exactly modelled on the Chinese prototype of Ch'ang-an. Yet a hundred years later, the Japanese embassies to the Chinese imperial court – already discontinued in 835 – were officially ended, and even earlier, in sculpture for example, there were signs of an independent non-Chinese style. The year 901 was the beginning of the Fujiwara period, an era characterized by a culture of sophisticated, aristocratic courtiers which aesthetically permeated and reshaped all aspects of life. Native talent flowed more freely, and in architecture, painting and calligraphy new, typically Japanese forms ('shinden-zukuri'; 'Yamato-e'; 'hirigana') came into being. [28] With the *Tales of Genji*, written in about 1000 by the lady-in-waiting, Murasaki Shikibu, Japanese prose was already at the peak of maturity. National self-esteem was born and was consciously contrasted with Chinese culture. [29] This severing of the links with China, this development of a separate, purely Japanese style are clearly discernible in the lacquer works of the first half of the Heian period, discussed here.

Eleventh and twelfth centuries: the golden age of Heian lacquerwork

DESPITE POLITICAL STRIFE AND CIVIL WARS, THE SECOND HALF OF THE
Heian period is characterized by the elegant courtly culture of the Fujiwara
era. The aristocracy at the Kyōto Court with its luxurious way of life,
dominated by aesthetic and sentimental considerations, marked the epoch
in the eyes of succeeding ages as the epitome of elegance, refinement and
lyrical beauty.

The spirit of this era is most vividly manifested in the numerous surviving examples of lacquerwork. Apparently there was a great demand for
lacquerwork in the eleventh and twelfth centuries – especially for items
which combined the white moonglow of mother-of-pearl inlay with a
black-lacquer ground and the gentle golden gleam of makie. The dreamlike
effect of such objects in the dimness of the living quarters or temple halls

Plate 21   Konjiki-dō. Interior view. 1124. Chūson-ji, Iwate province

must – as literary sources in fact confirm – have responded so exactly to the spirit of the period, with its craving for beauty, that one is indeed fully justified in speaking of an 'age of lacquer art.'

Almost all aspects of life were affected; the work of lacquermasters was everywhere: in Buddhist appurtenances like sutra boxes and altar bases, eating and drinking utensils, writing-boxes, bookshelves (tana), chests and tables, comb boxes and toilet cases, lamp and mirror stands, sword scabbards and saddles, in the frames of folding screens and sliding doors, even in the pillars, walls and ceilings of buildings.

Plate 22 Detail of a pillar in the Konjiki-dō. 1124

Though pure makie works still continued to be made, the dominant technique now is gold lacquer combined with mother-of-pearl. Two buildings decorated in this manner have survived, and what is more, their exact dates are known: the Phoenix Hall (Hōō-dō) of the Byōdō-in, to the south of Kyōto, was built in 1053, and the Konjiki-dō (Gold-Coloured Hall) of the Chūson-ji in the Iwate-ken in 1124 (Pl. 21). While in the Phoenix Hall the mother-of-pearl inlay was restricted to the altar base and in the course of time almost all of it has disappeared, the whole interior of the Konjiki-dō sparkles with gold lacquer, togidashi and mother-of-pearl. Kümmel said of the Konjiki-dō that it 'probably surpasses all other buildings in the world in sheer radiant magnificence.'[1] But this statement should be qualified to the extent that far from being cold, glittery and ostentatious, this small room (only about 5.5 m square), with its decoration of gold lacquer, mother-of-pearl, bronze mountings and inlaid precious stones (though few of them remain today) has a warmth, distinction and intimate beauty which can hardly be described in words. One's amazement at the decoration of this building, which was erected as a mausoleum for Fujiwara Kiyohira,[2] is all the greater when one realizes that the temple of Chūson-ji is not in Kyōto but in the far north of the country. Yet such was the influence of the culture of the capital that its radiance spread even to this remote region of the country, and Fujiwara Kiyohira strove to have his small residence compete in refinement, beauty and elegance with the metropolis. He brought artists and craftsmen from Kyōto to Hiraizumi, the place near which the Chūson-ji is situated; indeed, it was its very remoteness which, in contrast to Kyōto, prevented this area becoming a theatre of war and which kept the

Plate 23 Baldachin in the Konjiki-dō. 1124

temple with all its art treasures safe and intact, making it a kind of Shōsōin of the Fujiwara period.'[3]

The interior walls and ceiling of the Konjiki-dō are covered with gold leaf, peeling off in places, on a black-lacquer ground. Four free-standing round pillars support a vaulted baldachin above the central one of three altars. These pillars, horizontally subdivided by studded bronze brands, are decorated in the three upper zones with twelve large medallions depicting the Dainichi Nyorai (Vairocana), the incarnation of the Absolute and of the highest wisdom (Pl. 22); these medallions are executed in gold togidashi on a fine, densely sprinkled gold ground (ikakeji).[4] The entire line drawing inside the design shows the original black-lacquer ground without gold sprinkling, and the result is a delicate, very appealing contrast of black and gold.[5] The wedge-shaped areas between the medallions contain alternate geometric and scroll patterns, also in togidashi; separating the pictorial zones are wide bands decorated with hōsōge patterns in mother-of-pearl inlay.

In order not to expose this decoration – which is extremely difficult to effect on the curved surfaces of the pillars – to any possible damage that might result from the cracking of a solid wood core, a very intricate technique was evolved whereby the round pillars themselves were built up out of individual segment-shaped planks.[6] There are no other examples of such pillars decorated with togidashi and mother-of-pearl inlay in the whole of Japan. They are master works of the artist-craftsmen of the Chūson-ji and are the most beautiful feature of the Konjiki-dō.

The upper part of the altar base, particularly the beams of the baldachin (Pl. 23) are also very richly adorned with mother-of-pearl inlay. The contrast between the gleaming milky white of the mother of pearl hōsōge medallions of various sizes and the warm gold of the lacquer ground, and the now greenish patina of the bronze openwork mountings is of extraordinary beauty. The combined superb craftsmanship, elegance of individual forms and the way the different materials and colours harmonize with each other culminate in a unique decorative effect.

The technique employed for inlaying the mother-of-pearl varies according to whether it is used architecturally – as in the Phoenix Hall and Konjiki-dō – or to decorate objects such as boxes, chests, saddles etc. On the latter objects the cut mother-of-pearl is glued to the ground, the lacquer is then built up to the same height (in many thin layers), and finally the whole surface is polished.[7] For large-scale architectural decoration this method would have required far too much expensive lacquer; so instead, the shape of the piece of mother-of-pearl to be inlaid was first carved out of the wooden ground, the mother-of-pearl was then inlaid and the whole covered with lacquer. Finally the lacquer was polished down to the level of the mother-of-pearl surface.[8]

A number of articles made around the date of the construction of the Chūson-ji also show gold lacquer (generally heijin; see p. 27) in combination with mother-of-pearl inlay. These are: an altar base (Pl. 24: *Raden hakkaku-shumidan*), two tables (Pl. 25: *Raden heijin-an*) and a lamp stand (*Raden heijin-tōdai*). All have been declared National Art Treasures and all clearly illustrate the outstanding technique and elegance of style of early twelfth-century lacquerwork.[9]

In order to do no more than hint at the inexhaustible abundance of

Plate 24 Altar base in the sutra hall of the Chūson-ji. ca 1109. Ht 52.4cm, diam.
193.9cm. Chūson-ji, Iwate province.

beauty, graciousness and elegance of this period, and to demonstrate by comparison what was typical for the period of Chūson-ji lacquerwork, it is worth referring to an only slightly earlier work in a very different field of the arts. The *Sanjūroku-nin kashū*, an anthology of poems, dating from 1112, now in the temple of Nishi-hongan-ji, owes its gem-like perfection not only to its fine calligraphy, but also to a variety of beautiful papers decorated with background pictures painted in gold and silver.[10] Both works, the Konjiki-dō and the anthology, are remarkable expressions of the spirit and refined taste of the Fujiwara period.

Only a few years later, in 1131 at the latest, a ceremonial quiver (*Kasuga-taisha hirayanagui*) now in the possession of the Kasuga shrine, also decorated with lacquer and mother-of-pearl inlay, was made.[11] The technique used here is unusual in that the small groups of rocks with bamboo grass and flying birds were first engraved in the protruding back which consisted of a yellow metal sheath over sandalwood and then filled in with black lacquer. (To complete the decoration, the back board was given a yellow metal appliqué surround.) There are no other instances of this kind of lacquer inlay.

A particularly famous example of the late Heian lacquerware is the oldest surviving toilet case (Pl. 27).[12] Its exterior surfaces are decorated with wagon wheels lying in water, from which the box takes its name (*Katawaguruma makie-tebako*). This motif, based on fact – wheels were laid in swift-running water to harden the wood – was very popular in the second

Plate 25 Table with mother-of-pearl inlay. Early 12th c. 77.5:66.3:33.5cm. Chūson-ji, Iwate province

half of the Heian period and throughout the Kamakure period. It also occurs, for instance, in the background paintings of the *Sanjūroku-nin kashū*, the anthology referred to above, and in the painted sutra fans in the Shitennō-ji in Osaka.

Seen in plan, the sides of the box bulge slightly, and the overlapping lid curves gently from the dust ledge to its crown. The proportions are gentle and pleasing, both with respect to the overall relationship of height, width and depth and the ratio between the height of the box and the height of the lid. The arrangement of the wheels in groups of two to four is unaffected and decorative. The wheels are made partly of engraved mother-of-pearl, partly of gold togidashi; the waves are also in togidashi on a black-lacquer ground sprinkled with heijin. There is no mother-of-pearl in the interior of either the box or the lid; instead, gold and silver togidashi provide the element of contrast in the decoration of birds, butterflies and sprays of

Plate 26 Back board of a quiver. ca 1131. Ht 32cm. Nara, Kasuga-taisha

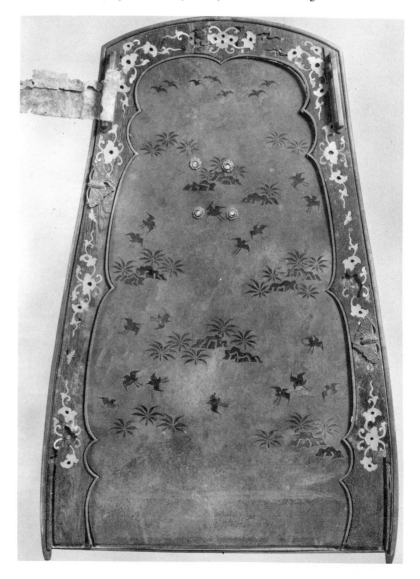

Plate 27 Toilet box with a motif of wheels in water. 2nd half (?) 12th c.
13:30.5:22.5cm. Tōkyō, Bunkazai Hogo Iinkai

Plate 28 Toilet box (see Pl.27). Detail of interior of lid

Plate 29 Chest with iris marsh and chidori birds. 12th c. 30.6:39.9:30.5cm.
Kongōbu-ji, Wakayama province

blossoms of various kinds (Pl. 28). [13] On the outer surfaces, where the colour accent is created by contrasting the gold lacquer and mother-of-pearl, silver dust has been dispensed with. There are, nevertheless, two distinct, though not strongly differentiated, shades of gold dust (yakigane and aokin).

Typical of this tebako and of eleventh- and twelfth-century pieces in general, are the rich yet gentle colour harmony, the way the decoration matches the quiet, well-proportioned shape with such apparent ease, the uncluttered rhythmic design and the elegance and finesse of style. How very different a box with the same motif, but made a hundred years later, was to look; how much more solid, incisive, metallic and cold (cf Pl. 56). [14]

Related to the katawaguruma toilet case by virtue of its colour harmony of gold, aokin and mother-of-pearl and the utterly Japanese style of the design and its entrancing beauty, is a small chest (barely 40cm long) decorated with irises, plantain and chidori birds, now in the Kongōbu-ji on the Kōyasan (Pl. 29: *Sawa-chidori raden-makie ko-karabitsu*). This chest, like the toilet case (Pl. 27), is considered one of the most important and characteristic masterpieces of the late Heian period even though neither can be more closely dated. The motif in its simple yet supremely elegant naturalism is completely Japanese: a close-up view of a straightforward, unassuming swamp landscape, spreading so naturally from the lid down the sides of the chest as if it had not been carefully composed. In few other works of art is the essence of the Japanese feeling for nature so clearly revealed. A. Soper has convincingly demonstrated how the difference between the landscapes of China and Japan engendered very different kinds of experience of nature in two peoples. Whereas for the Chinese the infinite extent and overwhelming majesty of his mountains, plains and streams is the determining factor, the Japanese stands in his more segmented and therefore smaller-scale landscape rather like a gardener observing his immediate surroundings with the gardener's affectionate eye for detail. [15] This intimacy, this gardener's proximity to nature can hardly be expressed more convincingly than in the decoration of this small chest.

The choice of motifs from nature as subjects for decoration and the pictorial style of execution are very characteristic of the second half of the Heian period. In ceramics, for instance, there are the incised autumn grasses and plants [16] of the roughly contemporary Tokoname ewer (Pl. 30), and in metalwork, the numerous mirrors decorated with landscapes. But in this iris chest, just as in the 'realistic' wheel motif of the katawaguruma box, Arakawa rightly points out that it is not a matter of simply copying nature, but rather that nature appears to be permeating the artist's heart through his eyes, thence to be reflected back like a dream. The image thus created is imbued with the spirit of poetry and gives the present-day observer some idea of the richness of feeling, craving for beauty and elegance of the late Heian period. The decoration of the chest might possibly have been inspired by a poetic work, the *Ise-monogatari*. The scene of one of the best-known episodes in the *Ise-monogatari* is an iris marsh; over the centuries, Japanese artists have again and again used it as a theme. In lacquer art the eight-fold-bridge writing box by Kōrin (Pl. 164) is the most famous example. Possibly the swamp landscape on the iris chest is one of the earliest pictorial treatments of this motif. [17]

Technically, the chest is a model of its kind. The decoration is mainly in togidashi, with gold and aokin dust providing the colour gradation. In addition, shading has been achieved by varying the amount of dust sprinkled – a technique called 'maki-bokashi' in Japanese – and applied principally on the patches of earth. Typical also of the late Heian period is the way finely engraved pieces of mother-of-pearl are inlaid here and there to enhance the lively colour effect.

Eleventh and twelfth centuries

Water, plantain and chidori are also represented on the outside of the richly decorated interior tray (kakego) of the chest (Pl. 31). Although the exact purpose of the chest is unknown, it may have been used to store cult implements. The black-lacquer ground of the floor of the tray (Pl. 32) is sprinkled with heijin and inlaid with openwork bronze-gilt rosettes and heraldic devices in mother-of-pearl. Both are of great stylistic interest and, again, are characteristic of the late Heian period. For they show how the complicated circular patterns of the Nara period are gradually simplified and developed into more distinct, tightly knit motifs resembling heraldic devices. [18] Already discernible in the scrolls of the early makie boxes, this

Plate 30 Ewer decorated with autumn grasses. 12th c. Ht 38.5cm

Plate 31 Tray from chest in Pl. 29

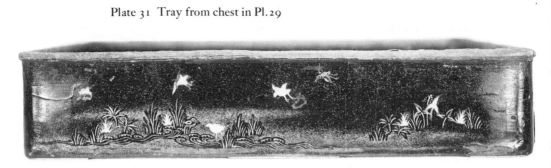

Plate 32 Floor of tray from chest in Pl. 29

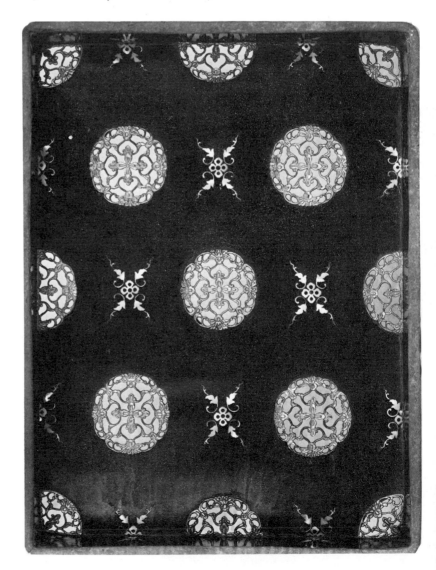

tendency appears everywhere by the eleventh and twelfth centuries.

A low, table-like priest's stool (Pl. 33), of the kind used at this time by the Shingon sect, shows this crest-like aspect in the lacquer decoration and in the metal mountings (*Rindō byakurō-makie raiban*).[19] The decoration is sprinkled in with a white powder, known as 'byakurō-fun,' made from an alloy of tin and lead. Byakurō is often mentioned in sources of the period,[20] and the paulownia and bamboo decoration on a sake bottle, attributed to the twelfth century,[21] is rendered in this powder.

Plate 33 Priest's stool. 12th c. 12.7:66:66cm. Tōkyō National Museum.

Plate 34 Chest with phoenix motif. End of 11th c. 59:92.3:67.7cm. Tōkyō National Museum

Circular patterns of this kind ('ban-e' in Japanese) are used to great effect as the sole decoration of another, considerably larger chest of the Heian period: the circular-pattern phoenix chest in the Tōkyō National Museum (Pl. 34).[22] The phoenix medallions are inlaid in a black-lacquer ground lightly sprinkled with heijin; the larger ones (on the lid and sides) are made up of several pieces of mother-of-pearl, the smaller ones (on six legs) are each cut out of a single piece. Again the lacquer ground inside the medallions is sprinkled with heijin, more densely in the large patterns than on the body of the chest, and so thickly in the small ones that it could almost be called ikakeji. Although the predominant impression of the black lacquer and mother-of-pearl contrast prevails, the apparently less important gold sprinkling has been carried out with great sensitivity to give those three distinct gradations. The bevelled edges of the legs are also densely sprinkled with heijin; this technique emphasizes their vertical aspect and their powerful supporting function in contrast to the heavy horizontal body of the chest. Such refinements demonstrate the artistic skill and precise planning that underlie the design of this chest.

Mizoguchi has pointed out that there is a literary reference, for the year 1029, to the decorative use in furniture of circular mother-of-pearl patterns in an ikake-ji ground.[23] And, since a study of the flower scrolls in gold and silver togidashi which decorate the inside of the lid of the chest reveals a

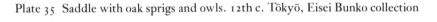

Plate 35 Saddle with oak sprigs and owls. 12th c. Tōkyō, Eisei Bunko collection

strong similarity to those on the lid of the sutra box in the Enryaku-ji, it is probably still justifiable to attribute the phoenix chest to the late eleventh century. The use of silver dust rather than aokin also argues against a later dating.

Four saddles from the end of the Heian period are decorated not with makie but exclusively with mother-of-pearl inlay in a lacquer ground. [24] Like almost all surviving saddles of the Heian and Kamakura periods, they are of the 'gunjin' type, that being the term for the robust saddles used in the field as opposed to the more elegant ceremonial saddles which are known as 'kara-gura.' They are the following:

Plate 35, saddle with oak sprigs and little owls (*Kashiwa ni mimizuki raden-gura*);
Plate 36, saddle with hagi sprigs (*Hagi raden-gura*);
Plate 37, saddle with peony decoration (*Botan raden-gura*);
Plate 38, saddle with rhomboid wave motifs (*Seikaiha raden-gura*).

In both the saddle with oak sprigs and owls and the peony saddle the decorative inlay consists not of compact pieces of mother-of-pearl, but either completely or in part, of a kind of detailed 'line' drawing in mother-of-pearl. This technically difficult process, which provides such a charming alternative to the plane nature of compact mother-of-pearl inlay, occurs for the first time in this period.

The rhomboid waves on the seikaiha saddle can be taken as a kind of *leitmotif* of the Heian period. They appear in the aforementioned *Sanjūrokunin kashū* anthology, and in the famous *Heikeno-kyo* sutra rolls of

Plate 36 Saddle with hagi decoration. Detail. 12th c. Tōkyō National Museum

1164, which are in the possession of the Itsukushima-jinja.[25] They also occur in another lacquer work of this period: the oldest surviving writing-

Plate 37 Saddle decorated with peonies. Detail. 12th c. Tōkyō National Museum

Plate 38 Saddle with wave motif. 12th c. Japan, private collection

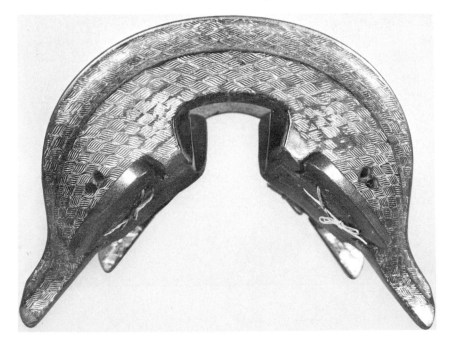

box (Pl. 39: *Suhama-u raden-suzuribako*)ᵢ It shows a pond in mother-of-pearl inlay in the centre of the lid; overlooking it a cormorant stands on a rock flapping its wings. The chidori birds, which fly around the pond singly or in groups, are sprinkled in with gold dust, and the decoration as a whole fits itself to the curve of the lid in an easy, natural manner.[26] Here, as in the katawaguruma box, the simple elegance and innate harmony between the shape of the object and the layout of the design are as remarkable as the way the inverted corners of the box echo the shape of the pond.

The stylized, rhomboid wave form is occasionally revived in the Muromachi period but is then generally festooned with the crinkly splashes of a wave-crest.

To a certain extent, the combination of gold lacquer and mother-of-pearl inlay may be considered typical of the second half of the Heian period. But at the same time, there are also pieces, the sole decoration of which consists of red or black lacquer, and others that are pure makie. In the former category belongs a 'takazuki,' a food stand, in the form of a small round table only 21cm high. Its supporting foot opens out below the table top into a chamfered carrying surface in the shape of a flower.[27] On its underside the table top is inscribed with the date 1165 and the name of a dignitary of the Tamukeyama-Hachiman shrine in Nara. Both in the Hachiman shrine and in the neighbouring Tōdai-ji, other objects bearing the same name have

Plate 39 Writing box with cormorant. 12th c. 5.8:27.3:27.3cm. Japan, private collection

survived. The food stand, now in a private collection, is in black lacquer, but the lacquer has flaked off in many places revealing the wooden substructure. Since it is not decorated at all, the takazuki is as useless from the point of view of the history of lacquer art as are numerous dated Negoro lacquers of the thirteenth and seventeenth centuries (cf. p.85); yet, on the other hand, like the latter pieces, its definite shape makes it important for a study of the development of the shapes of objects.

At the same time, their donor, Saeki Kagehiro, presented two small chests (*Matsugui-tsuru ko-karabitsu*) now also at Miyajima (Pl.40); the inscriptions on the undersides indicate that they were given as votive offerings to two subsidiary shrines of the Itsukushima-jinja; in other words, they are in the very place today for which they were made almost eight hundred years ago.[29] The robes of the Emperor Antoku (who reigned from 1180 to 1185) are said to have been kept in them.

Though very similar, the chests vary in the arrangement of their patterns, depicting flying cranes in gold and silver togidashi. The cranes carry pine twigs in their bills. This motif, which first occurs in the Heian period, is the Japanese adaptation of the phoenix biting on a neck ornament (cf. Pl.4) and the birds with flowering twigs in their bills (cf. Pl.7) – both used in China as early as the T'ang period. The 'pine-chewing crane' (matsugui-tsuru), however, is an exclusively Japanese motif. (The pine twigs originally indicated that the crane comes from or flies around the Hōraisan, the legendary mountain of immortality; they are, like the crane itself, symbols

Plate 40 Small chest with 'pine chewing cranes.' 1183. 21.8:31.8:25.1cm. Miyajima, Itsukushima-jinja

of longevity.)[30] These two chests are among the earliest instances of the use of this motif, which from then on was to occur frequently in Japanese art. Small pine twigs, in silver togidashi only, are scattered on the inside of the lids.

The elegant sophistication of the small iris chest (Pl. 29) was a matter of the past; the wars that had been raging between the Taira and Minamoto clans since 1156 had had a nefarious influence on the luxurious art of the Fujiwara period. Yet even these simple pieces show the same infallible good taste. An example is the way in which – in contrast to the lacquer decoration of the body of the chest – the six legs are inlaid with mother-of-pearl, thereby glowingly emphasizing their supporting function.

The following important twelfth-century works are decorated exclusively in makie, and make no use of mother-of-pearl:

Plate 41   Sutra box with Fudō representation. ca 1100(?). 5.8:19.1:31.2cm. Oku-in, Nara province

Eleventh and twelfth centuries

a sutra box in the National Museum Tōkyō with a symbolic representation of the Fūdō Myōō;

a number of dated (1175 and 1182 respectively) chests containing sutra boxes in the possession of the Nanatsu-dera, Nagoya;

a tebako with sparrows in a field, in the possession of the Kongō-ji, Osaka.

The sutra box in the National Museum (Pl.41: *Kurikara-ryū makie kyōbako*) must originally have had a tray between the lower section of the box and the lid. The lid is decorated with a dragon flanked by two attendants on rock bases in the sea, and the dragon itself is twisted around an upright sword. This strange representation points to Fūdō Myōō, a Buddhist deity, who is generally depicted with a sword in his right hand. Here, the god is represented by the dragon; its two attendants are Seitaku and Kongara. Falling lotus petals surround the figures and a lotus pool is depicted on the outer sides of the lower part of the box. The metal mountings for the tying cord are also in the form of lotus blossoms; the lotus as a Buddhist symbol plays a major role here. The box shows the slight bulge of the sides and lid typical of the second half of the Heian period; it is covered with black lacquer thinly sprinkled with heijin and decorated in gold and silver togidashi. The superbly composed representation on the lid is closely linked with Buddhist painting of the period; the shape of the box, lacquer technique and elegant brushwork point to a date of origin in the early twelfth

Plate 42 Intermediate lid of a sutra chest. 1175. Nagoya, Nanatsu-dera

century, possibly even a little earlier.

Between 1175 and 1182 a series of large chests designed to contain sutra boxes were made for the Nanatsu-dera (a temple in Nagoya). Each chest holds two sets of five boxes stacked next to each other and linked by a shared lid (not the lid of the chest but an intermediate lid fitting on the box tops proper). These intermediate lids have images of Yakushi Nyorai, Hannya Bosatsu or other Buddhist deities, each surrounded by sixteen to twenty minor beings of the Buddhist hierarchy (Pl.42). The dates are inscribed in red lacquer inside the lids.[31] These works, originating from 1175-1182, represent significant landmarks in the history of lacquerwork, inasmuch as here – for the first time – use is made of the hiramakie technique (cf. p.25) whereas in all earlier lacquer articles the sprinkled decor was togidashi. The 'old' technique, in this case silver togidashi, is still used for the wave design in the lower parts of the exterior of the sutra boxes (Pl.43). The lotus plants, however, are sprinkled on with relatively coarse gold dust without subsequent polishing down, so they are very slightly raised above the blackish lacquer ground. Gold hiramakie is also used for the decoration of the intermediate lids, in an unusual combination with red lacquer.[32]

The tebako with sparrows in a field (Pl.44: *Nobe ni suzume makie-tebako*), the fourth of these important pure makie works of the late Heian period, does not belong within the sphere of influence of Buddhist painting. The tebako is said to have been made for the personal use of Princess Hachijō-in (born 1137).

On the lid and the exterior faces of the box (extensively restored in places) a great artist has painted scenes from the life of the sparrow – strikingly observed and full of humour. The realistic treatment of the theme already heralds the approach of the Kamakura period. Yet the shape of the box, with its relatively flat, overlapping lid,[33] the heijin ground and the colour gradation of the rather coarse dust are still in the Fujiwara idiom. The alternation of gold and silver dust, in both the feathers of the birds and the grasses and plants, is remarkable and expressive, and the shading sprinkling technique (maki-bokashi) contributes to the lively ef-

Plate 43 Set of sutra boxes. 1175. Dimensions of the individual boxes 5.9:50.7:34cm. Tōkyō National Museum

fect of the patches of earth. Small plum twigs are depicted in silver togidashi inside the lid.

In reviewing the lacquerwork of the late Heian period and considering for this purpose three of its most important works – the Konjiki-dō (Pl. 21), the katawaguruma box (Pl. 27) and the small iris chest (Pl. 29) – the essential characteristics are: the purely Japanese style of the decoration, the finesse and elegance of the shape, and the sensitive gradation of the various shades of gold and silver, often used in combination with mother-of-pearl.

As far as style is concerned, from about the middle of the Heian period onwards three separate 'genealogies' can be distinguished: the continuing influence of the large circular designs of the Nara period, which gradually evolve into smaller and more crest-like shapes; the elements introduced from Chinese painting, which disappear temporarily, however, toward the end of the Fujiwara period, and lastly, the strong influence of Yamato-e. Owing to the latter, the largely ornamental decoration of the early Heian period is succeeded in turn by pictorial designs which sometimes show purely secular subjects even on items designed for religious use. Yet even when these motifs are taken from discernible reality, the representations remain far removed from crass naturalism – they are both simpler and more poetic than mere fidelity to nature could ever be.

In shape, the lacquerwork of the late Heian period is characterized by the gently curved boxes with their slightly domed lids. Already in the early Heian period the corners were generally rounded off, and the lid rose in a delicate S bend from the chiri-i, the dust ledge. But its top remained flat.

Plate 44 Toilet box with sparrows. Mid 12th c. 18.5:42:28.5cm. Osaka, Kongō-ji

Towards the end of the period, however, the lids are usually slightly domed. This domed lid, an important formal characteristic, the Japanese call 'kōmori.'

A simultaneous and parallel characteristic is the development of the slightly bulging sidewalls ('dōbari' in Japanese). The rectangular plan of the box seems to be breathing and stretching and, in so doing, assuming a slightly inflated shape. Kōmori and dōbari combined to give the boxes fuller, gentler outlines. Visually, the resulting impression is one of elegant flowing forms, on which harshness and angularity have been softened; in tactile terms, the shape now fits more snugly and naturally into the curve of the hand: the boxes are really made to be used. Also, their wooden substructure is composed of very thin laths, so that delicacy of form is matched with physical lightness. In contrast to the lively energy of the Nara period, which continued to be felt throughout the ninth and tenth centuries, the late Heian period produced lacquerwork of a more delicate, reticent nature, perfectly matched to the sensitive, aristocratic concept of beauty of that age.

Technically, typical characteristics are: the heijin grounds in which black lacquer is still important; the combination of gold, silver and frequently aokin dust, as well as the shading-off sprinkling technique of maki-bokashi; but primarily the combination of colour-differentiated makie with mother-of-pearl inlay, and the first use of hiramakie. Written sources of the period also frequently mention ikakeji, that is, a densely sprinkled gold ground. But apart from the round pillars of the Konjiki-dō, only a few such works have survived; for example a portable shrine (mikoshi) in the Hachiman shrine, Wakamiya-ken.[34]

Technique still remains uncomplicated, despite the excellence of the workmanship; the dust used for sprinkling is still not very fine-grained. Yet in the most admirable manner, the given technical means achieve and enhance complete harmony of form and decoration. This late Heian period lacquerwork – in itself never loud or coarse – is constantly entrancing to look at. Here, a peak of perfection has been achieved which cannot be surpassed in this particular line of endeavour. But already in some works a new spirit is manifest, and the lacquerwork of the Kamakura period applies itself to new and different objectives.

Kamakura period

4

IN ANY MEANINGFUL APPRECIATION OF KAMAKURA LACQUERWARE, THREE prime factors, which interact and enhance each other, must be taken into account: the tendency to realism apparent in all spheres of Japanese art in the thirteenth century; the masculine spirit of the new age, which strongly distinguishes itself from the lyrical elegance of the Fujiwara period; and lastly – in the craftsmanship proper of lacquer art – a great enrichment and refinement of technical skills. This newly developing technical standard is in itself the prerequisite for realistic representation.

In order to depict an object exactly, one must be able to show its contours sharply and clearly. That had not yet been possible with the lacquer techniques of the Heian period – which in any case, did not have that objective in view – because up to the end of the twelfth century, the gold used was not gold dust as such but consisted of the so-called 'yasuri-fun,' that is, fine gold and silver filings. These filings were by nature irregular in shape and uneven in size.[1] Consequently, no sharply defined outlines could be achieved, and if examined through a magnifying glass, a lacquer object of the Heian period clearly reveals a blurring and fuzziness of the edges.

In the Kamakura period the technique changed. More uniformly grained and finer dust was produced, and the particles were graded according to size. The so-called 'hirame-fun,' literally 'flat-eye dust,' represents the first step in this development. To make hirame-fun, the gold and silver fillings were scattered onto a copper plate, and copper rods, about 2.5cm in diameter, were rolled back and forth over the filings under pressure. When in this way the filings had been flattened out and expanded, sieves were used to grade the dust according to size. This hirame-fun is used from the Kamakura period onwards, especially for sprinkling the ground (hirame-ji). If this dust, which is still irregular in shape, is reduced even more, it becomes 'nashiji-fun.'[2]

Specifically, after a time, genuine, round-particled, comparatively fine gold dust was successfully manufactured, thus making possible the production of clearly defined outlines in sprinkling. The implements used to make this dust were a metal pestle or hammer with file-like grooves and a roughened metal plate as a base. By scattering the flattened gold filings onto the metal plate and grinding them with the pestle, they were further reduced in size and, even more important, rolled into a round shape.

Incidentally, also charcteristic of lacquerwork of the Kamakura period is the almost exclusive use of gold dust; the gentle harmony of the different shades of gold, aokin and silver, typical of the Heian period, is now replaced by the more assertive monochrome gold. At first, variety was achieved only by the use of different materials (mother-of-pearl, hyōmon) resulting in stronger contrasts. Towards the end of the Kamakura period, it is true, the gold colour was made to appear less uniform: a new kind of polychrome effect was obtained by using variously sized particles of gold dust, and by grading the density of the sprinkling (maki-bokashi). An almost total absence of silver may also be noted during the entire Muromachi period.

If the fine, even-grained dust of the Kamakura period made it possible to draw clearly defined contours, so, too, hiramakie and takamakie (see p.25) answered the demand for 'realistic' three-dimensional surfaces. Takamakie made its debut only towards the end of the era, to meet the requirements for ever greater precision and realism in representation. The same end was served by 'tsukegaki,' a process whereby fine raised lines were drawn with viscous lacquer on togidashi or hiramakie and then sprinkled with gold dust. From the middle of the Kamakura period onwards, this technique was popular and used frequently to depict waves or the details of feathers, blossoms, etc.

Kamakura period

Nor was it only in the decorative use of lacquer that three-dimensional values were introduced: but in the use of mother-of-pearl as well, here and there, thick inlays alternate with thin ones to make the surface more responsive to the touch.

But all these technical innovations, with their potential for naturalistic depiction, developed only gradually. The transition from the Heian to the Kamakura period did not take place abruptly. Even under the rule of the new war lords echoes of the court art of the late Fujiwara period remained, just as, conversely, works of the late twelfth century had already heralded the realistic technique of the Kamakura period (cf. Pl.44).

An excellent example of this unbroken transition is provided by the autumn field tebako in the Izumo shrine (*Akino ni shika makie-tebako*), a toilet case with a flush-fitting lid (Pl.45) and two interior trays. The lyricism, indeed the whole mood of the landscape depicted – which the deer and the hagi shrubs show to be autumnal – clearly echoes the Heian tradition. The simple elegance and poetry of the composition still bears comparison with the small sawa-chidori chest (Pl.29). Both works also have much in common

Plate 45 Toilet box with autumn field decoration. Lid from above (see Pl.46)

in their distribution of colour and in their predominant use of gold togidashi and mother-of-pearl.

But the shape of the box is now in a new idiom (Pl. 46): the bulging of the sides and of the lid (dōbari and kōmori) is more pronounced than in the Heian period, and instead of gradually rising in a gentle S bend from the dust ledge to the top of the lid, the cover now rises directly in a forceful curve.

The lid no longer overlaps, as it generally did in the Heian period, but sits flush on the box; its sides are directly above those of the box, thereby emphasizing the vertical tendency. Also, the box itself is now appreciably higher in relation to the lid, which gives an impression of stability and weight. This shape clearly foreshadows the heavy, powerful boxes made at the height of the Kamakura period.

The gold dust is still rather coarse. But what is new is the idea of varying the manner of sprinkling by using nashiji as a new shade of gold within the decoration itself; in this case for the rocks and the fur of the roe-deer.[3] Later in the Momoyama period, very similar use was made of 'picture-nashiji' (e-nashiji), whereas in Muromachi lacquerwork nashiji only occurs in the form of ground sprinkling.

The manner of the representation – the way the deer hold their heads and the movement of some of the birds – is based on close observation of nature, something not yet common in the more poetically generalized designs of the Heian period. (In this respect the sparrow tebako in Plate 44, which dates from the end of the Heian period, is definitely a herald of the future.) A comparison of bird subjects of the Heian period with those of the Kamakura period shows that the earlier birds do not really seem to be flying but rather to be hovering in an uncertain way. Only beginning with the Kamakura period (that is, starting at the end of the twelfth century) is movement understood and represented as such.[4]

Plate 46 Toilet box with autumn field decoration. ca 1200. 16:29.7:22.8cm. Izumo-taisha, Shimane province

Despite the exact observation of nature indicated by these details the actual size relationship between the deer, birds, insects and hagi bushes is blithely ignored – a characteristic shared by the Yamato-e painting of the period (and like so much else, it is taken up again in the Momoyama period).

This picture is not simply one of roe-deer and bushes; it has the extraordinary power of suggestion which makes the mood of autumn take complete hold of the observer. The simple and irresistable way in which this happens is characteristic of the most beautiful Japanese works of art. Even among the best boxes of the Kamakura period, this *Akino ni shika-tebako* occupies a position of pre-eminence.

Also still closely linked with the Heian tradition is the surviving fragment (Pl. 47) – now mounted as a lid for a small box – of what was very likely quite a large lacquer object, probably made in the first decade of the thirteenth century.[5] The fragment shows a section of the 'Western Paradise' with buildings and Bodhisattvas, probably closely related iconographically to the woven cult image in the Taima-dera (see p. 22). Representations of Buddha are very rare in lacquer art: next to the Tamamushi shrine (whose lacquer painting cannot really be likened to the makie of the fragment), only the sutra box depicting the good deeds of the Buddha (Pl. 19), the representations of the Buddha on the round pillars of the Konjiki-dō (Pl. 22) and the Kurikara-ryū sutra box (Pl. 41) have survived – not counting a few small fragments, probably dating from about 1200, which were at some stage made up into a small box (now in the Boston Museum of Fine Arts). In K. Tomita's opinion, the latter originally formed part of a representation of the Amida Raigō.[6]

The fragment in Cleveland is admirably worked almost exclusively in gold dust of a single shade. But, by varying the density of the sprinkling onto the black ground, the result manages to suggest several different shades. The soft, velvety impression of this example of makie is very different from the metallic quality frequently seen in gold lacquer objects produced at the height of the Kamakura period.

Another work of the beginning of the Kamakura period, the Sumiyoshi

Plate 47 Fragment of a representation of the Western Paradise. ca 1210. 14.7:7.8cm. The Cleveland Museum of Art

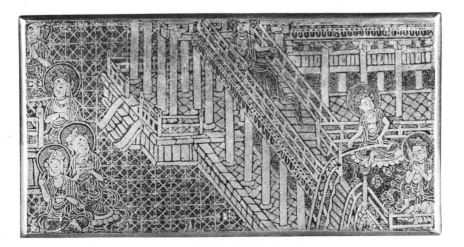

tebako in the Rinnō-ji near Nikkō (Pl.48: *Sumiyoshi makie-tebako*),[7] is inscribed with the date 1228. The decoration on the lid and outer sides of the box shows a moonlit night on the pine-clad coast of Sumiyoshi near Osaka, with the 'torii'[8] of the Sumiyoshi shrine and the mountainous island of Awaji in the background. The decoration is rendered in silver togidashi and silver hyōmon and, probably as a result of adding tin to the silver dust, is heavily corroded. Nor is the black lacquer ground well preserved. Surprisingly, the lacquermaster used red lacquer to represent the torii, so in both technique and colour this box is something of an exception.

Its proportions still correspond to the tebako shapes of the twelfth century: the lid takes up about a quarter of the total height. In later Kamakura boxes it was reduced to a fifth as the lower parts of the boxes gradually grew larger and sturdier.

The box is particularly interesting from the iconographic point of view since it is the earliest surviving example in lacquerwork of a representation of the Sumiyoshi landscape. Some fifty years before the box was made, Minamoto Yorimasa (1105-1180) died. His Sumiyoshi poem, 'Peering through the pines of the River Sumi I see the moon setting over the island mountains of Awabi', provided a constant source of inspiration for Japanese artists of the Kamakura and particularly of the Muromachi period. The decoration of this tebako might also be based on the poem but this cannot be established with absolute certainty.[9] The representation is simple, both in overall composition and in individual details yet for all its simplicity it has a certain dignity and distinction.

Plate 48 Toilet box with Sumiyoshi representation. 1228. 17:33:26cm. Nikkō, Rinnō-ji (reproduced from Casal, *Japanese Art Lacquers*)

In addition to this box of 1228, two more dated works have survived from the first half of the thirteenth century: the two three-part doors of the Mandara shrine in the Taima-dera (*Renchi makie-tobira*), dated 1242 and decorated in makie, and the base of the shrine, dated 1243 (*Taima-mandara-zushi no raden-shumidan*), richly inlaid with mother-of-pearl. The doors, made when the shrine was already more than four hundred years old (see p.22), are decorated with the Buddhist motif of the lotus pool (Pl.49)[10] and bear a long inscription, also in makie. It records not only the date of origin, 1242, but also the names of many of the donors – including that of the Shōgun Fujiwara Yoritsune – and the name of the lacquermaster Fujiwara Sadatsune. This is interesting for two reasons. First, it demonstrates why the Fujiwara style continued right into the middle of the thirteenth century: members of the Fujiwara clan continued to commission and carry out such work. Second, the inscription makes it possible to link a

Kamakura period

Plate 49 Fujiwara Sadatsune: doors of the Mandara shrine. 1242. 353:189cm. Taima-dera, Nara province

specific piece of lacquerwork, that is, the doors, with the name of a specific lacquermaster, which is very unusual for this period. Though contemporary written sources do in fact quote the names of about thirty lacquermasters, there is no indication of which particular objects they made. [11]

The doors show waves, lotus plants and numerous petals, seemingly floating down from the sky, all in gold togidashi on a black-lacquer ground. Nashiji is also occasionally used within the decoration itself. The lotus blossoms are depicted both in profile and head on; the leaves, too, vary in shape. Nevertheless, the overall composition remains serene and uncluttered and admirably suited to the large format – the doors being more than 3m high. Most recent research has proved, surprisingly, that the present decoration of the doors is not the original of 1242, but an exact overpainting (or sprinkling-in). With the aid of infra-red rays one can make out the original design under the present black-lacquer ground. The present decoration, probably carried out some fifty to one hundred years later, does largely correspond to the original design, but in places its lines stray by a few millimetres. The lowest waves and the topmost written characters have been partially lost as a result of the later over-lacquering. [12]

The mother-of-pearl decoration on the base of the Mandara shrine (Pl. 50) appears, at first sight, not to tally with the date of 1243, also inlaid in mother-of-pearl at the base, since the large, completely unnatural hōsōge flowers are themselves at variance with the naturalistic taste of the Kamakura period. Also the tendency towards pattern, the way in which the plants are shaped into a decorative device capable of enlargement in every direction, would indicate a much earlier date of origin. But this relationship

Plate 50 Base of the Mandara shrine. Detail. 1243. Taima-dera, Nara province

with forms of the Nara period is the result of a kind of Nara renaissance to be found also in other instances of the art of the Kamakura period. In the thirteenth century many old temples destroyed during the wars of the Heian period were being rebuilt, and the resulting close contact with works of art of past eras stimulated the revival of certain stylistic elements of the Nara period.[13] That in lacquerwork this renaissance should manifest itself more strongly in mother-of-pearl than in makie work may be attributed to the nature of the material itself. Mother-of-pearl is definitely less easy to use for realistic representation than makie, but probably not all that difficult for stylized hōsōge scrolls etc.

The lotus pond motif that was employed for the doors of the Taima shrine recurs on a sutra box in the Kajū-ji temple in Kyōto (Pl. 51: *Renchi makie-kyōbako*) – that is, again within the sphere of Buddhism.[14] The box consists of three superimposed sections and a lid. Still in the tradition of late Heian boxes are the very slight curvature of the sides and lid, the gentle S-shaped initial rise of the lid, the heijin-sprinkled ground and the additional use of silver togidashi for the waves and for the lotus petal decoration inside the lid and all three tiers of the box.

The obviously deliberate parallel arrangement of the stalks, however, and the neat regularity in the distribution of the drifting petals, show a

Plate 51   Sutra box with lotus pool. 1st half of 13th c. 20.3:21.2:33.9cm. Kyōto, Kajū-ji

degree of conscious rationalization which argues for a date of origin in the Kamakura period. Furthermore, a comparison with earlier lotus representations (Pl.43) reveals the greater realism, for example, in the drawing of the leaves.

Probably the sutra box was made a little earlier than the doors of the Taima-dera, that is, in the first half of the thirteenth century. Its 'old-fashioned' characteristics, reminiscent of the Heian period, again bear witness to the continuing influence of the Heian style, but they probably also owe something to the conservative attitude often apparent in Buddhist decorative art. In the temples and monasteries new fashions were largely ignored in favour of given forms; once established as ideally suited for religious use, it was not abandoned lightly.

Still dating from the beginning of the thirteenth century is the famous writing-box with chrysanthemums by a fence (Pl.52: *Magaki-kiku raden ikakeji-suzuribako*), now in the possession of the Tsurugaoka Hachiman shrine in Kamakura. Next to the Suhama writing-box (Pl.39) it is the oldest surviving suzuribako, and since all its accessories – water-dropper, ink stick, ink container, brush cover, paper piercer, scissors, etc. – have sur-

Plate 52 Writing-box with chrysanthemums by the East Fence. Early 13th c. 5.5:24.2:25.8cm. Kamakura, Tsurugaoka Hachiman-gū

vived, it is very important from the point of view not only of art history, but also of cultural history. Both its shape – the overlapping lid is only slightly curved – and the style of the mother-of-pearl inlay indicate a date of origin in the early Kamakura period.

With the utmost artistry, the motif of the chrysanthemums by the East Fence – originally derived from a Chinese poem[15] – is first magnificently stated on the lid (inlaid with mother-of-pearl on ikakeji ground) and then repeated in variations on all the other parts: inside the lid, on both trays to the right and left of the ink stone, even on the floor of the box under the trays and indeed also on the water dropper.

The oldest surviving examples of mother-of-pearl inlay in the densely sprinkled gold ground known as ikakeji are the pillars of the Konjiki-dō (cf. Pl. 22); this writing-box is, therefore, in no sense an innovation. But the radiant glow of the ikakeji is particularly appealing to the ardent vitality of the Kamkura period. There is a group of ikakeji-raden lacquer objects, beginning perhaps with this writing-box, which were to become characteristic – in a variety of styles – of the mid-Kamakura period. Two of these objects, a quiver (Pl. 53: *Ikakeji gyōyō raden hirayanagui*) and a sword

Plate 52a Writing-box with chrysanthemums by the East Fence (cf. Pl. 52); opened box

scabbard,[16] were made at much the same time as the writing-box. Both have an apricot leaf design of mother-of-pearl on ikakeji ground, and both, like the writing-box, are in the possession of the Tsurugaoka Hachiman gū.

Although temple tradition links them with Minamoto Yoriyoshi (998-1075), both – like the chrysanthemum writing-box (allegedly a gift from the ex-Emperor Goshirakawa to Minamoto Yoritomo, 1177-1199) – are now generally accepted as works of the early Kamakura period. They were probably made in about the last decade of the twelfth century.

Related to them in time is a suebako in the Daigo-ji,[17] a lidless box used by Buddhist priests to store items of clothing. (The box also has a smaller companion piece.) Here, too, the more heraldic than naturalistic shapes of the mother-of-pearl inlay, which are related to the decoration on the low front section of the quiver, suggest a date hardly later than 1200.

For all their rich, golden glow, these four pieces – writing-box, quiver, sword scabbard and suebako – possess a serene beauty and almost reticent

Plate 53 Quiver with mother-of-pearl inlay. ca 1190. Ht 43.4cm. Kamakura, Tsurugaoka Hachiman-gū

elegance; yet, typical of the middle of the Kamakura period and produced by the same technique, is a more powerful, colder, more metallic appearance. The courtiers' distinction no longer prevails in lacquerwork; instead, the warlike spirit of the aristocracy of the sword is now in the ascendant.

A group of toilet boxes illustrates this style at the height of the Kamakura period. First is the tebako with butterfly decoration (Pl. 54: *Chō raden-makie tebako*), which probably still dates from the first half of the thirteenth century. The powerful masculine spirit of the Kamakura period is quite unmistakable. The shape and technique no longer owe anything to the Heian period, and, stylistically as well, only a few individual scrolls are reminiscent of the past. The first impression created by this tebako is one of radiant strength and magnificence: the consequence, mainly, of the materials used and the admirable workmanship. The box seems to speak with three voices: gold togidashi, mother-of-pearl inlay and silver hyōmon; each technique, each material is of equal validity, equal importance in the lavish decoration. The nashiji ground[18] bears a dense pattern of peony scrolls and butterflies: the scrolls and leaves in togidashi, the butterflies and blooms in sheet silver or mother-of-pearl. The silver and mother-of-pearl are themselves decorated with gold lacquer and have in addition, particularly the wings of the butterflies, an exquisitely delicate engraving which in turn has gold dust rubbed into it. Neither togidashi, hyōmon nor raden are new

Plate 54 Toilet box with butterfly decoration. First half of 13th c.
21.2:35.1:26.4cm. Tōkyō, Hatakeyama Museum

techniques. What is new is their simultaneous use in a way which does not fuse their individual identities in a common expression but rather allows each to realize fully its own potential.[19] Visually, this 'multitude of voices' is almost too strong (a photograph does not adequately convey the effect of the different materials), yet the impression of fiery splendour is overwhelming. And the shape of the box, with its relatively high bottom section and lowset metal mountings for the tying cord, gives a feeling of stability and strength which admirably matches the decoration. The low setting of the mountings is characteristic of the fully developed Kamakura style; a comparison of the butterfly box with the Sumiyoshi tebako (Pl.48), demonstrates the effect of this lowering of the optical centre of gravity.

The small patterns which decorate the wings of the butterflies also merit particular attention. A wealth of different round patterns are used: commas, spirals, circular stamped patterns, nine-ring patterns (kuyō), even

Plate 55 Hand guard of a suit of armour. 13th c. Nara, Kasuga-taisha

wheels and plum blossoms. Every single one is carefully and 'realistically'
worked, but the application is by no means even remotely naturalistic – such patterns are quite definitely not found on real butterflies.
This element of fantasy, also manifested in the arbitrary-size relationships
of the autumn field box in the Izumo shrine (Pl.45), in the otherwise realistic style of the Kamakura period was by no means restricted to lacquerwork. One of the most convincing examples and a close parallel to the
butterfly box is the hand guard from a knight's suit of armour (Pl. 55): in the
midst of naturalistic chrysanthemums, it shows a butterfly whose wings are
covered with designs based on pure fantasy. [20] This combination of fact and
fantasy is typical of the Kamakura period; it is not found in either the
preceding Heian or the following Muromachi periods. In this respect, too,
the butterfly tebako is an excellent and unmistakable example of Kamakura
art.

The most famous work of this period and, indeed, one of the best-known
items of Japanese lacquerwork is the *Katawaguruma-tebako* in the Tōkyō
National Museum (Pl.56). Here too is mother-of-pearl in gold lacquer, but
how compact and virile it is compared with articles made around 1200. A
comparison of this tebako with the one in Plate 27, which is decorated with
the same motif of wheels in water but was made about a century earlier,
most vividly illustrates the enormous difference between typical Heian
and typical Kamakura pieces. The former is a low, 'gentle' box with overlapping, barely curved lid, and rich in nuances: on the outside the delicate
gradation of gold dust and aokin on black-lacquer ground sprinkled with
heijin combined with mother-of-pearl; on the inside gold and silver togidashi. The latter has the bold, precipitous, mid-thirteenth-century

Plate 56 Toilet box with a motif of wheels in water. Mid 13th c. 21:35.5:27.3cm.
Tōkyō National Museum

shape, enhanced by the low-set mountings and the powerfully domed, flush-fitting lid; its colour is pure, unbroken gold, without any gradation, contrasting with the accents of gleaming mother-of-pearl. Such is the Kamakura style: solid, clear-cut and masculine – even the lacquerwork of this knightly age seems to evoke the cold metal of weapons of war.

Plate 57 Toilet box with fusenryō patterns. Mid 13th c. 21.5:36:26.6cm. Tōkyō, Suntory Gallery

Plate 58 Diary of Murasaki Shikibu. Detail. 1st half 13th c. Tōkyō, Gotō Museum

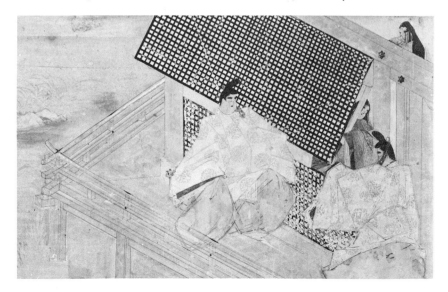

Plate 59 Toilet box with plum trees and geese. Early 14th c. 19.7:34.5:25.8cm.
Mishima-taisha, Shizuoka province

Contemporary, if not slightly earlier, is a tebako in the same spirit, with round patterns (Pl. 57: *Fusenryō-mon makie-tebako*). Originally used for textiles only, 'fusenryō-mon' gradually became a standard term for all large, circular patterns. It is certainly no coincidence that such patterns appear in lacquerwork around the middle of the Kamakura period, for, since about 1230, the influence of Chinese weaving of the Sung period had given Japanese textile art in Kyōto fresh impetus,[21] and circular patterns of this kind were apparently very fashionable for the clothes of the nobility, as can be seen in many contemporary paintings. It is not surprising that the lacquer artists who worked for the nobility should have adapted this popular motif for their own purposes (Pl. 58).

Many different flowering plants and grasses are represented in gold togidashi inside the lid. Such motifs were also frequently used for lid interiors in the Heian period, but whereas decorative, stylized elegance was the dominant characteristic then, this lid is almost like a botanical textbook in its very life-like depiction of flowers, leaves, grasses and twigs. If in the Heian period the love of nature was expressed in terms of mood transcended by human emotion (cf. the iris chest, Pl. 29), then in the Kamakura period it is expressed through exact, objective observation and description. (Reference has already been made to the elements of fantasy that sometimes mingle with pure realism.)

The 'metallic' katawaguruma and fusenryōmon tebako epitomize the style of the mid-Kamakura period, a style which probably only lasted until about 1280 (when the Mongol invasions were repulsed). A toilet box with plum-tree decoration (Pl. 59), the *Ume makie-tebako* of the Mishima-taisha shrine, seems nearer to the end of the era. It is one of the great masterpieces of Japanese lacquerwork and a standard work of its period. No definite date can be put to it, but Okada is probably right in attributing it to the beginning of the fourteenth century.[22]

The decoration of the lid and the side walls shows the edge of a pond planted with two kinds of plum tree – one with single, the other with double blossoms – and, on the water and in flight, a flock of wild geese. The inside of the lid has a similar subject (with pines instead of plum trees, Pl. 60), and the portrayal of the geese and their different patterns of motion, on land, on water and in the air, is even finer and more varied here than on the outside. This is the realism of the Kamakura period at its beautiful, triumphant best. Two trays, which fit one inside the other, repeat the geese motif.

Incorporated into the design on the lid are six written characters taken from a poem by the Chinese poet Po Chü-i (772-846). The design is, therefore, an example of 'uta-e,' that is, a picture into which a few individual written characters are scattered and more or less integrated within the representational scene.[23] Such characters, never giving the complete text of the poem they are taken from, evoke to the erudite connoisseur the mood of a particular poem. The representational lacquer decoration need not be an exact 'illustration' of the poem; rather the characters, evoking the poem in the spectator's mind, give an additional and deeper meaning to an otherwise independent and self-sufficient decoration. It is not surprising that a Chinese poem was chosen for this box, since, by this time, strong currents of Chinese culture had long ago re-entered Japanese thinking through the intermediary of Zen Buddhism.

Although this tebako is the earliest example of takamakie, the unknown lacquer-artist applies many other techniques as well: ikakeji, togidashi, tsukegaki, silver hyōmon, as well as all kinds of gold-dust sprinkling like maru-fun, hirame, and nashiji. In contrast to the relief technique of the takamakie (for the trunks of the trees, the double blossoms, the wild geese etc.), the hyōmon used for the single blossoms and the written characters is recessed in the ground, one layer deeper than the surrounding ikakeji. This three-dimensional layering, hitherto unknown, results in an enormous enrichment, in both visual and tactile terms. The surface, very much alive with its relief patterns, produces new accents and gradations of light and dark, which themselves create intricate but pleasing effects.

This tebako from the Mishima-taisha shows that all the sprinkling techniques up to and including takamakie were now fully developed towards the end of the Kamakura period and that the lacquermasters were in full control. Equally evident is the fact that these various processes were now used in a carefully worked-out, pre-planned manner to obtain the desired effect. (A definite step forward from the butterfly tebako in Pl. 54.) It should be noted that this absolute mastery of techniques, this studied, rational basic attitude, is as essential a characteristic of Kamakura lacquers as is the 'realism' of representation and the power, austerity and incisiveness.

Two trays in the tebako are fitted out with a complete set of toilet articles: a mirror, a mirror case, powder boxes, small containers for the

Plate 60 Toilet box (see Pl. 59). Interior of lid

blacking used to colour the teeth, boxes for perfume, combs, hair pins, scissors and tweezers. The trays, small boxes and containers are all decorated with the same subjects as the tebako, but corresponding to the size of each container, in a simplified form for both the motifs and the techniques.

The rational element, quite unmistakable already in the *Ume-makie tebako*, was so intensified towards the very end of the Kamakura period that it culminated in strictly mathematical exercises in some toilet boxes made at that time. The examples illustrated clearly reveal this mathematical element: the tebako in the Tōkyō National Museum (Pl.61: *Hiōgi-mon-chirashi makie-tebako*) with its decoration of clusters of hinoki-wood fans, by the regular four-lobed central form; the box with painted fans (Pl.62: *Ōgi-chirashi makie-tebako*),[24] by the emphasis on the four corners. The decoration in both cases is directly related to the shape of the box, the corners are emphasized and a central field is created. Though the artists most elegantly avoided complete regularity, nevertheless there is a clearly manifested desire for order in accordance with definite laws.

At the same time, the rather cold, metallic colour harmony, which had been so typical since the middle of the period, was now replaced by a warmer effect with richer nuances. Although in these boxes, too, only pure gold dust is used, the lacquermasters manage to achieve shading of great sensitivity by varying the density of the sprinkling (maki-bokashi) and the fineness of the grain; hirame-fun and nashiji-fun are used in addition to maru-fun. This colour gradation also prevents the lobed fields[25] of the Hiōgi tebako and similar boxes from becoming tediously schematic.[26] A

Plate 61 Toilet box with decoration of hinoki-wood fans. Early 14th c. 17:30.3:23.6cm. Tōkyō National Museum

changing sense of beauty is reflected in this desire for obtaining varying colour effects from gold. The full awareness of technical possibilities and the virtuosity in applying them is revealed in both the composition and the calculated use of the numerous technical resources at the artists' disposal.

Takamakie is no longer used on these boxes: only togidashi and light hiramakie are employed. [27] The Ōgi-chirashi tebako–most attractive for the graceful life-like precision of the decorative fan motifs–features a new element, technically speaking: the use of kirigane – sheet gold cut into small squares and individually inlaid. Although later, in the Muromachi period, they are used in groups to distinguish areas of light and shade, to emphasize the pictorial structure or to give the impression of greater volume, here, they are purely decorative: occasional highlights and accents.

As in the Ume-makie-tebako (Pl.59), the decoration of this tebako is further enriched by the use of written characters, though only inside the lid. The willow and the plum tree motif is not intended to illustrate the poem to which the characters *chō-sei-den* (Hall of Long Life) refer. Visual representation and literary association are essentially independent of each other, with no, or at most only a tenuous, connection between them.

The Kamakura period witnesses changes not only in the decorative principle and the nature of the colouring, but also in the proportions of the boxes. When a comparison is made of various tebako in the sequence so far

Plate 62 Toilet box with motif of painted fans. Early 14th c. 14.3:29.7:22.8cm. Tōkyō, Ōkura-Shūkokan

determined by reasons of style and technique, the following relationships of width to height are established:[28]

HEIAN
| Katawaguruma-tebako | (Pl. 27) | w:ht = 2.35 |
| Sparrow tebako | (Pl. 44) | w:ht = 2.27 |

KAMAKURA
Autumn field tebako	(Pl. 46)	w:ht = 1.85
Sumiyoshi-tebako	(Pl. 48)	w:ht = 1.94
Butterfly tebako	(Pl. 54)	w:ht = 1.65
Fusenryōmon-tebako	(Pl. 57)	w:ht = 1.67
Katawaguruma-tebako	(Pl. 56)	w:ht = 1.69
Plum tree tebako	(Pl. 59)	w:ht = 1.75
Hinoki-wood fan tebako	(Pl. 61)	w:ht = 1.78
Painted fan tebako	(Pl. 62)	w:ht = 2.07

It can be seen from the above figures that, beginning with the Heian period, the ratio of width to height at first decreases steadily: the boxes gain in vertical bias. The 'metallic' tebako of the mid-Kamakura period represent the peak of this development; then after gradual decline, the box with the painted fans (in which the metallic effect has also completely disappeared)

Plate 63 Kōgō.. 13th c. Tōkyō National Museum

finally returns to the flatter proportions of the twelfth-century boxes; the bold, powerful style of the Kamakura period is a matter of the past.

The tebako are such a characteristic *leitmotif* of the Kamakura period that one can trace in them the whole development of makie. Of course there are also a great many other items decorated with gold lacquer: the writing and sutra boxes already mentioned, some comb boxes (kushibako),[29] and a large number of small boxes and containers some of which probably were originally parts of the tebako, but which today are generally described as kōgō (incense boxes; Pl.63).[30] They too tend to have squat, sturdy shapes and are usually decorated with life-like vegetable or animal motifs in togidashi or hiramakie, sometimes on ikakeji. The compositions of simple, uncluttered aspects admirably suit the small format of the boxes. Later in the Muromachi period the designs, even on the small kōgō, are frequently much more intricate.

A small comb box decorated with fine, careful makie work (Pl.64: *Sumiyoshi makie-raden-kushibako*), was probably made about the same time as the Ogi-chirashi tebako (Pl.62) at the end of the Kamakura period.[31] The comb box is only 16 cm long and its shape appears to be typical of comb boxes in general: it has rounded corners and an overlapping lid, which, in order to provide a better grip, has had a tri-lobate section cut out of the bottom edge of the long sides. Only two comb boxes of this kind have survived the late Kamakura period; a third probably dates from the later fourteenth century. On the top of the lid is a view of the Sumiyoshi shrine (Pl.65; cf. Pl.48); inside the lid is a coastal scene with fishermen pulling in their nets. The exteriors of box and lid are decorated with a number of different kinds of autumn plants, all skillfully harmonized with each other. The individual forms are simple but the large variety of motifs is amazing. Technique and colour effect also combine richness and fine gradation: al-

Plate 64 Comb box with Sumiyoshi decoration. Early 14th c. 9.5:16.1:13.2cm. Japan, private collection.

though togidashi on a nashiji ground is dominant, details are variously presented in ikakeji, silver dust, mother-of-pearl, hiramakie and tsukegaki. This kushibako is a good example of the very high standard of artistry achieved by the lacquerworkers of the time. So sure is the sense of style the lacquermaster exercises over his great repertoire of techniques that, for all its richness, the intended clarity and simplicity in the representation of nature have been fully achieved. The effect of these lacquerworks is so convincing that at first glance one might almost overlook the exact balance of their proportions, the subtlety of the composition and the great technical quality.

Just as the sprinkling techniques come to full flower in this period, so too, at the end of the Kamakura period, the standard of pure (that is, unadorned) mother-of-pearl inlay in a lacquer ground is truly masterly. The most famous example is the *Shigure* saddle (Pl.66), which takes its name (autumn shower) from the text of the poem that inspired its decoration.[32] Some written characters of the poem are included among the storm-tossed pines of the design; this literary association gives the content of the picture a depth that extends beyond the purely visual. The dry, brittle mother-of-pearl has been cut and inlaid in the curved walls of the saddle with consummate skill. The alternation of rigid and flexible lines, cut openwork and solid inlays is superb; equally splendid in this connection is the way in which the colour is distributed in the black-lacquer ground. A saddle with cherry blossom decoration (Pl.67: *Sakura raden-gura*) is in much the same spirit as the *Shigure* saddle but appears to have been made somewhat later, perhaps around the beginning of the Muromachi period. Both saddles represent the absolute zenith of the art of mother-of-pearl inlay in a lacquer ground.

Plate 65 Comb box with Sumiyoshi decoration. (See Pl.64). Lid from above.

To the lacquermasters of the time, makie and raden were old, traditional techniques which were constantly improved upon. Towards the end of the Kamakura period, however, new developments appear: the beginning of what is known as Negoro-nuri and perhaps also of Kamakura-bori. (For Kamakura-bori see the following chapter.)

Negoro-nuri does not really come into its own until the Muromachi period, and will be dealt with more fully in a later chapter. But it originates in the last decade of the thirteenth century. In 1288 Bishop Raiyu Sōjō and his pupils moved down from Mount Kōyasan to the nearby temple of Negoro, and the name Negoro-nuri derives from the lacquer objects the priests subsequently made there for their daily use.[33]

The term is, in fact, used not so much to describe the implements made in the temple proper (not a single surviving Negoro lacquer can be traced back to the temple), but rather as a generic name for a group of undecorated lacquerwares distinguished by the peculiar character of their red-lacquer coatings. The term designates objects with a characteristically thick 'tough' layer of red lacquer which has been worn away in places by long use, revealing irregular patches of the underlying black lacquer. The colour effect of such pieces can be outstandingly beautiful; it is particularly prized in Japan today and deliberately produced in modern works. The name also includes objects in which the red lacquer is used in combination either with transparent lacquer on a natural-wood base or with black lacquer; the black lacquer in this case is not used as a foundation beneath the red lacquer.

As a descriptive term, therefore, 'Negoro-nuri' is not clearly defined.

Plate 66 Shigure saddle. ca 1300. Tōkyō, Eisei Bunko collection

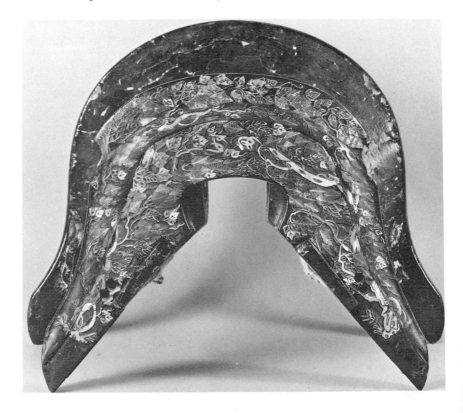

Nor is it any more precise from the point of view of dating, since it is used in an unhistorically broad sense both for objects which were made before 1288 and for objects that were made after the destruction of the Negoro temple in 1585.

Red or red and black lacquered furniture and utensils already existed in the Heian period and, in spite of its early date, a red-lacquer table made in 1164 is regarded today as an example of Negoro lacquerwork. [34] The colour and character of the lacquer skin are the decisive factors.

The dates on the Negoro lacquers of the Kamakura period correspond to the years 1261, 1262, 1298, 1305, 1307, 1330 and 1332. The majority, and certainly the most beautiful specimens of this type of work, were only made after the end of the Kamakura period. Almost without exception they are utensils for eating and drinking, vegetable hampers, oil jars (Pl.68), serving dishes, etc., often in sets of several pieces.

Experts in Japan make a distinction among Negoro lacquers in a purely Japanese style, those in a Chinese-influenced mixed style and, finally, those in a Chinese style. [35] (The latter were not made until the Muromachi period.) In all these completely undecorated objects the style is determined by shape alone. The simple round shape of a plate dated 1298 is purely Japanese. [36] But other items made at almost the same time clearly reveal Chinese influence – perhaps in the way the handle sits on the vegetable container in the illustration (Pl.69: *Negoro-nuri sai-oke*), in the curve of the legs and rims and, particularly, in the blossom-shaped lobed outlines of plates and dishes. These lobed plates are common in the Muromachi period, but one bears a date as early as 1261. [37] Though of no further

Plate 67 Saddle with cherry blossoms. 1st half 14th c. Japan, private collection

significance for the history of lacquer art, this plate is interesting as one of the earliest lacquer objects to show the influence of Chinese decorative art.

The influence of China on the textile arts of Japan has already been mentioned (see p. 77). Similarly, the magnificent Chinese works of the Sung period clearly served as models for Seto ceramic wares in the thirteenth century. After the Japanese priest Eisai returned from China in 1191, tea was cultivated in Japan, and the custom of tea drinking spread. As a result, a need arose for suitable tea ceramics which were initially imported from China because of the overwhelming Chinese superiority in this field. But in 1223 the Japanese potter Katō Shirozaemon went to China for six years to learn the techniques being used there. Once back in Japan, he settled in Seto and from that moment on Seto pottery improved so dramatically that Shirozaemon – better known under the name of Tōshirō – became the 'father of Japanese ceramics.' The Chinese influence on the decoration of

Plate 68 Oil jar. 1330. Ht 43.4cm. Nara, Tōdai-ji

many Seto pottery wares of the late Kamakura period can be proved beyond doubt.[38] In lacquerwork and metalwork, on the other hand, Chinese influence is comparatively rare and weak in the thirteenth century. Although the subject for a lacquer design is occasionally taken from a Chinese poem, this fact has a greater literary than artistic significance, since such works – the writing-box with Chrysanthemums at the East Fence (Pl. 52) and the tebako from the Mishima-taisha (Pl. 59) among others – are purely Japanese in style and technique. There are no Chinese makie works of this kind, either then or later. The gold-lacquer techniques, developed by the Japanese lacquermasters from the Nara period onwards, and based on the sprinkling-in of the dust, were independent Japanese achievements. Naturally they could serve a variety of styles, but even the takamakie of the late Kamakura period does not yet show any sign of links with Chinese stylistic elements. The realism of the representation derives from Yamato-e, not from Chinese painting.

Initially it is the shape of Negoro lacquer wares, such as the blossom-shaped plate of 1261 and the vegetable container of 1307 to which the influence of Chinese models can be traced: very late and limited in extent compared with textiles and ceramics. Nor is this surprising, for while these arts were relatively underdeveloped and the craftsmen had much to learn from the Chinese, in the Heian period lacquer art had become the leading Japanese craft; in the Kamakura period only metalwork achieved comparable status. The Japanese lacquer artists, whose work had been sought after in China and Korea for three hundred years, were unequalled anywhere in

Plate 69 Vegetable bucket. 1307. Japan, private collection

their gold and mother-of-pearl lacquer wares.[39] Consequently foreign styles influenced them relatively late.

Of course, there is evidence of the new dialogue with China in the Negoro lacquers, but so far it is insignificant in lacquerwork in general. Whereas for the historian the Kamakura and the Muromachi periods are one, and are referred to as the 'Japanese Middle Ages,' for the art historian the Kamakura period is much more closely linked to the preceding late Heian period. The work of all the Japanese lacquermasters up to the end of the Kamakura period is part of one vast evolution from 'Chinese' beginnings rooted in T'ang culture to the purely Japanese lacquer art. Naturally there are important differences between the elegant, refined forms of the Heian period and the heavier, more powerful ones of the Kamakura period; between the gentle, delicately graduated colour harmonies of the earlier works and the harsher tone of the pure gold-lacquer in the later ones; and only the Kamakura period initiates the trend to precise observation and realistic representation of nature, and to rational, almost mathematical composition. But the overall development is uniform, the sophistication and refinement of the technical methods proceed without a break, and all Japanese lacquer wares from the late Heian period up to the end of the Kamakura period are pure Japanese expressions of art.

An attempt to find what distinguishes the Kamakura lacquers from the Heian period wares – despite all their common points – results in the following conclusions. The tebako is the most important feature. Its lower section increases in height, the box as a whole takes on a vertical bias and is more pronouncedly curved. The lid rises from the dust ledge not in a gentle S bend but in an uncompromising arc. The metal mountings are set lower than in the Heian period.

The techniques become more refined (different grades of gold dust) and richer (hiramakie, takamakie, e-nashiji, and finally kirigane). Relief adds a spatial dimension, adding new effects of shadow, light and dark, while the colour differentiation is replaced by pure monochrome gold or restricted to variations in the density of the sprinkling.

The style is characterized by a realistic attitude to nature; it is objectively representational, but occasionally combined with elements of fantasy. The works created at the height of the Kamakura period are powerful and lavish, 'metallic' and virile. Towards the end of the period those characteristics decline, and are replaced by a rational element resulting from the mathematical nature of the composition and the carefully calculated use of technical methods. But this rational element does not become predominant, for apparently it is only now that one sees uta-e (the integration of scattered written characters within a representational scene) beginning to be used to any appreciable extent in lacquer art. (The plum tree tebako in Pl.59 provides the earliest surviving example of uta-e.) The literary associations thus evoked seem closer to the courtly spirit of the Heian rather than the more robust Kamakura culture, and indeed it is in Heian painting that *uta-e* makes its first appearance. But in the late Kamakura period, this technique is commonly used for lacquerwork as well. This linking of decorative art and poetry manifested *expressis verbis* by written characters should be stressed as being a purely Japanese way of decoration.

Muromachi period I: Nambokuchō period to Higashiyama period

AS CAN BE SEEN FROM THE PRECEDING CHAPTERS, IT IS NOT TOO DIFFICULT to get a comparatively clear overall picture of the history of Japanese lacquerwork up to the end of the Kamakura period. Starting with the Nara period, when Chinese lacquerwork first appeared on the scene and was taken over and adapted by Japanese craftsmen, technical advances and numerous changes of style lead up to the late Kamakura period in a relatively uniform progression. The next 250 years, however, are not as easy to analyse.

Nor is this simply because dated works, which represent the solid pillars of a bridge spanning this period of time, are comparatively rare. Admittedly this does make analysis more difficult, but the main difficulties come from another quarter; from the lack of uniformity, the dichotomy, indeed the multiplicity, of the tendencies which now manifest themselves in the art of lacquerwork. True, these different directions can be established but cannot as yet be traced as clearly in their development as might be hoped.

Only seventy years of relative peace and the flowering of the arts stand out against the heavy fighting and civil wars at the beginning and end of the Muromachi era. On the basis of extant works it is possible to hazard a guess at the kind of developments that took place in lacquer art before and after this interval, but there is no conclusive evidence. There are quite a number of groups of lacquer objects with very different stylistic emphases, but it is not possible to trace a consistent line of development. Just as for ceramics, metalwork and textiles, so too for lacquerwork is the Muromachi period an era of comparative darkness for long stretches of time.

The Ōnin war (1467-1477) divides the era into two very different halves. Taking the period before 1467 first, the historical background should be briefly considered.

Towards the end of the Kamakura period a war flared up between two lines of the Japanese imperial house, each with a valid claim to the succession; it ended only in 1392 after the 'southern line' was subjugated. (In Japan this period is known as Nambokuchō, that is, 'southern and northern dynasties.') As early as 1333 Kamakura had been taken and destroyed. The government subsequently returned once more to Kyōto, and the Muromachi district, in which the new Shōgun Ashikaga Takauji established his seat of government, gave its name to the epoch of the Ashikaga shōguns. By the end of the war Shōgun Ashikaga Yoshimitsu was the strongest power in the land. But although he abdicated some three years later, in reality he continued to hold the reins of government until his death in 1408.

Up to the beginning of the Muromachi period the imperial court had fostered the arts; in the Nambokuchō wars the temples in particular had patronized artists. But these long wars of succession had so completely impoverished the court that it no longer had the means for artistic undertakings of any kind; instead, the role of Maecenas fell to Yoshimitsu as the first of the shōguns in Kyōto. He promoted trade with China not only for financial reasons, but also because he so loved things Chinese that, for example, he often dressed himself in Chinese clothes and had himself carried in Chinese sedan chairs. During his reign the luxurious Ashikaga culture developed.

This culturally highly significant period lasted only about seventy years. Perhaps because people were tired of the long struggle that had just

ended (or possibly because they wanted to close their eyes to the new wars
that were already threatening), a style of life developed in the ambience of
the shōguns in Kyōto, the luxury of which, at first somewhat 'nouveau
riche,' later frequently tended towards a sophisticated yet very expensive
simplicity. None of the Ashikaga were strong rulers, but whereas
Yoshimitsu, in spite of his great love of art, still concerned himself with
affairs of state, Yoshimasa (1435-1490; Shōgun 1443-1474) dedicated himself completely to his aesthetic inclinations. While the land suffered famine,
he surrounded himself with a group of aesthetes, artists, monks and art
lovers of all kinds, who were largely responsible for the flowering of
Higashiyama culture.

From the point of view of art, the first half of the Muromachi period
bears witness to an insatiable love of things Chinese. In addition to Chinese
paintings and ceramics, large quantities of lacquerware were imported at
that time.

From the warlike Nambokuchō period, which preceded the rule of the
Ashikaga proper and was hardly conducive to the arts and crafts, not many
examples of lacquerwork have survived.[1] As far as dated items are concerned, apart from thirteen undecorated pieces which are not very
significant from the art-historical viewpoint,[2] we know of only three makie
works, made in 1342, 1357 and 1382 respectively. In addition there is a
small group of undated items which, on stylistic grounds, should probably
also be ascribed to the fourteenth century. These few surviving lacquer
objects of the Nambokuchō period can be divided into first, those that
continue the Heian-Kamakura tradition; second, those that, influenced by
Chinese painting, show a new mixed style made up of Japanese and Chinese
elements; and third, at least one article in the new technique of Kamakurabori.

The small box in the Kongōbu-ji (Pl.70: *Shinobu-kazura makie-raden
bako*)[3] belongs to the traditional, conservative group: its still extant deed of
gift states that 1342 is the year it was made. Its decoration is diagonally
subdivided twice into four fields; two with delicate leaves of polypodia in
hiramakie, the other two with mother-of-pearl scrolls inlaid in ikake-ji. The
distinct, logical structure corresponds to the geometric tendency of late
Kamakura lacquerwork (cf. Pls 61 and 62), but the way the decoration
consciously aims at contrast does not. Nevertheless a comparison with a
much older work is not entirely irrelevant: the decoration of the jewel box in
the Ninna-ji (cf. p.30, Pl.16), which dates from the first half of the tenth
century, shows a similarly contrasting composition. And since initially,
after the overthrow of the Kamakura shōgunate (1333), it was indeed the
aim of the imperial court in Kyōto to re-establish the pattern of court life as
it had existed in the Engi era (901-922),[4] this polypodium box may perhaps
with some justice be regarded as evidence of an attempt at such a link.[5] The
elegance and detail of draughtsmanship and technique harmonize well with
the graceful form of the box. In spite of its slightly domed lid, it has none of
the sturdiness and weight of typical Kamakura boxes, and the inverted
corners – already present in the jewel box in the Ninna-ji – are indeed a
favourite device of the Muromachi period. A comparison with the comb
box from the late Kamakura period (Pl.64), emphasizes the slackening of
the curvature and, figuratively speaking, the greater calmness of the overall
form.

The conservative works also include a tebako (Pl.71: *Semmen-chirashi makie-tebako*), undated but definitely made in the fourteenth century. Its decoration of scattered fans immediately brings to mind the ōgi-chirashi tebako (Pl.62). But whereas the latter, a work of the late Kamakura period, is characterized by the clarity of its decorative forms and its logical composition, here the sense of order is less certain and the lacquer artist is no longer in full control of the all too numerous decorative elements. Also, the outlines of the box are not as markedly defined, the proportions are less obvious. The link with Kamakura lacquerwork is unmistakable and the motifs on the fans, which derive from Yamato-e, serve to further underline this link; but both the sturdiness and greatness of the Kamakura period and the elegance and finesse of the Heian period are missing. A degree of technical richness, manifested in the use of togidashi, hiramakie, takamakie, nashiji and tsukegaki, cannot conceal the lack of artistic taste amounting, indeed, to a certain decadence.. Finally, also in the purely Japanese tradition are objects like the small kōgō (incense box) in Plate 72. The decoration and technique evoke works of the Kamakura period, but the flat, elongated shape, devoid of any tension, indicates that it belongs to the Muromachi era.

Amidst the unrest of the Nambokuchō period a chest was made bearing the date 1357 (Pl.73); its design, consisting of the Sumiyoshi landscape (*Sumiyoshi makie-karabitsu*)[6] under a full moon, is carried out in togidashi, hiramakie, silver hyōmon and mother-of-pearl inlay. It shows many inconsistencies in technique and style: for example, while the trunks of the trees

Plate 70 Box decorated with polypodia and scrolls. 1342. 13.6:28.4:21.5cm. Kongōbu-ji, Wakayama province

are in togidashi, the thin pine needles are in relief; nor is the representation of the birds on the lid very successful. What makes this chest interesting, however, is that it is the first example showing the clearly recognizable influence of Chinese painting. This influence can be seen in iconographic details, like the sharp-edged rocks pierced in places by holes (a favourite Chinese motif), in the way the tree trunks cross each other, and in the fine but somewhat self-conscious representation of the water. The Chinese influence is also seen in the new relationship between the decoration and the dark lacquer ground, which gives the representation its pictorial character. A comparison with the Sumiyoshi tebako of 1228 (Pl.48) shows that the empty background now plays a larger, more active role – it now constitutes an element of the composition and is no longer just simply the side of a box to be decorated.

From the point of view of style this chest is not much different from an undated, much better quality tebako (Pl.74) with a moon and plum branch decorative motif (*Baigetsu makie-tebako*) that also belongs to the early Muromachi period and was probably made around 1400.[7] Again the influence of Chinese painting is indicated by the empty ground effect which is reminiscent of ink paintings. The way the branches are drawn, with their calligraphic curves and rich intersections, points to Sung and Yüan painting. To appreciate the change that has taken place, it is worth contrasting this baigetsu (plum and moon) tebako with the tebako from the Mishima-taisha (Pl.59) made in the Kamakura period. How much simpler and more spontaneous the earlier representations of plum branches appear in com-

Plate 71 Toilet box with scattered fans. 14th c. 14.7:29.7:22.6cm. Tōkyō National Museum

parison, and how much more deliberate the drawing of the Muromachi period!

In addition to the Chinese influence, the baigetsu tebako also illustrates other essential characteristics of Muromachi lacquerwork. (Though often more pronounced in later works, they are already definitely used in this relatively early box.) Above all there is the 'mood,' that feeling of night stillness, loneliness and impermanence consciously evoked by the design of the plum tree in the moonlight, by the broken-off twigs and falling petals. The effect is heightened by the literary associations inherent in the use of the written characters cut out of sheet silver and set into the picture. Written characters of this kind had already been employed in the decoration of Kamakura lacquerwork (cf. Pls 59 and 66), but the Muromachi period witnesses a significant increase in their importance. The emphasis shifts from the factually represented, visual aspect of the decoration towards the specific content of the poem to which the characters refer.

The (in a certain respect) naïve realism of the Kamakura period is succeeded in the Muromachi lacquers by a vastly more sophisticated representation of nature that combines objective observations with poetic mood, and is closely linked with literature and poetry. The lacquer works of the fourteenth to fifteenth centuries cannot be fully grasped by hand and eye alone: they reveal their full meaning only to the literate.

This increasing complexity and refinement of content would appear to be almost antithetic to the development of the artistic means, that is, the devising of virile, sculptural, sumptuous new techniques. Thus, in the baigetsu tebako, the raised takamakie, itself further adorned with kirigane, and the heaviness of the sheet silver for the moon and written characters, are

Plate 72 Kōgō with chrysanthemums by the East Fence. 14th-15th c. Tōkyō National Museum

almost too overpowering for the poetic motif.

Such robustness, in particular the preference for strong sculptural relief decoration is often as much a characteristic of many Muromachi lacquerworks as the Chinese-influenced forms and the literary content. While at the height of the Kamakura period the predominant impression was of overwhelming power, this was primarily the result of the shape and proportions of the boxes themselves and, above all, of kōmori and dōbari; the effect did not depend on the weight or mass of the individual elements of the decoration. In the Muromachi period, however, the tight, bulging fulness of form no longer plays an important role – on the contrary, the curvature of lid and sides lose their strength and the shapes tend to become slack.[8] The decoration, on the other hand, becomes richer, more detailed, massive and sculptural, a development in which the frequent use of relatively thick gold or silver kanagai and the growing popularity of kirigane, skilfully applied in considerable quantity, are as significant as the takamakie itself.

The baigetsu tebako, therefore, provides an early example of characteristics which, even if not always used simultaneously, occur again and again in Muromachi lacquerwork – namely, the pictorial relationship between the ground and the decoration; the Chinese-influenced forms; the

Plate 73 Shami Kūkagu: chest with Sumiyoshi decoration. 1357. 51:73.2:54.6cm.
Tōkyō National Museum

strong literary influence on the content and the emphatically sculptural nature of the individual decorative elements.

When dealing with the early Muromachi period, apart from conservative lacquer works which continue the Kamakura tradition on the one hand, and items the style of which is influenced by Chinese painting on the other, mention must also be made of those pieces executed in the new techniques of carved lacquer and Kamakurabori, techniques either borrowed from or inspired by China.

As a result of the numerous links established with China through Zen Buddhism and renewed commercial activity, large numbers of Chinese works of art arrived in Japan. Besides pictures, specimens of calligraphy, poetry, porcelain and brocades, beginning at the very latest with the fourteenth century a great many Chinese carved-lacquer objects reached Zen temples and the court of the shōguns. An inventory for the year 1363 of the temple of Enkaku-ji in Kamakura[9] already records an astonishingly large number of such pieces, including plates, dishes, incense boxes, medicine and seal cases. Apart from these articles, contemporary portraits of Japanese Zen priests often show chairs, foot-rests and sceptres of carved lacquer. Chinese carved-lacquer articles for use in the ritual ceremonies, in the tea ceremony or for purposes of interior decoration were particularly popular because nothing comparable existed in Japan.

Contemporary Japanese sources contain references to the many uses to which objects of this kind were put; the Japanese enjoyed constantly inventing new names for the different varieties of carved lacquer. The most common term is 'tsuishu,' which means 'heaped-up red,' a very apt description. In carved lacquerwork of this kind the substructure – which generally

Plate 74   Toilet box with plum blossom and moon. ca 1400. 13.6:30.3:23.8cm. Tōkyō National Museum

consisted of wood, but sometimes also of metal of various types – was
coated first with several layers of lacquer, then reinforced with fabric as a
whole or in part (rim), and again coated with many more thin layers of
lacquer until, finally, a skin of lacquer several millimetres thick was formed
around the object. The design was then carved into this thick lacquer coat.
As red lacquer alone was used for a great many of these articles, the name
heaped-up red is very appropriate. There are also many other varieties of
carved lacquer with successive layers of different coloured lacquer which,
when cut, either appear as fine coloured veins on the sides of the incisions or
form a colour ground which contrasts with the surface layers. The wealth of
descriptive terms which the Japanese invented for these different variants
clearly illustrates how popular Chinese carved-lacquer works were
– indeed, for Japanese collectors of the period, they must have been among
the most sought-after objects. A letter from the year 1407, written at the
command of the Chinese Emperor Yung-lo, to Ashikaga Yoshimitsu, gives
some idea of the quantities in which these items came to Japan: accompanying this letter, Yoshimitsu received a gift of twenty large carved-lacquer
plates and thirty carved-lacquer boxes.[10] Most of the names both of different forms of carved lacquer and of various objects are recorded in the
Kundaikan sayu chōki, a manuscript written by Nōami in 1475, which represents a kind of catalogue raisonné of the collection owned by Ashikaga
Yoshimasa.[11]

Though it was probably not long before Japanese lacquermasters tried
to imitate these much admired objects, our actual knowledge of the origins
of Japanese carved lacquerwork is non-existent; the earliest information we
have is a reference to the Ōnin-Bunmei era (1467-1487) when a Kyōto
lacquermaster by the name of Monnyū found fame through his carved
lacquerwork. Not a single object from his hand is known to have survived
today, but he and his followers are said to have worked much in the style of
Chinese models.[12] This might explain why, when considering early carved
lacquerwork, it is very difficult today to distinguish Japanese works from
Chinese. Partly as a result of finds made in graves in China in recent years,
Chinese carved lacquer has re-entered the mainstream of discussion at the
time this is being written. Any new evidence arising from these researches
might also shed fresh light on the question of Japanese carved lacquerwork
of the Muromachi period. For the time being all that can be said with
certainty is that, according to Japanese sources, carved-lacquer objects
were manufactured in Japan at least since the time of Monnyū, that is, since
the end of the fifteenth century, and that they probably adhered closely to
Chinese prototypes; but we cannot identify any of these early works with
certainty (see also p. 166)

Our knowledge of Kamakurabori is a little better. The name, which
derives from the most important place of manufacture,[13] describes a way of
imitating genuine carved lacquer whereby the artist spared himself the time
and trouble of applying the numerous coats of lacquer. In Kamakurabori it
is not a thick layer of lacquer that is carved but the actual wooden surface of
the object itself, after which it is covered with lacquer. With early
Kamakurabori works the intention must certainly have been for the finished
object to resemble genuine carved lacquer as closely as possible. Fairly soon
though – there are no exact dates – this aim must have become secondary,
because on later examples of Kamakurabori there is no pretense of thick

layers of lacquer; instead, the wood itself is the dominant element (see p.135).

There is a Japanese tradition that Kamakurabori first occurred as early as the middle of the thirteenth century when the sculptor Ko-un, drawing his inspiration from Chinese carved lacquers of the Sung period, made Buddhist utensils for the temple of Hokke-dō.[14] This tradition is refuted by Japanese experts today, and it is not known whether Kamakurabori objects were in fact made in the thirteenth century at all. If they were, they must be deemed lost. A large kōgō in the temple of Nanzen-ji in Kyōto (Pl.75: *Botan Kamakurabori-kōgō*) is now taken to be the oldest surviving example of the Kamakurabori technique; there is some controversy about its exact date of orgin, but possibly it was made towards the end of the fourteenth century.[15] The influence of Chinese prototypes in the composition and in the relationship between the relief areas and the ground are unmistakable. The box has a deep powerful cutting which is regarded as characteristic of early Kamakurabori. In this context, 'early' is also used to describe the fifteenth century: the Kinren-ji in Kyōto, for example, contains a kōgō (Pl.76) of the same size with equally deep cutting, bearing the inscription 'Bunmei 13th year' (1481) in red lacquer, and the small box in Plate 77 is also ascribed to the fifteenth century. Both pieces clearly demonstrate how Kamakurabori was able to achieve effects far beyond the mere imitation of genuine carved

Plate 75 Incense box. Late 14th c. Ht 9.1cm, diam. 32.6cm. Kyōto, Nanzen-ji

lacquer. But apparently most of the surviving Kamakurabori lacquers were made only after the end of the Muromachi period (see p. 135).

Nor was the imitation of genuine carved lacquer by means of lacquered-over wood carving necessarily a Japanese discovery: it is said to have been in use in China as early as in the Ming period. [16] It is also true, though, that the technique had been employed in Japan some time previously for architectural details, [17] admittedly in a completely different style and context, and without the least intention of simulating carved lacquer.

At any rate, it is probably safe to say that, in the first instance, Kamakurabori was made with the express aim of imitating genuine carved lacquer; the Nanzen-ji kōgō was clearly meant to be taken for tsuishu. But the function of Kamakurabori did not remain restricted to that of a substitute; in due course a certain change in its essential character was to transform it into a typically Japanese lacquer technique.

The three tendencies which could be distinguished in the lacquerwork of the very beginning of the Muromachi (or of the Nambokuchō) period continue into the fifteenth century. These were: the 'conservative' style, based on the Heian-Kamakura tradition; the 'modern' style, strongly influenced by Chinese ink painting; and, lastly, the new technique inspired by Chinese models. But now makie work influenced by Chinese painting moves into the foreground.

Objects in the conservative style, that is, free of all Chinese influence, occur very seldom in the fifteenth century, and even then apparently only in the form of temple implements. In technique and decoration they often continue the tradition of earlier works and consequently do not always escape the dangers of stylistic stagnation and impoverishment, characteristics which one can also observe in contemporary Buddhist metal implements.

Plate 76 Kamakurabori-kōgō. 1481. Ht 7.2cm, diam. 28.5cm. Kyōto, Kinren-ji

There are no major differences between Buddhist lacquer articles of the fifteenth century and those of the Nambokuchō period. If one compares a rosary box of 1382 (Pl. 78: *Tokko-mon makie-gōsu*) with a sutra box (Pl. 79: *Rimpō makie-kyōbako*) of 1409,[18] what they have in common is immediately apparent: a plain shape, and Buddhist motifs for decorations. In Muromachi lacquerwork, the Buddhist figurative subjects of the Heian and early Kamakura periods (Pls 19, 41, 42, 47) are no longer used; around the year 1400 representations of symbolic cult implements seem to have been preferred. Accordingly, the rosary box is decorated with the 'tokko,' a sceptre-like object which was used in the rites of the Shingon sect; the sutra box repeats the motif of the 'rimpō,' the symbol for 'the wheel of Buddhist doctrine.'

The sutra box is worked in hiramakie. Both the technique and the mathematical regularity of the arrangement in the design are conservative, belonging to some extent to the traditional fund. New and typical of the early Muromachi period, however, are the pure black-lacquer ground, which – apart from the decoration – is contrasted here with simple gold-sprinkled borders or flat areas (for example on the feet),[19] and the 'harigaki' technique for the fine interior linework of the decoration. Before the Muromachi period these thin lines were left free when the preliminary lacquer drawing was made, so as to avoid any gold dust adhering to them while sprinkling. In harigaki ('needle drawing'), on the other hand, the

Plate 77 Kamakurabori-kōgō. 15th c. Ht 3.5cm, diam. 7.5cm. Wuppertal, Dr Kurt Herberts

whole decoration is first sketched with lacquer, sprinkled with gold dust, and only then, before the lacquer is dry, the interior linework is picked out with a needle. Thus harigaki lines are always of the same width, while the linework in older lacquers may vary in thickness. The rimpō kyōbako is the earliest dated example of the harigaki technique; because of its simplicity it would be used very frequently in later periods, above all in the Momoyama period.

Another quite simple example of conservative lacquerwork from the Muromachi period is dated: the sacrificial table of the Kasuga shrine (Pl.80: *Matsugui-tsuru makie-sammaibon*), of the year 1467. As the Japanese name, 'sammaibon'[20] indicates, in certain ceremonies rice was heaped up on tables of this kind and then scattered. Since the objects themselves were purely

Plate 78 Rosary box. 1382. Ht 9.7cm, diam. 16.5cm. Reproduced from *Tōji and Its Cultural Treasures*

Plate 79 Sutra box with rimpō decoration. 1409. 15.5:35.2:17.5cm. Biwako Bunka-kan, Shiga province

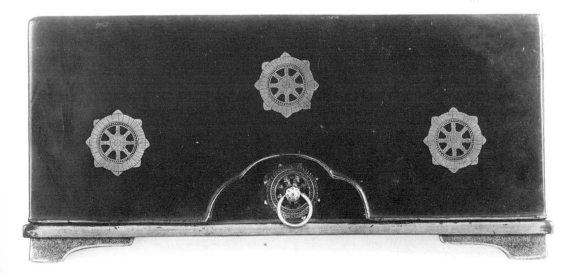

functional, the decorative techniques were also simple. The motif of pine-chewing cranes had been used since the Heian period (cf. Pl. 40).

In contrast to the small number of Muromachi lacquers in the Heian-Kamakura tradition, there are a host of Chinese-influenced ones. The effects of Chinese ink painting on Japanese lacquerwork first became apparent in the Sumiyoshi chest of 1357 (Pl. 73) and the plum blossom tebako (Pl. 74). A work in which traditional and new elements as well as Japanese

Plate 80 Small sacrificial table. 1467. Nara, Kasuga-taisha

Plate 81 Toilet box with autumn field decoration. ca 1400. 15.3:33.2:25cm. Japan, private collection

and Chinese elements are combined in a somewhat contradictory manner is the autumn field tebako in the Tōyama collection (Pls 81, 82: *Akino makie-tebako*). Typical autumn plants,[21] sometimes tossed by the wind, had been a very popular motif, especially in the Kamakura period, and at first glance this box appears to be closely linked to the old tradition. Also, specific details, like the outline of the hill on the left side of the lid and the patches of earth still derive from Yamato-e. But if this tebako is compared with Kamakura versions of the autumn field motif, as for instance in Plate 45, 64, or an autumn field tebako in the Nezu Museum, Tōkyō,[22] the new and different element is immediately apparent. The Chinese influence is revealed most strongly in the shape of the rocks and in the curiously inter-twining design of the branches. Clearly the calligraphic brushwork of many ink paintings served as models but the result is somewhat confused and cramped. For instance, the branch on the right of the lid starts by growing outwards, then forks into two smaller branches, one of which is bent downwards, the other upwards, and finishes with the latter curving back inwards to produce a corkscrew effect completely alien to Kamakura art. Furthermore, although the branches and plants are bent over by the storm wind – as on the box in the Nezu museum – some of the grasses are bent in the opposite direction in an almost mannered way.

If the lines are overly complicated in themselves, then the technique adds to the feeling of unrest – for example, by the inappropriate way of using mother-of-pearl for some of the pine needle clusters. Compared to

Plate 82 Toilet box with autumn field decoration (see Pl. 81). Lid from above

hiramakie, these inlays look more like small bare twigs rather than pine needles. The strong takamakie of the rocks and tree trunks, and the numerous written characters scattered in the decoration, add to the complexity. This box seems to abound with contradictions and is proof of the fact that the lacquermasters did not always find it easy to come to terms with the modern, much-admired Chinese stylistic principles. [23]

Much more harmonious in its effect is the so-called *Nagi-makie tebako* (Pl.83) in the Kumano Hayatama shrine, [24] a box now generally attributed to the fifteenth century. It belongs to a group of eleven tebako still extant in this shrine. Previously they had been given the date 1390, based on an entry in one of the shrine inventories, [25] but today the relevant section of the text is regarded as a later addition. The boxes, which have survived with all their interior fittings such as trays intact, are admirably worked. [26] The nagi box, like most of the others, has a not too densely sprinkled nashiji ground, on which the trees (one on each side), sparse, large-scale and stylized, are represented in medium to high takamakie with mother-of-pearl inlay. What is new is the way in which bold tsukegaki lines are used to pick out in gold the veins of the mother-of-pearl leaves. The Chinese influence is particularly evident in the shape of the rocks. Here, as well as for the sloping edge of the bank, kirigane is employed quite deliberately to add character to the structure, and not simply to enliven the decorative surface, as was done in late Kamakura lacquerwork.

Although the effect of the box is traditional in many respects, it is obvious that the earlier finesse and exactness of representation have been replaced by simpler forms using bolder and more generous techniques. A comparison with typical Kamakura lacquers (Pls 59 and 64) makes this abundantly clear. This tendency to decorative simplification is something

Plate 83 Toilet box with nagi decoration. 15th c. 22.3:34.3:25.6cm. Kumano Hayatama-jinja, Wakayama province

not frequently encountered before the Ōnin war; but towards the end of the Muromachi era and, above all, in the Momoyama period it is more commonly used. Among the lacquer objects made in the first half of the Muromachi period it is difficult to pick out any one work which approximates the style of this box – almost all of them are more complicated and much more strongly influenced by literature. Quite possibly, related items have been lost; at any rate, it is not feasible today to trace a straight progression from the nagi tebako to works of the sixteenth century. Nevertheless a note is sounded here which is taken up again in the Momoyama period – albeit in an altered form.

Probably because of this relationship to later works, it has occasionally been suggested that the date of origin of the nagi tebako should be moved up to the end of the Muromachi period. Among other things, the use of mother-of-pearl in the traditional raden technique argues against this. In the late Muromachi period raden drops competely from sight and is replaced by much thinner mother-of-pearl inlays; but, as there is no sign of this change here, the fifteenth century is the mot likely date.

A writing-table depicting the coastline of Hamamatsu (Pl.84: *Hamamatsu makie-bundai*) also gives the impression of being relatively serene. Here, the curving shoreline, the shape of the rocks (the one deriving from Yamato-e, the other from Sung and Yüan painting), and the decoratively twisted trunks and branches of the trees are more in harmony with each other. Just as in an unrelated and probably somewhat later writing-box decorated with a similar subject,[27] one is struck by the remarkable way in which the waves, which consist of a series of tightly parallel curves, look as if they had been cut off with a knife at the bottom and occasionally at the top. Consequently, the finely sprinkled ground appears to be jutting into the sea in the same way as in Yamato-e the streaks of cloud run into the sky.

The Hamamatsu writing-table may date from about the same time as an eight-lobed mirror case in the Atsuta shrine (Pl.85: *Hōrai makie-kagami-bako*). The decoration of the box, like that of the mirror that goes with

Plate 84 Writing-table showing the coast of Hamamatsu. Mid 15th c. 9.5:58:33cm. Japan, private collection

it, donated in 1445,[28] consists of a landscape with pines, bamboo plants, rocks, cranes and a tortoise. This means that it refers to the island (or mountain) of Hōrai – the legendary land of the blessed. The Hōraisan motif is very frequently used in the Muromachi period,[29] above all on mirrors. Decorations on mirrors also provide the readiest parallels to the somewhat precious, self-conscious manner in which the cranes are depicted on this box.

The dialogue between Japanese tradition and Chinese influence can, therefore, be clearly discussed in many lacquer works of the fourteenth and even the early fifteenth centuries. Since they are heterogeneous elements, the different stylistic tendencies conflict with each other when brought together in the same work. But sometimes – perhaps particularly in the second and third quarters of the fifteenth century – the contrasts resolve themselves, and the Japanese and Chinese components are synthesized with apparent ease. Works of absolute beauty were created: objects which would be unthinkable without the influence of China, but which nevertheless are completely Japanese and, indeed, represent some of the highest achievements of Japanese lacquerwork. One of these masterpieces is a writing-table in the National Museum, Tōkyō (Pl. 86); the decoration shows a flowering plum tree on a river bank at night (*Baigetsu makie-bundai*). In the composition of the design, the individual pictorial elements are exquisitely

Plate 85 Mirror box with Hōrai motifs. 1445. Diam. 27cm. Nagoya, Atsuta-jinja

attuned to each other; thus, the branch which extends far out to the right is balanced by the leftward motion of the small waves, and the thin crescent moon above by the stone rising out of the water below. The gentle alternation of hiramakie and nashiji is just as carefully balanced as the effect of the uncluttered, undecorated black-lacquer surface on which the branches are inscribed with such great calligraphic beauty.

Okada has said that there is scarcely another example of lacquerwork which so breathes the very spirit of the Muromachi period and which – obviously influenced by Zen Buddhism – so strongly expresses the feeling for stillness, solitude, indeed the sense of being lost.[30] The decoration of this writing-table does not include any written characters nor is the representation inspired by any specific poem. Yet a seemingly inexhaustible richness of mood, the whole world of 'yūgen,'[31] is contained here. This apparent simplicity of the work belies its profound significance and fascination.

Another eminent work of the fifteenth-sixteenth centuries also shows the union of Chinese influences with Japanese mastery of lacquer at its most felicitous: a writing-box with cherry blossom decoration (Pl.87: *Sakura makie-suzuribako*) in the possession of the National Museum, Tōkyō. It too is admirable in the way it combines a superb, precisely worked-out composition with a desire for sophisticated simplicity. This economy of decoration – only one single branch for the whole surface of the lid – first occurs in the Muromachi period; here again, the influence of Zen painting is apparent. The numerous gradations of hiramakie and takamakie, gold and silver dust (the latter for the blossoms) and the kirigane accents are skilfully handled, but nowhere is the technique obtrusive. The cherry blossom motif is beautifully varied, in the sense that it becomes increasingly more

Plate 86 Writing-table with plum tree and moon. Mid 15th c. 10:60:35cm. Tōkyō National Museum

refined and intensified. Whereas the entire top of the lid is more or less filled by a strong branch rendered in relief, the inside (Pl.88) shows only a small spray of blossoms and the tray for the brushes is sparsely decorated with a bud, a rear view of a blossom with only three remaining petals, and a few scattered petals. This treatment amplifies the symbolic nature of the cherry blossom, which represents the way in which a noble human being departs this life easily and without resistance – as easily as the cherry blossom from the twig. Accordingly, the fallen petals have a greater significance than the branch still decked in full blossom. This gradual build-up of the inner content, which the user of the writing-box sees and experiences when he opens the box, admirably matches the inner concentration and composure that should precede every use of the brush.

Such variations of the design occur frequently in writing-boxes of the Muromachi period, even if they are seldom as finely realized as they are here. It is true that in the tebako of the Kamakura period the small interior trays had also often taken up and improvised on the decorative themes of the main box (see p.79). But whereas there only the motif and its repetition were involved – a consideration, therefore, of form alone – in Muromachi

Plate 87 Writing-box with cherry blossom decoration. 15th-16th c.
4.5:22.2:24.2cm. Tōkyō National Museum

writing-boxes, the concern is very often with varying and intensifying the emotional content.

Lacquers like the plum tree writing-table in Plate 86 and this cherry-blossom writing-box must have been greatly admired not only in Japan but also in China. It is an accepted fact that in the fifteenth century the Chinese acknowledged the superiority of Japanese lacquerwork and tried to learn from it. Thus, for example, the Chinese book, *Huang Ming wen tse*,[32] states that during the Hsüan-te era (1426-1435) Chinese craftsmen had been sent to Japan to learn 'gold-lacquer painting" (meaning makie). And, referring to the same period, the *Tung hai chi* records that 'The father of Yang Hsüan ... used to send people to Japan to learn the techniques of lacquer sprinkling and lacquer painting. On their return Hsüan adopted these methods and further enriched them with his own ideas ... .'[33] Surviving fifteenth-century Chinese lacquer works in fact show that at that time attempts were made in the Middle Kingdom to imitate the Japanese sprinkling techniques of makie.[14] Furthermore, in the Muromachi period, Japanese lacquer articles decorated in makie, nashiji and kanagai were shipped to China in considerable numbers, partly as tribute, partly by way of trade, for the very reason that they were so highly prized there.[35]

In addition, unlacquered items were likely sent on occasion from China

Plate 88 Writing-box with cherry blossom decoration (see Pl.87). Interior of box

to Japan to be decorated by Japanese lacquermasters. This possibility is suggested by a plate which is purely Chinese in shape yet has Japanese lacquer decoration (Pl. 89: *Momo raden-makie rinkagata-bon*). Furthermore, since the peach blossom motif is also more Chinese than Japanese, it might, perhaps, have been a case of a Japanese lacquermaster carrying out a Chinese commission. Or it may have been commissioned by a Japanese collector who was particularly fond of Chinese forms; plates of this kind were unusual in Japan. [36] Probably the plate belongs in the second half or even at the end of the fifteenth century.

But in their dealings with China, Japanese lacquermasters by no means always found themselves in the role of teacher: from China came not only the highly prized carved lacquers but also the 'ch'iang-chin' technique and a new form of mother-of-pearl inlay. In Japanese ch'iang-chin (Chinese term) is known as 'chinkinbori'; a process in which the decoration is not sprinkled in (makie), inlaid (raden) or carved (Kamakurabori or genuine carved lacquer), but in which the pattern is engraved with fine lines into the lacquer ground and then gold is rubbed into them. [37]

The technique had been in use in China at least since the Yüan dynasty, and at the end of the thirteenth century the master, P'eng Chün-pao, from Yanghui in the district of Chia-hsing is said to have specialized in

Plate 89 Lobed bowl with spray of peach blossom. End of 15th c. (?) Ht 11.2cm, diam. 47cm. Japan, private collection

ch'iang-chin lacquerwork.[38] Three Chinese sutra boxes in this technique have survived in Japan, all, according to their inscriptions, dating from the year 1315.[39]

In fact it is not known when works of this kind first reached Japan; the earliest reference to them is not until 1433, the year in which the Chinese Emperor Hsüan-te sent a number of gifts, including a set of ch'iang-chin lacquers, to the Shōgun Ashikaga Yoshinori.[40] Although there are two further references to such works for the year 1435,[41] these engraved lacquers are not mentioned in Japanese sources nearly as frequently as the much prized carved lacquerwork. Numerous Japanese chinkinbori objects in the Chinese style are said to have been made in the Muromachi period, yet very little has survived.

Best known is a tebako in the National Museum in Tōkyō (Pl.90: *Hōraisan chinkinbori-tebako*), which probably belongs to the sixteenth century.[42] With its steeply rising but flat-topped lid, it closely resembles Chinese ch'iang-chin sutra boxes in form. Where it differs from them completely, however, is that, apart from the actual pictorial areas, it has a red lacquer ground sprinkled with nashiji. Also the engraving is different from the Chinese examples: instead of being fluid and elegant as they are, it is more simple and straightforward. The subjects depicted on the box have remarkably little connection with each other: while the lid and the front are decorated with Hōraizan scenes, the back shows three people in an interior,

Plate 90 Toilet box in chinkinbori technique. Detail. 16th c. Overall dimensions 24:34.7:22.5cm. Tōkyō National Museum

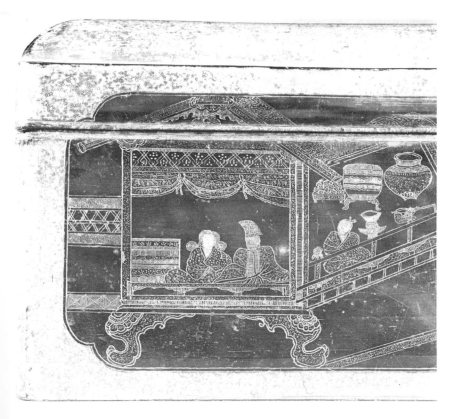

and the side walls mussel and crab motifs. It is worth mentioning that the people's faces have been painted with a kind of white oil paint – the first instance since the Nara period of the use of this Chinese technique in Japan (cf. mitsuda-e, p.15).

In the area of mother-of-pearl inlay as well, important influences emanated from China. After centuries of mother-of-pearl lacquerwork appearing to be a purely Japanese domain, there was a new flowering of this art in China during the Yüan dynasty (1280-1368), which made use of very much thinner mother-of-pearl than had ever been used before. In Japan the old raden technique had continued to decline since the end of the Kamakura period, but now under the influence of the new Chinese mother-of-pearl lacquers, Japanese masters also turned their attention to the inlay of thinner, finer mother-of-pearl (aogai). A good example of this is the saddle in Plate 91 which dates from the fifteenth century (*Matsu ni tomoe-mon raden-gura*). In shape it is still very much in the tradition of the famous Kamakura saddles, but the new Chinese influence can be seen not only in the technique but also in the design, the circular shape of the pine-needle cluster.

The most important works not only of the fifteenth century but of the whole Muromachi period are the so-called Higashiyama lacquers, a rather well-defined group of objects owned by Ashikaga Yoshimasa (or were made in the style of such articles) and take their name from Yoshimasa's residence at the foot of Mount Higashiyama in Kyōto. (Yoshimasa was shōgun from

Plate 91 Saddle with pines and tomoe motifs. 15th c. Tōkyō National Museum

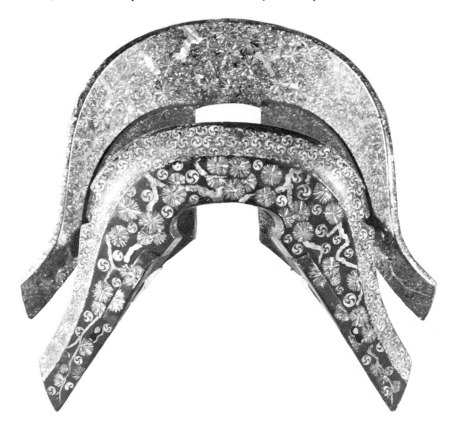

1443 to 1474; he died in 1490.) Among this Higashiyama lacquerwork, three writing-boxes have survived; they are documented as having belonged to Yoshimasa: the *Kasugayama makie-suzuribako* in the Nezu Museum in Tōkyō,[43] the Mikasayama suzuribako in the Konoike collection, and the Sumidagawa suzuribako in the Ohara collection in Kurashiki. The Kasugayama writing-box (Pl.92) will be described in detail below since in form, technique, iconography and style it shows all the typical characteristics of the Higashiyama lacquers.

Its shape may, indeed, be considered the norm for writing-boxes of the Muromachi period. It is almost square and has an overlapping lid (kabusebuta in Japanese) with bevelled upper edges. While the earliest Japanese writing-boxes, the shape of which we get some idea of from pictorial scrolls of the Heian period, appear to have had flush-fitting lids (known as awasebuta, inrōbuta or aikuchi-zukuri), the oldest surviving pieces (Pls 39 and 52) already have overlapping lids. This is also the more common form for the many surviving writing-boxes of the Muromachi and Momoyama periods. Flush-fitting lids only occur occasionally. In the Edo period both types were produced; the flush-fitting variety may even be

Plate 92 Kasugayama writing-box. 2nd half 15th c. 4.9:22:23.9cm. Tōkyō, Nezu Museum

more common. There are also a very small number of individual examples
of okibuta, that is, lids which consist simply of a board held in place by
means of guide ledges on its under side. In general, therefore, overlapping
lids are preferred for writing-boxes, while tebako – with the exception of
those of the Heian period – almost always have flush-fitting lids. In
Muromachi writing-boxes the water container and inkstone are generally
placed along the central axis with the trays for brushes, ink and other
accessories to the right and left of them.

The top of the lid now assumes a new shape. While in boxes of the Heian
and Kamakura period it rises from the dust ledge in a more or less domed
shape, in Muromachi writing-boxes it is generally flat. Bevelled edges,
often delicately decorated with hiramakie or kirigane, lead from this horizontal plane to the vertical sides of the lid. In the Kasugayama writing-box
these bevelled edges are joined at right angles; in other pieces this sudden-
ness is softened by bevelled corners (sumikiri). Rounded-off or inverted
corners (sumimaru and irizumi respectively), which occasionally had been
used in earlier periods, were used more frequently in the Muromachi era.

The favourite technique employed in the Higashiyama lacquers is a rich
takamakie now often deliberately contrasted with togidashi. The combined
use of these techniques is known as 'shishiai-makie.' In the Kasugayama
writing-box the autumn plants, the deer and the stones, for example, are in
takamakie, the ridge of the hill, on the other hand, is in togidashi. The full
moon is inlaid in silver kanagai – the preference for kanagai being typical of
the Muromachi period.

The delicate and precise accuracy which distinguished the Hiramakie of
the Kamakura period is, of course, no longer part of Muromachi lacquerwork, with its rather emphatic relief. Instead, the lacquermasters of the
Higashiyama era were stimulated by novel techniques they devised to
produce new, rich, and sometimes rather complicated effects – especially
by combining several of these processes in one object. In these articles the
technical aspect of the decoration is sometimes so obvious and self-assertive
that the observer is immediately struck by the sheer ingenuity of the workmanship. This is new, for in the lacquers of the Heian and Kamakura
periods, technique had so evidently been the means to the end of surface
decoration that it scarcely had any independent significance, any weight of
its own. The Higashiyama lacquermasters give greater prominence to
technique; yet in so doing they are by no means simply toying with technical problems nor do they give the sort of conscious display of technical
virtuosity which makes many lacquer articles produced later in the Edo
period seem so barren and superficial.

The preference for takamakie implies that the ornamental element of the
lacquer is no longer necessarily subordinate to the shape of the box. Although it is perhaps somewhat of an exaggeration, one might say that there
is now a risk of the object or its surface being reduced to a mere vehicle for
decoration. Decoration in such obvious relief can no longer be subservient
to the lively, taut, almost breathing surfaces; it cannot emphasize or accen-
tuate them; at best it can merely dominate them. It is therefore quite logical
that the process of flattening out domed lids and side walls of the boxes that
had begun in the late Kamakura era, should further accelerate with the rise
of takamakie. Thus, the impression created by these lacquer objects is
altogether and very decisively changed: while the boxes of the Heian and

Kamakura periods often appeal directly to the sense of touch, even when not actually held in the hand, Muromachi lacquerwork is directed primarily at the eye.

The decoration, therefore, develops from the subordinate or possibly integrated ornamentation of surface areas to an actual 'picture' with its own validity; it established its own autonomy. In precisely this type of pictorial decoration the influence of Chinese ink painting with its accentuated brush-strokes is displayed to best advantage. The diagonal division of many Chinese pictures – the so-called 'one-corner' style – also appears to have affected Higashiyama lacquerwork. It is quite possible that the high regard in which Chinese painting and its stylistic characteristics were held was a major factor in the development of takamakie. [44] (Theoretically it might be assumed that the popularity of Chinese carved lacquer had inspired the desire for relief decoration. But this hypothesis must be rejected on the grounds that in the fifteenth century the decoration of Chinese carved lacquerwork continued to be largely determined by the shape and surface of the object, and as such very definitely did not create any independent pictorial design.)

Although in itself the relief mode of representation makes possible a higher degree of realism than its two-dimensional equivalent, the Higashiyama lacquers are no more naturalistic in effect than those of the Kamakura period. The emphasis on mood and the literary associations of these works of the Muromachi period, their yūgen content, tends to give the subjects depicted a rather unreal poetic character. Almost all the motifs represented on the famous Muromachi writing-boxes originate from Japanese poems: accordingly, they are examples of uta-e. [45] In many instances, individual characters of a specific poem are interwoven with the representation, as, for instance, in a very restrained form, among some of the grasses and tendrils on the Kasugayama writing-box. This quality of poetic mood, which in the writing-table with the plum tree and moon motif (Pl.86) had already shown itself to be so essential in Muromachi lacquerwork, is captured much more strongly in the Higashiyama works than the Western observer – who does not know the poems on which they are based – can possibly realize. To Western eyes the representation on the Kasugayama writing-box merely shows red deer in an autumn landscape, but for the Japanese observer it literally brims over with a magical mood of dream-like unreality. It immediately arouses in him the feeling of the poem on which it is based:

> What is as lonely as a mountain village in autumn?
> I am woken by the cry of the red deer. [46]

In the Kamakura period one can legitimately compare the realistic representations to botanical studies (cf. p.77), but with their fifteenth-century equivalents (Pl.88, for example) no such comparison is possible. The close links with poetry and all the associations thereby evoked indicate that the lacquerwork of the Muromachi, and particularly the Higashiyama, periods were pointed in an altogether different direction. Never before and never since has the link between poetry and the art of lacquerwork been as close as it was then. The aim was not to represent the outer world but to touch upon and express the inner world, the world of emotion. It is not so strange that man, with his capacity for feeling, should now also appear in the landscape: the inside of the lid of the Kasugayama writing-box (Pl.93) shows a human form in a thatched mountain hut, apparently listening to 'the cry of the red deer.' This is not, however, the earliest non-religious representation of the human form within a lacquer decoration: a work of the late Kamakura period (the comb case in Pl.64) depicts fishermen with nets in a coastal landscape within the lid. But these have more of a decorative effect – they completely lack the emotional emphasis typical of the Muromachi period.

In the *Hana-no-Shirakawa* writing-box (Pl.94), a man is shown occupying the central position on the top of the lid. At first glance, it is apparent that, although this box also belonged to Yoshimasa, [47] it cannot be included in the Higashiyama group of lacquers. Although it is a work of the fifteenth century it stems from an older tradition. The charming shape of the box with its curved ground plan, domed lid and inverted corners, is not typical of the Higashiyama lacquers; also the technique – pure togidashi – is unusual for the fifteenth century. The picture shows a nobleman standing at the foot of an old cherry tree and turning thoughtfully towards the falling petals. The characters 'hana,' 'shiro' and 'kawa' refer to a poem by Fujiwara Masatsune which is dedicated to the cherry blossoms at Shirakawa. [48] The

Plate 93 Kasugayama writing-box (see Pl.92). Interior of lid

interior of the box is decorated with scattered petals.

Although this box is so very different from typical Higashiyama lacquers, it could hardly have been made – as was assumed earlier – before the fifteenth century. Not simply because of the linking of Chinese with purely Japanese stylistic elements – the tree could come straight from a picture by a Kanō painter, while the clouds and the figure of the courtier are in the Yamato-e tradition – but, above all, because the design is saturated with literary and emotional content. The design is simple, yet, for all its beauty, it lacks the careful elegance of earlier works. On the other hand, it clearly expresses the poetic, somewhat melancholy mood which is a recurrent theme in the decoration of fifteenth-century lacquer objects. In the emphasis given to man as the focus for the romantic mood, the Hana-no-Shirakawa writing-box is unique in the art of Japanese lacquerwork; it was possible only in this century when subjectively experienced landscapes so often served as motifs for lacquer decoration.

Beside the Kasugayama writing-box, mention should be made of another major example of Higashiyama lacquerwork: the *Shionoyama-suzuribako* in the National Museum in Kyōto (Pl.95).[49] The Shionoyama motif, so popular in the Muromachi period, is depicted here with great

Plate 94 Hana-no-Shirakawa writing-box. 15th c. 4.5:20.6:22.7cm. Tōkyō, Nezu Museum

clarity. This is another typical uta-e: seven characters, the beginning of a poem about the Shionoyama landscape, are woven into the design of the landscape.

Besides these sumptuously made, princely writing-boxes, there are simpler, contemporary examples of lacquerwork which, though perhaps not specifically made for Yoshimasa, are nevertheless very close in style and mood to the major works.[50] All these lacquers of the Higashiyama period, the sumptuously rich and the simpler items alike, belong together not only because of the predominant technique of takamakie but also because of the content expressed by this technique, and because of the literary basis of their landscape representations and the depth of human feeling that permeates them. Regardless of whether the decoration derives from a specific poem as in the numerous uta-e lacquers, whether, less often, the motifs are taken from tales of the Heian period (as, for example, the motif of the ivy path from the *Ise-monogatari*), or whether the representation expresses this typical relationship to nature only in quite general terms without reference to a specific literary antecedent, the close link between poetry and decoration is an essential characteristic of Higashiyama lacquerwork. One might

Plate 95 Shionoyama writing-box. 2nd half 15th c. 4.8:22.7:26.7cm. Kyōto National Museum

almost be tempted to refer to these works as 'having two voices,' since they appeal both to the eye and to the literary mind of the observer. It is all the more admirable that the lacquer decoration does not sink to the level of merely illustrating the poems, but that, with its own means and within its own terms, it translates poetic feeling into form.

Two lacquermasters who worked for Yoshimasa are known from written sources: Kōami Michinaga (1410-1478) and Igarashi Shinsai (dates unknown). No extant item can be attributed to either of them; but they were the founders of two schools of lacquermasters, members of which worked from now on for generations for the shōguns and the nobility, both schools in their own individual style (a subject which has not yet been sufficiently researched).

Two writing-boxes, which also qualify as examples of Higashiyama lacquerwork, approximate to the Kōami style and might possibly have been made for Yoshimasa by Michinaga or his son Michikiyo (1433-1500).[51] They are the Otokoyama writing-box in the National Museum in Tōkyō (Pl.96) and the Sagayama writing-box in the Nezu Museum (Pl.97). The latter is particularly interesting because of the remarkable contrast between the decoration on the outside and that on the inside of the lid. The exterior shows one of the large kettledrums used in official Court music, executed on

Plate 96 Otokoyama writing-box. Late 15th c. 4.8:21.1:22.3cm. Tōkyō National Museum

black-lacquer ground in takamakie, colour-graded dust and sheet-gold inlay. The inside of the lid shows a landscape typical of the Higashiyama style. Some characters from the pertinent poem are depicted in the interior of the box itself. Under the influence of Zen and the tea ceremony, it became the custom at this juncture to adorn the interiors of the writing-boxes more lavishly than the exteriors,[52] and the strangely contrasting decoration of the Sagayama writing-box could perhaps be considered within the context of this development.

The bevelled edges of the lid show very delicately and finely worked scrolls and dragons on an ikakeji ground. While takamakie dominates on the exterior of the lid, the interior offers a veritable compendium of different lacquer techniques: shishiai-makie (see p.114), maki-bokashi, harigaki, tsukegaki, black-lacquer drawing, tin-dust sprinkling, kirigane etc. This very combination of different technical possibilities is characteristic of lacquerwork of the Muromachi period.

Not until more precise research has been carried out can this suzuribako

Plate 97 Sagayama writing-box. Interior of lid. Late 15th c. 6:24.8:27.8cm. Tōkyō, Nezu Museum

be considered as the point of departure for all subsequent Kōami lacquers, yet it is obvious that the representation is smaller in scale and more detailed than either the Kasugayama or the Shionoyama writing-boxes. The box does not appear to possess the generous virility of the typical Higashiyama lacquers; instead, it is worked in that very neat but somewhat dry manner which is not unusual, later, in the work of the Kōami school.

A series of dated objects which, apart from their covering of red or black lacquer, show no further decoration, have also survived from the Higashiyama period, or, more precisely, from the years 1452 to 1482. Their shape clearly reveals Chinese influence, but since they are not particularly significant from the point of view of the actual history of Japanese lacquer-work, they are only briefly alluded to here.[53]

Muromachi period II: from the end of the Higashiyama period to 1567

THE GLITTERING PICTURE OF THE HIGASHIYAMA COURT MERELY SHOWS
the lighter side of that period. While in Yoshimasa's innermost circle art and
culture reached a lavish and costly zenith, economically and politically the
country was careening headlong towards chaos. Even in Yoshimasa's reign
(1443-1474) there were four popular uprisings demanding the general re-
mission of debt; the terrible famine of 1454 cost thousands of people their
lives; and finally, in 1467, the great civil war known as *Ōnin no ran*, which
was to last ten years, began. During its course, in the late sixties, Kyōto
became the scene of terrible battles, which left it a desolate wasteland of
ruins. The war ended in 1477, but by 1490 the country once more became
the scene of conflict; the next hundred years were subsequently described
as 'Sengoku-jidai,' the era of the Civil Wars. The imperial court and the
shōgun were soon stripped of all their power, and when the Emperor
Go-Tsuchimikado – the same man for whose coronation Yoshimasa had
commissioned Kōami Michikiyo to fashion a number of lacquer articles
– died in 1500, it took forty-four days to scrape together enough money
to defray the burial costs.

Kyōto, destroyed, ceased to be the source and focus of all art. Instead,
the large daimyo clans of the Ouchi, the Hōjō, the Shimazu and the Kikuchi
invited the scholars and artists to their provincial seats. In those places that
were spared by the war which raged back and forth, there arose small local
centres of culture. As far as lacquerwork is concerned, they included the
following: Yamaguchi to the southwest of Hondo (until 1557 the seat of the
Ouchi clan), Odawara southwest of Tōkyō (ruled until 1590 by the Hōjō),
and Sakai, a port in the neighbourhood of Osaka, which in the Muromachi
period managed to attain a considerable degree of independence.[1]

It is understandable that in this century of general upheaval neither the
luxurious execution of the Higashiyama lacquers nor their high artistic
quality could be maintained. Later, in the more peaceful era of the
Tokugawa shōguns, conservative lacquermasters again harked back to the
works of the Higashiyama period which, to a large extent, became model
and yardstick of the period. But the sixteenth century, something of a dark
age, witnessed first a lessening of quality and then also a change in style.

Naturally, though, echoes of the Higashiyama style can still be recognized in the first decades of the Sengoku period, and a surviving lacquer
work of this kind, a small box for incense wood (Pl.98: *Chidori makie-
jimbako*) now owned by the University of Art (Geijutsu Daigaku) in
Tōkyō, even provides us with a fixed point in time. It was made in the
second decade of the Eishō era (1504-1520). The second number of the year
has been so worn away that it is no longer recognizable; accordingly, it
could refer to any year from 1514, the eleventh of the era, to 1520, the
seventeenth and last of the era. On the lid and sides chidori (golden plovers)
are represented above waves; the beach is indicated by a few patches of rock
and grass; a full moon shines above. This is no longer a complex landscape,
depicted in depth, nor is there the impact of the thematically related
Shionoyama design on the Kyōto writing-box (Pl.95). Nevertheless, this
much simpler little box still reflects some of the beauty and culture of the
Higashiyama lacquers.

The chidori flock motif picks up a theme which had already been used
occasionally in the Kamakura period, but which is particularly characteristic of the lacquerwork of the Muromachi period. In the grouping and the

rhythm of the flight pattern, the birds not only are eminently suitable for purposes of composition, but also can be used, as in this instance, in the context of a more pictorial form of decoration. There are several poems to which such chidori pictures could be linked, but apparently this small box does not refer to any specific verse. In its very economy the little box retains much of that feeling of nocturnal solitude and tranquility which is characteristic of many Muromachi lacquers.

The moon and some sections of the rocks are inlaid in silver kanagai; it has already been pointed out that the combination of makie and kanagai was particularly popular in the Muromachi period. The subject and technique, therefore, conform to what was usual in lacquerwork of the period. Furthermore, certain details are also typical: for example, the shape of the wings of the chidori with their precise, rectilinear outlines and parallel feathers, which look like the teeth of a comb. In Heian and Kamakura lacquerwork the chidori wings have more gently curved contours and differently shaped feathers (cf. Pls 31 and 45); later, in the Edo period, they freeze into a stereotyped hardness.

Swallows and willow branches adorn a saddle (Pl.99) which bears the date 1516 and was therefore made at much the same time as the small box above (*Yanagi ni tsubame makie-gura*). Whereas the magnificent saddles of the Kamakura period were decorated throughout with raden, those of the Muromachi period often have kanagai as well as the new 'Chinese' technique of aogai (see Pl.91). Makie does occur occasionally from the fourteenth

Plate 98 Small incense box. ca 1515. Ht 8cm, diam. 14cm. Tōkyō Geijutsu Daigaku

century onwards, but up to the Momoyama period it is rarely used for the designs (as opposed to the grounds) of the saddles.[2] In this respect, this makie saddle has a certain interest, even if its quality is not particularly remarkable.

It has proved impossible so far to give an exact date to certain of the lacquer articles produced in the second half of the Muromachi period. They retain the multiplicity of techniques apparent in Higashiyama lacquerwork as well as the preference for takamakie and kanagai. Often, however, further three-dimensional elements are added, like small silver studs hammered in to represent dew drops and sometimes also metal inlays in such strong relief that the essential character of pure lacquerwork is almost lost. Items like the *Magaki-kiku-tebako* (Pl. 100), for instance, could almost be described as a combination of lacquer and metalwork.

Stylistically, there is a noticeable eclipse of Chinese elements in the sixteenth century. Just as the late Heian and the Kamakura periods were marked by the assimilation and adaptation of the Chinese models that had been so readily accepted in the Nara period, in the second half of the Muromachi period the tendency is toward a fresh Japanization, a transformation of Chinese stimuli into a native style. This is expressed as much in the overall conception of the decoration as in specific details. The Japanese feeling for the beauty inherent in the simple and the unadorned gains the upper hand, almost certainly influenced by the spirit of the tea ceremony, which finds its ultimate form at the end of the Muromachi period. (A parallel development can be observed in metalwork.) Indeed, the very 'Japaneseness' of sixteenth-century lacquerwork emphasizes the extent to which the early Muromachi period had opened itself to Chinese influence.

Plate 99 Saddle with swallows and willows. 1516. Japan, private collection

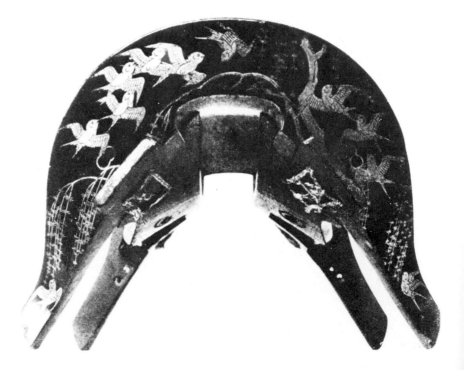

How does this self-awareness, this new breakthrough of Japanese tendencies, manifest itself specifically? The first thing worth noting is the fact that painting has now virtually ceased to serve as a model. There are exceptions, of course, but in general we no longer find any independent pictorial representations, particularly the type of landscape stretching far into the distance that were favourite subjects in the Higashiyama lacquers. Instead there is a new flatness making use of planes both in composition and in style. For purposes of composition, the subject matter chosen is limited to motifs depicted in the foreground or in close-up view. Again, the decoration becomes denser and covers the entire surface area, no longer leaving so much empty pictorial space. In many works of the early Muromachi period this very emptiness had suggested a kind of atmospheric depth even where there was no background design whatever, as for instance in the writing-table in Plate 86. In their denser covering of the surface to be decorated, many late Muromachi lacquers resemble works of the Kamakura period.

To this general compositional principle is added a further specific stylistic device: the decorative elements, above all blossoms and leaves, are now invariably depicted full-on: severely flattened out on every plane as if they had been pressed for a botanical album. This manner of decoration seems to be increasingly prevalent during the sixteenth century. A work such as the *Kiri makie-tebako* (Pl. 101), on which the leaves are almost all shown full-on and flat – which makes them appear to crowd together in the topmost 'spatial plane' – already approximates in principle to the Kōdai-ji lacquers of the Momoyama period. (It is interesting to compare the Kiri tebako with the

Plate 100   Toilet box with chrysanthemums beside a fence. 16th c. 22.5:34.5:26cm.
Kumano Hayatama-jinja, Wakayama province

fifteenth-century Nagi tebako (Pl.83) which likewise came from the Kumano Hayatama-jinja. In the latter there is also a general tendency to flatness, but several leaves are quite deliberately twisted round to break

Plate 101   Toilet box with kiri tree. 16th c. 23.4:35.2:26.8cm.
Kumano Hayatama-jinja, Wakayama province

Plate 102   Toilet box with pine and plum blossom. 16th c. 15.1:30.9:23.9cm.
Nagoya, Tokugawa Museum

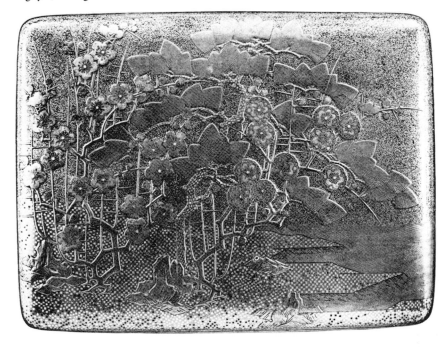

through the plane and point both forwards and backwards into 'space.') Very closely related to the Kiri tebako in its severe flattening-out of the decorative elements is a tebako with plum blossoms and pine trees (Pl. 102: *Nashiji matsu-ume makie-tebako*) in the Tokugawa Museum, Nagoya; it provides an excellent illustration of this stage of stylistic development.

Full-on representations do, of course, occur much earlier, but never so consciously, never with the deliberate aim of making everything two-dimensional and representing it as such. This flatness, which is an essential characteristic of the decorative nature of more recent Japanese art, also reappears in the painting of the same period, as Robert T. Paine has so appositely pointed out with reference to three crane pictures by the Kanō masters Masanobu (1434-1530), Motonobu (1476-1559) and Eitoku (1543-1590).[3] The tendency to flat planes opens up decorative possibilities, which in the Momoyama period play an important part in the new flowering of the art of lacquerwork. The Kiri tebako and – though not quite so obviously – the superb *Kiku makie-tebako* (Pl. 103) and other related pieces point in that direction. But technically, they unmistakably still belong to the Muromachi period, particularly the Kiku makie-tebako with its numerous kanagai inlays.

Lacquers like the so-called *Genji Yūgao-tebako* (Pl. 104), which shows a motif from the *Genji-monogatari* on the top of the lid, are difficult to date. Classical literature of the Heian period is turned to for the first time, as far as lacquerwork is concerned, in the Muromachi period; nor is the peculiar way of depicting pine needles as spokes of a wheel to be found in earlier work (cf. the saddle in Pl. 91). between the clusters of needles, bare, dried-up twigs are visible in places: these can be traced back to Chinese painting;

Plate 103 Toilet box with chrysanthemums by a stream. 16th c. 16.5:31.5:23cm. Japan, private collection

they reflect the aesthetic concept of 'wabi.' The style and format of the design – attention is deliberately focused on the immediate foreground – argue against an early date: that is, still in the Higashiyama period. Also, little free space has been left between the individual objects depicted; the space no longer has a function of its own, either as a 'pictorial surface' or suggesting spatial depth. The primary aim of the decoration is ornamental, not pictorial. Then again, the somewhat unmotivated, strongly emphasized plasticity of the roots and lower sections of the branches on the trees also points to the sixteenth century. The inside of the lid is decorated in a more traditional manner reminiscent of earlier autumn-field representations or of fifteenth-century mirrors. This combination of the old and the new suggests a dating no earlier than the second half of the Muromachi period.

The writing-box with the Ogurayama landscape (Pl. 105) probably also belongs right at the end of the Muromachi period. It is taken to be a work of the Igarashi school ands still clearly shows echoes of the Higashiyama lacquers. At first glance the landscape depicted on the lid is strongly reminiscent of the Otokoyama and Sagayama landscapes of the Higashiyama writing-boxes (Pls 96 and 97). For this reason the Ogurayama writing-box is even now sometimes grouped with Higashiyama lacquerwork,[4] especially since an inscription on the box in which it was kept (but which certainly was made in the Edo period) specifically describes it as 'Higashiyama-gomotsu.' The traditional technique with 'shishiai-togidashi' (the combination of takamakie and togidashi), maki-bokashi, nashiji and kirigane would not contradict such an early dating. (The particular stylistic characteristics of the Igarashi school will be discussed later; see p. 195.) However, the curious reversal of the size relationship, in which

Plate 104 Toilet box with a motif from the *Tales of Genji*. 16th c. Japan, private collection

the trees in the background are much larger than those in the immediate foreground, argues against the Higashiyama period and in favour of the sixteenth century. While Higashiyama lacquermasters had a fondness for spatial depth, not only because of its link with the mood of ink painting, but also because it matched the world-renouncing, nature-loving aspect of the poems that had inspired them, the reverse perspective of the Ogurayama writing-box, in spite of the separation of the ranges of hills, in fact cancels out the effect of depth. By distorting the size relationship, distant objects are brought quite emphatically into the foreground and the spatial effect is reduced to two dimensions. It would be inconceivable for this unusual technique to have been used unintentionally; if it was intentional, though, it matches the tendencies – mentioned earlier – of the second half of the Muromachi era, and the striving for a new, two-dimensional effect.

An iconographic detail also points to a dating in the sixteenth century: the design of the flower-bearing raft inside the box. This motif became popular at the end of the century and was used in textiles as well as in lacquerwork (for example on the steps of the Kōdai-ji; see p.151). There is no instance of the use of this motif in the Higashiyama period.

Plate 105 Ogurayama writing-box. 16th c. 4.2:22.8:25.5cm. Tōkyō, Suntori Gallery

Free from the Higashiyama tradition, however, is a writing-box, made in about 1550, which shows a long-tailed bird on a branch of flowering cherry (Pl. 106: *Sakura-sanjaku makie-suzuribako*). The box is unsigned, but the Kōami family chronicle confirms it as a work of Kōami Sōhaku (1485-1557); a certificate of authenticity written in 1713 gives the age of the box as 170 years. The Kōami masters, who had been working for the shōguns since the school was founded by Michinaga, are time and again described as being important lacquermasters, but until the end of the seventeenth century there are very few works that can positively be linked with a specific master.[5] In this respect the Sakura-sanjaku writing-box is an important document.

Beyond this, the box tells a great deal about the style of the late Muromachi period. Henceforth, there would be no more retracing of links to lacquer works of the Higashiyama period with their complex techniques and strong literary emphasis, although the echoes of Chinese painting can still be perceived. The technial execution is neither particularly fine nor careful (for example the pewter kirigane on the breast of the bird), but the design is superb. There is great mastery in the composition of the essential parts: the branch, the various clusters of blossoms, and the bird are beautifully spread across the top and well-balanced with an acute sense of the rhythm of the various directions they move in. If this design is compared with works of the early Muromachi period – perhaps with the baigetsu writing-table (Pl. 86), which cannot be praised too often for the masterpiece it is – the change is obvious: the earlier work is infinitely more refined in its elegance and is imbued with a deep, soulful, poetic mood. These characteristics disappear in the sixteenth century; instead there is a more robust creative spirit no longer connected to literature, but which applies itself, if less lovingly, quite forcefully and with great skill to the decorative tasks at hand. Like the Kiri-tebako (Pl. 101) this writing-box – very definitely still a

Plate 106 Kōami Sōhaku: writing-box with a bird on a branch of flowering cherry. ca 1550. 4.6:20.9:21.8cm. Japan, private collection

work of the Muromachi era – already points ahead to the Momoyama period, not so much in the individual forms as in the change in the overall artistic conception.

The interior of the box is equally interesting. Next to the Shionoyama writing-box, it is one of the earliest surviving instances where the inkstone and water container are set to the left of the central axis while the right-hand side is taken up by the tray for the brushes.[6] Very charming, and again determined by purely decorative reasons, is the design of this tray, consisting of pine twigs inlaid in aogai. The positioning of the twigs and the stylized arrangement of the needles make the design look more like an ornament than a naturalistic representation. Incidentally, aogai is also used on the lid for some of the cherry blossoms and the 'peacock's eyes' in the tail feathers of the bird.

Two simpler works are also worth mentioning in this context. According to their inscriptions both pieces, a black-lacquer box with shishi decoration[7] and a votive tablet with a horse design (Pl. 107), were donated to the temple of Chūson-ji in 1564 by a man called Kimura Yūbei. Of course, there were and still are simple, mass-produced votive tablets, but lacquer works can hardly be included in this category and quite definitely not if, as in this case, they were commissioned pieces. Accordingly, the unmistakable tendency towards simplicity and a two-dimensional decorative effect, through the use of straightforward techniques, cannot adequately be explained by the hypothesis that this is not 'art.' The decorative simplification should be considered in the overall context of stylistic development.

Mention has already been made of the lacquer utensils produced in the temple of Negoro for the personal use of the priests and monks, the so-called Negoro-nuri (see p.84). The origins of these undecorated red- or

Plate 107 Votive tablet. 1564. 30:23.3cm. Chūson-ji, Iwate province. Reproduced from *Chūson-ji*

red-and-black-lacquered wares are in the thirteenth century, but the main flowering of Negoro-nuri appears to have occurred at the end of the Muromachi period. (The temple was then at the height of its power; in about 1570, 5900 monks were attached to it.) As it happens, the number of inscribed and dated pieces is considerably smaller in the sixteenth than in the fourteenth and fifteenth centuries, but this could simply have been a question of fashion and need not necessarily be taken as evidence of either the quantity or the quality of the Negoro lacquers produced. [8] Among the most beautiful items ascribed to the sixteenth century is a small medicine jar only 8.1cm high (Pl. 108). The lively, entirely self-contained shape, which perhaps still owes something to Chinese Sung ceramics, is an outstanding example of the turner's art. But the true beauty of its form is fully revealed only by the soft glow of its lacquer skin. The rounded shape combined with the soft lustre – of which no illustration can accurately convey the delicacy – is inevitably reminiscent of a pearl.

The fact that the red-lacquer coating is so worn away and rubbed off in many places, and that the underlying black lacquer shows through, gives that sense of age, history and venerability so esteemed by the Japanese teamasters. In spite of the freshness of the colours, this small container is pure 'wabi.' Like so many Negoro lacquers it is in complete accord with the ideal of refined simplicity which, through the intermediary of the tea ceremony, has had such a far-reaching influence on Japanese taste. Even the

Plate 108 Medicine box. 16th c. Ht 8.1cm. Japan, private collection

Western connoisseur of lacquerwork, whose eyes are dazzled by the gold glitter of makie, cannot fail to be struck by the beauty of this simple jar; its renown among Japanese experts is universal.

It is scarcely by coincidence that a great deal of Kamakurabori work was produced at this time, but in a style clearly distinct from early examples of the technique. Even though initially Kamakurabori had merely provided a substitute for genuine carved lacquer, its subsequent development took a different direction. No longer was any attempt made to simulate a thick, hard skin of lacquer: on the contrary, the carved wood itself became increasingly evident as such. At the same time, as in the Negoro lacquers, the black lacquer was often allowed to show through the partially abraded layer of red lacquer. This is not necessarily always the case: there are also pure red and pure black Kamakurabori works, but the others are more common. Already, the small container in Plate 77, which is ascribed to the fifteenth century, is quite evidently carved from wood, not from a basically textureless build-up of numerous successive layers of lacquer. It seems that in the course of the sixteenth century Chinese carved lacquers, which had been so highly prized in the Higashiyama period, had lost some of their universal appeal; also, the time-consuming nature of their production was probably hampered by the civil war. Yet it appears, on the other hand, that potential and charms beyond the straightforward imitation of carved lacquerwork, were now discovered in the technique of Kamakurabori. When Chinese carved lacquer and Japanese Kamakurabori are set side by side, it is immediately obvious that the carved lacquer looks more elegant, sophisticated and artistic, and that in contrast, the Kamakurabori possesses an artless grace. But it was this very simplicity that made Kamakurabori appeal so strongly to all levels of Japanese society – an appeal it maintains to this day. Genuine carved lacquerwork, however, despite the initial enthusiasm for items imported from China, does not really appear to have found its place in Japanese art until the nineteenth century (see pp. 166ff.).

One particular variant of Chinese carved lacquer known in Japanese as 'kōka-ryokuyō' (red blossoms – green leaves) was nevertheless often imitated in Kamakurabori toward the end of the Muromachi period. In Chinese works made with this technique, multicoloured layers of lacquer were uncovered by varying the depth of the carving so that the finished decoration showed red-lacquer blossoms over or among green-lacquer leaves. In the Japanese imitations, as in all Kamakurabori, the decoration is carved not into the lacquer, but into the underlying wood; the subsequent lacquering-over in different colours presents no problem.

This multi-coloured Kamakurabori was particularly popular for the large, portable wooden boxes carried by itinerant Buddhist priests like a kind of rucksack. Several such wooden rucksacks (oi) have survived, and sections of others were later used for sliding doors in small cupboards and wall shelves.[9] A rucksack from the Jigen-ji (Pl. 109: *Tsubaki-mon kamakurabori-oi*) provides a good example of this vigorous, simple and very effective technique. The display side is divided into three horizontal zones bearing a motif of red camellias with green leaves on a black-lacquer ground. The thalami and stamens of the flowers are accentuated with superimposed gold leaf and the leaves are very decoratively arranged in low relief. The narrow marginal fields show chrysanthemums (the lowest over a mere allusion to the beloved 'East Fence'), while a diaper pattern in the lowest zone serves as a solid and unifying base.. The numerous carved dew drops in both the central and the marginal fields add a light touch to the overall composition.

The powerful construction of the wooden rucksack, the simple, large-patterned decoration and the use of a limited range of contrasting colours match beautifully. Ornamental composition and bold simplification definitely reflect the style which was also manifesting itself in other types of sixteenth-century lacquerwork; at the same time they show the very Japanese nature of this style. Of course, it is true that works of this kind are peripheral in the art of lacquerwork – the lacquer playing only a minor role as it does, say, in Negoro-nuri.

It appears that at about the same time as the wooden rucksacks, a whole series of kōgō were made in the Kamakurabori technique. Two of these are dated and show the so-called 'guri' pattern borrowed from China. The guri kōgō from the temple of Chion-in in Kyōto has a diameter of about 25 cm

Plate 109 Wooden rucksack. 16th c. Ht ca 80cm. Tōkyō National Museum

and dates from 1564; a year later, the second box (Pl. 110), in the Enkaku-ji in Kamakura, almost identical in size, carries on its underside a dedicatory inscription on red lacquer with the date 'Eiroku eighth year,' that is, 1565.[10] In the remarkable shallowness of its relief this kōgō to some extent reflects the tendency to flatness in the sixteenth century (noted above); it lacks the imposing vigour of earlier Kamakurabori works and the best Chinese guri lacquers.

Finally, at the end of the Muromachi period, mention should be made of a new type of lacquer box with an overlapping lid, the so-called 'sumi-aka' ('corners red'). Individual specimens appeared in the middle of the fourteenth century, but the real popularity of the box, which it retained throughout the Momoyama and Edo periods (see Pl. 142), dates from the end of the Muromachi era. In a sumi-aka, which come in different sizes, the top section of the box and the lower section of the lid are decorated with a red-lacquer border, narrow along the sides and wide at the corners in a manner that looks not unlike metal edging. Frequently these parts are first covered with coarse cloth onto which the red lacquer is applied without grounding, leaving the texture of the cloth to impart an accent of its own. With the exception of the red corners and the narrow linking zones, the boxes are generally lacquered black and decorated with makie. The simple colour contrast which matches their shape so well, gives sumi-aka works a certain power and freshness far removed from the refined elegance of earlier lacquer boxes. The decoration does not usually play a very significant role in these pieces but this situation of course varies in the Muromachi, Momoyama and Edo periods according to the respective stylistic conventions. (The piece illustrated belongs in the early Edo period, an annotation gives its date as the fifth year Genna, or 1619.)

Plate 110 Kamakurabori-kōgō. 1565. Diam. 25.4cm. Kamakura, Enkaku-ji

Let us attempt to summarize the general characteristics of Muromachi
lacquerwork as a whole.

Although the tradition of late Kamakura lacquerwork is continued in a
few individual items especially of the fourteenth century, the bulk of the
lacquers of the early Muromachi period (that is, of the fourteenth and
fifteenth centuries) show a strong Chinese influence. Most easily recognizable is the influence of Chinese painting which manifests itself in the choice
of subject and composition, in the relationship of the decoration to the
pictorial ground, in the style of calligraphic lines and in the quest for spatial
depth. But Chinese arts and crafts also directly affected the shape of
Japanese lacquer works of this period, as many Negoro lacquers attest.

Especially characteristic of the fifteenth century, and in particular of the
Higashiyama period, is the intimate relationship between lacquerwork and
poetry. Almost all the outstanding lacquer works of this era can be directly
connected with a poem. This strong literary content, together with the
influence exercised by painting and the technique of takamakie, provides
another reason for the temporary relaxation of the close link between the
shape and the lacquer decoration of an article, resulting in an independent
lacquer 'picture.'

Towards the end of the Muromachi period, in the sixteenth century, the
Chinese elements in lacquerwork decline – they have been assimilated and
Japanized – and the Japanese feeling for two-dimensional design and
rhythmic-decorative effect reasserts itself. Spatial depth and literary associations, so characteristic of Higashiyama lacquerwork, disappear in the
course of this evolution, or at any rate become much rarer. In late works one
can clearly discern a tendency towards greater simplicity, stylized com-
pression of individual forms previously depicted in fine detail (blossoms
and pine needles, for example), and emphasis on two-dimensional designs.
But at the same time, even if less evident, the traditional custom, based on
the Higashiyama lacquers and in the final analysis on the work of the
Kamakura period, continues. Even the new elements still remain within the
framework of what, as far as lacquerwork is concerned, is an imprecise,
ambiguous term: the Muromachi style.

Hence, it would be tempting to divide Muromachi lacquers into the
following categories: an early style strongly influenced by Chinese painting
(for example Pls 73, 74, 81, 86); the fully developed style as characterized
by the takamakie stage of development of the Higashiyama lacquers (here
the links with poetry are at their closest; Pls 92, 95, 96, 97); and a late style
in which emphasis on the decorative replaces the elements derived from
painting and poetry (Pls 101, 102, 106). But such a classification would be
an oversimplification, since it creates the mistaken impression of a
chronological sequence that is non-existent in this pure form. The main
tendencies are as indicated, of course, but that is not to say that the various
stages do not overlap.

As far as technique is concerned, the following can be said: the old raden
technique, which had played a significant role since the late Heian period,
was abandoned in the Muromachi period, and under Chinese influence
attention shifted to thinner aogai inlays. Chinkinbori, carved lacquer and
Kamakurabori were also stimulated by Chinese models and expanded the
range of Japanese lacquers, but in the purely Japanese sphere of makie there
are no new developments. All the sprinkling techniques employed in

Muromachi lacquerwork were already known, at the latest, by the time the plum tree tebako in the Mishima-taisha (Pl. 59) was made. The only innovations were that such prominence was given to takamakie, kanagai and kirigane; that different techniques were now more often used in combination (for example the simultaneous use of takamakie and togidashi); and that, as a consequence of the resulting impression of technical complexity, the observer became much more or perhaps for the first time, fully aware of the craftsmanship of the lacquermasters and of a certain element of artistry.

Accordingly, it is hardly possible to talk in terms of a uniform development of lacquerwork during the Muromachi period. The continued influence of tradition, the eager affinity for Chinese prototypes and, in technique, all sorts of experiments and combinations combine to demonstrate that works of a very different nature can stand side by side. The luxurious Higashiyama lacquers and the simple Negoronuri works exist simultaneously, yet have nothing in common; nor is there necessarily a great time gap between articles as different as the Hana-no-Shirakawa and the Kasugayama writing-boxes.

The prime task confronting the Muromachi period, and its area of greatest achievement, lay not in technique but in style; in coming to terms with the wave of Chinese influence, adapting and transforming it. In this respect the Muromachi lacquermasters faced a situation very similar to that experienced by their predecessors in the Heian period.

Momoyama period

THE GREAT CIVIL WAR THAT HAD DEVELOPED FROM THE DETERIORATION OF
the political situation in Japan since the end of the fifteenth century had
radically altered the existing balance of power in the sixteenth century. The
imperial court and the shōgunate were divested of their authority, many a
flourishing princely line died out or sank into oblivion, and many a previously insignifiant family rose to play a leading role. To survive these strug-
gles, not ancient lineage but real power was the decisive factor, and only the
most powerful could, by suppressing the other factions, succeed in gradually re-uniting the ruined country. The three men who, succeeding one
another, saw this great work to fruition were Oda Nobunaga (1534-1582),
Toyotomi Hideyoshi (1536-1598) and Tokugawa Ieyasu (1542-1616). The
interval between the victorious entry of Oda Nobunaga into Kyōto in 1568
and the final establishment of the Tokugawa shōgunate by the taking of
Osaka castle (the years between 1568 and 1615), is known as the Momoyama period.[1] (The name derives from a place to the south of Kyōto,
where Hideyoshi built his famous Fushimi Castle.) The Momoyama period
lasted only forty-seven years, yet it was of paramount importance for both
the history and art of Japan.

It was a time of new men, newly developing political unity and social
strata, and new, powerful self-assurance. Vigour, great activity, new prosperity, and an affirmation of life mark the spirit of these decades; freedom,
broadmindedness, and a receptiveness to outside influences are the forces
which animated this era, causing it to break away from the Middle Ages in
one great vital sweep and seek new, more modern modes of existence.
Trade and shipping prospered and there was new wealth for the citizens.
After the destructive wars of the Muromachi period an unprecedented urge
to reconstruct created numerous magnificently appointed castles and
palaces; many devastated temples were restored. Through the Portuguese,
the Spanish and the Dutch, Western ideas were introduced; through the
wars against Korea Korean influence was felt; both were quickly and ea-
gerly assimilated by Japanese artists.

This era is so vital, manifold and rich in new ideas that many find their
ultimate form only in the Edo period, while others merely flare up briefly,
only to be snuffed out by the altered circumstances of the later era. Yet
despite the freeing from medieval patterns and the turning to new modes of
expression, not every link with the past was severed. In lacquerwork, too,
much of the old tradition remains in both subject matter and technique; not
so much, it is true, in the sense of carrying on as before but through
rethinking and reinterpreting in an unbiased modern spirit. The strength of
this conservative, traditional tendency should not be underestimated. But
more striking and typical of the Momoyama period are lacquerworks of an
altogether new variety.

The central figure of the Momoyama period is Hideyoshi. Just as he
himself had risen from tying Nobunaga's sandals to become the most powerful man in the country, other men, whose minds had not been shaped by
the literary erudition or sophisticated spirit of the Muromachi period had
achieved positions of authority. For the masterwork of the Higashiyama
period, a poem about a lone, autumnal mountain village with its mood of
withdrawal from a noisy, turbulent world, had been both literary premise
and intellectual background (see p.115). To the new type of ruling men,
such literary associations meant very little; reticence, seriousness and

muted feelings were not to their liking. Their mentality is reflected in the art of their own time: easily understood, very appealing, generous and unfettered. It rejoices in magnificence, richness, colour and life. In painting, the radiant gold-ground sliding doors and screens of the Momoyama period succeed the sober Zen-inspired ink paintings of the Muromachi period; in pottery, the simple artless products of the previous centuries are followed by the first full flowering of the craft with such fresh, original works as the Shino- and Oribe-wares; the textile arts (largely dependent on China in the Muromachi period) in creating the magnificence of Nō and ceremonial costumes achieve something entirely novel in Japan; metalwork becomes multi-hued (*cloisonné*)² and lavish, and the art of lacquerwork as well is thoroughly imbued with this new spirit. In lacquerwork too, there remains an undercurrent, which, in accordance with the ideals of the great teamaster Rikyū (1521-1591), favours a severity and clean-cut simplicity but it is obscured by the prevailing love for a beauty that is strikingly decorative and intellectually undemanding.

It has become standard practice to group the lacquerwork of the Momoyama period into three large categories: items in the traditional style; the particularly characteristic group of the Kōdai-ji lacquers; and the so-called Nambam lacquers. But not everything fits into these main groups, nor are they strictly mutually exclusive. All three are imbued with the same vigorous, generous, broadminded, ebullient spirit, which is why there is much overlapping and interaction between the different types of Momoyama lacquerwork.

A saddle with matching stirrups (Pl. 111: *Ashi no ho makie-gura*) owned

Plate 111 Saddle with decoration after Eitoku. 1577. Tōkyō National Museum

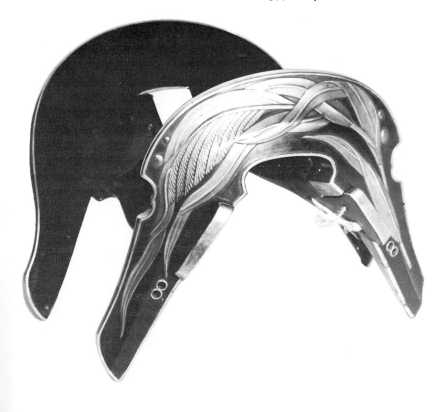

by Hideyoshi is a classic example of a work in the traditional group, as well as being the earliest of the small number of dated lacquers of the Momoyama period. The saddle itself is old (an inscription on the underside gives the date 1445), but it was redecorated in 1577: on the fore-bow there is the date fifth year Tenshō (1577) in Chinese ink and the kakihan of Hideyoshi. The design for this new lacquer decoration, which shows a full reed panicle covered with dew drops, is said to have been made by the most famous artist of the time, Kanō Eitoku (1543-1590).[3] This tradition cannot be substantiated, but Kanō Eitoku had carried out other commissions for Hideyoshi: he had provided paintings for both his castle in Osaka and the Yurakutei palace in Kyōto. It was certainly quite usual, from the Muromachi period onwards, for famous painters also to make preliminary drawings for lacquer articles.

The panicle is worked in prominently raised gold takamakie on a black-lacquer ground; sheet gold and silver inlay are used for the veins of the

Plate 112 Sumiyoshi writing-box. Late 16th c. Japan, private collection

leaves and the dew drops. Accordingly, the technical execution is traditional, since takamakie and metal inlays (kanagai) were the favourite lacquer techniques of the Muromachi period. But the simplicity of the subject – a single reed without any literary significance – and the bold confidence in using this motif to achieve the desired decorative effect, are born of the spirit of sweeping generosity of the Momoyama period.

A writing-box which is still clearly in the Muromachi tradition (Pl. 112: *Sumiyoshi makie-suzuribako*) was probably not made before the Momoyama period. The exterior of the lid shows, on a black-lacquer ground, the entrance to a Shintō sanctuary (as the scene on the interior of the lid confirms, it is in fact the Sumiyoshi shrine), with a somewhat strange representation of a frog on the shore in front of it. On the inside of the lid, the buildings that make up the shrine are sketchy rather than represented in detail; the interior tray continues the theme. The design inside the lid is closely related to the representation of the Sumiyoshi shrine (Pl. 105) inside the lid of the Ogurayama writing-box, which is taken as a work of the Igarashi school. Further peculiarities in this Sumiyoshi writing-box also indicate the work of an Igarashi master: for instance, the largely undecorated black-lacquer ground. The iconography, among other things, argues in favour of a relatively late date of origin, that is, in the Momoyama period: the mussel and seaweed motif (kai to kaisō) does not occur in the Muromachi period but is a favourite theme in the Momoyama period, and particularly at the beginning of the Edo period. This motif appears in much the same form, for example, on a small box of the early Edo period (Pl. 137). Around 1600, other forms of aquatic life also seem to have been favoured motifs. The Tokugawa Museum in Nagoya, for instance, has a yukata (a type of cotton summer kimono) of the Momoyama period, which is decorated solely with large crayfish.[4]

Yet another lacquer article bearing the traditional Sumiyoshi landscape, a table in the temple of Ninna-ji (Pl. 113: *Sumiyoshi makie-tsukue*), may well have been made around 1590. Hideyoshi is said to have given it to the Emperor Goyōzei, and, since he ruled from 1586 to 1611, and Hideyoshi died in 1598, the date of origin can be narrowed down to a specific period.

Plate 113 Writing-table with Sumiyoshi decoration. ca 1590. 26.7:90.2:38cm. Kyōto, Ninna-ji

Here too is seen the combination of takamakie, kanagai and kirigane so particularly popular in the Muromachi period; the ground is of densely sprinkled nashiji. But how strongly the powerful spirit of the Momoyama period with its love of magnificence emanates from this work; what a fine sense of rhythm in the allocation of visual accents and of large, two-dimensional, almost abstract patterns! How thoroughly the traditional elements of subject and technique have been rethought and reinterpreted, and, how purely Japanese the decoration is: there is not a hint of the love of China so characteristic of the Muromachi period.

A bookcase decorated with 'Three laughing sages in the Tiger Valley'[5] (Pl. 114: *Kokei-sanshō makie-dana*) shows the traditional Muromachi techniques still more clearly, although it was probably made later than the table. Written sources indicate that the lacquermaster Kōami Chōgen (1572-1607)

Plate 114 Bookshelf with 'The three laughing sages.' Early 17th c. 65.2:73.3:32.7cm. Tōkyō National Museum

Plate 115 Manuscript box with autumn grasses. Late 16th c. 26.5:50.2:31cm. Kyōto, Kōdai-ji

Plate 116 Tansu with autumn grasses. Late 16th c. 37.1:33:23.6cm. Kyōto, Kōdai-ji

was commissioned by the teamaster Furuta Oribe (1544-1615) to decorate a bookcase with this motif; a detailed description of the bookcase has survived. There are six so-called Oribe bookcases with kokei-sanshō decoration in existence today, but none exactly matches the old description. The bookcase in the National Museum in Tōkyō, which on its second shelf shows the three sages crossing the bridge, comes closest in its technical execution (takamakie, gold and silver kirigane, kanagai) to the traditional lacquer techniques. Consequently it is taken to be the earliest of the six. It is probably a contemporary copy of the original kokei-sanshō bookcase made by Kōami Chōgen. This type of bookcase with a small cupboard and a sliding door is known as a 'zushi-dana,' that is, a cupboard-bookcase.

Plate 117 Hot water jug. Late 16th c. Ht 12.9cm. Kyōto, Kōdai-ji

Plate 118 Spice jars. Late 16th c. Ht 7cm, diam. 22cm. Kyōto, Kōdai-ji

Throughout the Momoyama period, therefore, in addition to the lacquer works in the new modern style – which will be discussed later – numerous items were also produced which are still completely conservative in technique. The works of this type form part of an unbroken tradition leading from the Muromachi period to the famous trousseau which Kōami Nagashige created (see p. 189) in the early Edo period (1639) for the wedding of Tokugawa Iemitsu's daughter and Tokugawa Mitsumoto, the Prince of Bishū.[6] But while this stylistic tendency, though by no means untouched by the generous, broadminded spirit of the Momoyama period, produced nothing genuinely new, other forces were nevertheless at work. There were lacquermasters who burst the bonds of traditional subjects and techniques and created lacquer objects of a completely different kind to match new needs and new tastes.

The so-called Kōdai-ji lacquers show this new style in its purest form; together with the large decorative sliding doors and painted screens of the period they represent the most characteristic achievements of Momoyama art as a whole. They are particularly closely linked with Hideyoshi since a large proportion of them were made for his personal use; Hideyoshi and his wife are said to have particularly prized them.

The name 'Kōdai-ji-makie' derives from the Kōdai-ji temple in Kyōto, which Hideyoshi's widow ordered to be built in 1605 or 1606, and in which more than thirty such lacquer articles have survived to this day. But the term also covers works in this style in other collections.

Among the objects in the temple are the following: a writing-box (Pl. 115: *Akikusa makie-bunko*), a portable box for small volumes of poetry (Pl. 116: *Akikusa makie-kasho-tansu*), a hot-water can (Pl. 117: *Akikusa*

Plate 119 Tray with fans and grasses. ca 1600. 32.7:20.5cm. Japan, private collection

makie-yu-oke) and a matching set of spice containers shaped like a flower (Pl. 118: *Kaede-kiri-kiku-mon makie-yakumi-tsubo*); privately owned Kōdai-ji lacquers include, for example, a tray (Pl. 119: *Semmen-susuki makie-bon*) and a writing-box (Pl. 120: *Misu-matsu makie-suzuribako*). The date of origin of these items is unknown, but inside the Kōdai-ji itself, there is an unequivocal clue which gives the date of their origin.

As mentioned above, the temple was built on the orders of Kitano Mandokoro, Hideyoshi's widow; and as it happens, sections of Hideyoshi's former Fushimi Castle were incorporated in the structure. The truly magnificent castle was built in 1594 but was badly damaged only two years later by an earthquake. It was restored immediately by Hideyoshi only to be destroyed again after his death, in 1600. Although Ieyasu restored it again in 1603, large sections of the castle were transported to new localities and incorporated into other structures, such as the Kōdai-ji.[7] Many of the original buildings of the Kōdai-ji were later destroyed by fire, but the Kaizan-dō and the Mitamaya (ancestor hall or mausoleum) survived, the latter being of particular significance for the art of lacquerwork.

In the Mitayama there is a kind of dais with four steps leading up to it flanked by banisters (Pl. 121). On the dais, right and left, are two shrines

Plate 120 Misu-matsu writing-box. Early 17th c. Japan, private collection

containing wood carvings of Hideyoshi (right) and Kitano Mandokoro (left). The stairs, banisters, the base and doors of the shrine are decorated in glowing makie on a black-lacquer ground; the banisters and base show musical instruments; the stairs depict so-called 'hana-ikada' (wave-tossed rafts bearing flowers). The door panels of the Hideyoshi shrine are decorated on the outside with susuki grasses and kiri crests (on the inside with maples, chrysanthemums and kiri crests), and those of the Kitano Mandokoro shrine with pines and bamboo inside and out.

In 1939 and 1955, two small harigaki inscriptions were discovered in the makie decoration at the inside of the Hideyoshi shrine's door and at the base of the left staircase railing. These inscriptions, very difficult to read, were first interpreted as 'Bunroku 5th year, 12th month, made by Kōami Kyū.' But, according to later research, the artist's name should read Kōami Matazaemon.[8] The date 'Bunroku 5th year,' written on the door, proves that the doors were made in 1596, a decade before the Kōdai-ji was built; that means that they were made for the Fushimi Castle and later transferred from there to the Kōdai-ji. In addition to Matazaemon's name[9] written in harigaki, more signatures were found during a restoration in 1955-1956. They were written in black lacquer on the underside of one of the railings and give the names of Shinjirō, Iemon and Wakaemon, who probably also belonged to the Kōami school.

Momoyama period

Plate 121 Mitamaya. View of interior. Built 1606, lacquer work 1596. Kyōto, Kōdai-ji

There is no doubt, therefore, about either the date of origin of these items originally made for the Fushimi Castle and then transferred to the Kōdai-ji or about the lacquermasters who produced them. Other lacquer-decorated, architectural details, which came from Fushimi and which match those in the Kōdai-ji in style and technique, are now in the main hall of the Tsukufusuma-jinja[10] (two pillars, beautifully decorated with autumn grasses, chrysanthemums, kiri crests, etc., which have been designated National Treasures) and in the Sambō-in of the temple of Daigo-ji near Kyōto (a tokonoma threshold decorated with autumn plants.)[11]

Since the decoration of these architectural parts signed by Kōami masters matches the lacquer wares in the Kōdai-ji in technique, inconography and style, it may be assumed that the latter were also made by members of the Kōami school. It is fair to say that these articles and the architectural details were both part of the same master plan for the Fushimi Castle and thus they were made sometime after 1594, although the style continued into the early Edo period (see p. 170).

What are the characteristics, the peculiarities of Kōdai-ji lacquers? Quite a few will have to be mentioned here. From the iconographic point of view, there is first of all the *leitmotif* of autumn plants, which also include susuki grasses; often associated with these in Kōdai-ji lacquers are chrysanthemums, pines and bamboo; after that come the kiri and chrysanthemum crests which Hideyoshi frequently used. All autumn plants are depicted neither as part of an autumn landscape nor in conjunction with roe deer, insects and birds as they are in Kamakura lacquerwork. Instead, the decoration of the Kōdai-ji lacquers – except for a few patches of earth, which are more important from the point of view of composition than as subject representation – consists solely of the sprigs of blossoms, grasses and tendrils themselves. These are depicted with a totally new freedom dedicated solely to expressing their natural beauty and rhythmic swaying. The drawn line, its movement and direction, are given a new decorative emphasis.

Not only are the plants not part of any landscape, they do not have any deep symbolic or literary allusive significance either – as the plum and cherry blossoms of Muromachi lacquerwork did. Kōdai-ji decoration reproduces only the sensuous, eye-appealing image of plants, the 'beautiful aspect' of nature. The unambiguous motifs, which even the uneducated parvenu of the time could easily comprehend, are arranged in bold compostions, determined by a strong feeling for rhythm and line, which harmonize well with the shape of the article.

This simple beauty of line – so fascinating because of the rhythmic motions that seem to arise spontaneously from the designs of grasses, branches and tendrils – is repeatedly contrasted in Kōdai-ji lacquers with static elements that derive their effect not from the line but from well-filled, flat surface areas. Primarily, the large kiri crests (stylized *paulownia* flowers) serve this aim. They occur on a large proportion of the Kōdai-ji lacquers, but on the items illustrated here are visible only on the hot-water can and the door of the Hideyoshi shrine. In their heraldic compactness and immobility they are contrasted with the lightly swaying grasses and stalks, Here, not only line and flat area, but to an even stronger degree natural forms and stylized images are contrasted. An equally striking contrast can be seen in the tray in Plate 119 where large, curved blades of grass dotted with dew drops are surprisingly juxtaposed with finely decorated fan motifs which are, even more surprisingly, depicted in a most outlandish size relationship.

Particularly popular in Kōdai-ji lacquers is the contrast which makes the manuscript box in Plate 115 and the writing-box in Plate 120 so compelling: the diagonal dovetailing, on one or more sides of the article, of two fields differing from each other in colour, motif and rhythm. The manuscript box is probably the most famous example of this style; on each of the outer sides a black-lacquer field with curved, lightly swaying autumn plants meets a nashiji field with austere, vertical, parallel bamboo shafts. In the writing-box the contrast is between chrysanthemums and water-chestnut tendrils on a black-lacquer ground on the one hand, and a golden bamboo curtain (misu) with a pine tree and three kiri crests on the other. The way the stalks and tendrils – loose, isolated and full of movement and curves – are contrasted with the rigid horizontal and vertical grid of the curtain, and the firmly rooted quality of the pine tree; the way the flat values of the black ground and the areas of gold balance each other, all these evidence not only a most sophisticated inventiveness but also a highly developed, sensitive artistic awareness. The zig-zag dovetailing of the opposing fields in both boxes enhances their very special dynamics.

These compositions, so effective because their rich contrasts come as almost a physical shock to the eye, are by no means the prerogative of the Kōdai-ji lacquermasters. In the Momoyama period they occur even more frequently in textiles and ceramics, which at that time were enjoying a renaissance, and which were consequently less strongly hemmed in by tradition. Indeed, it might have been from them that Kōdai-ji lacquerwork derived this type of composition. In textiles this love of contrast resulted, for example, in the so-called 'katami-kawari' kimonos, in which, front and back, pieces of cloth in different colours and materials are juxtaposed to great effect. It can also be seen in patterns of interlocking wedge shapes extending over the whole width of the kimono, alternating naturalistic motifs of small scattered flowers with geometric patterns of small dots.[12] In

Plate 122 Oribe box and cover. Late 16th c. Japan, private collection

ceramics, Oribe wares rely for their effect chiefly on contrasts of colour and form (Pl. 122). All these works, in all these different branches of applied art, express the same feeling for decorative effect, for lively imagination and complete unconventionality that are so typical of the Momoyama period. Precisely because these elements, common to every sphere of art, are the basic characteristics of the Kōdai-ji lacquers, they must be considered the prime exponents of Momoyama lacquerwork.

Another essential trait of Kōdai-ji lacquerwork is its technique. The simple themes and uncluttered designs are matched – and this represents a complete departure from the rich and complex traditional processes – by a deliberately simple technique. The decoration is carried out almost exclusively in gold hiramakie, but contrary to usual practice, it is not polished after the sprinkling (so-called maki-hanashi). The desired degree of colour differentiation is obtained either by varying the density of the sprinkling or, very often, by means of 'e-nashiji,' that is, nashiji used in the decoration itself and not simply for the ground. It makes a very charming colour contrast with the usual sprinkled gold dust and the black-lacquer ground. In earlier periods lacquermasters had, in fact, also employed this technique, but only occasionally and for small areas; not until the Momoyama period did e-nashiji become a decisively important, much-used component in the decoration.

To maki-hanashi and e-nashiji was added, in the Kōdai-ji lacquers, a third, equally simple technique: 'harigaki,' which involves picking out fine lines with a needle in the gold-sprinkled lacquer surface before it has dried. This process was not new either,[13] but only at this time did it come into regular use. It makes it possible to form fluid, mobile lines as in drawing; in the veining of the leaves and the internal details of the blossoms, these lines contribute significantly to the grace and charm of the Kōdai-ji lacquers.

Thus, decorative forms, composition and technique combine harmoniously in creating an easily discernible, very ornamental style of radiant freshness and beauty. In their naïve, generously uncluttered splendour, the Kōdai-ji lacquers are indeed a prime expression of the new unconventional spirit of the time; they wholly correspond to contemporary works in ceramics and textiles.

The third large category of Momoyama lacquerwork – the so-called Namban lacquers – is more closely related to the Kōdai-ji lacquers than are the traditional works.

'Namban' was at that time used to describe everything that came from foreign countries lying to the south of Japan, from the Philippines, Java, Borneo etc. Since the Portuguese, Spanish and Dutch came to Japan from these southern regions, they were called the 'Namban-jin,' or 'southern barbarians.' Namban lacquers consist, in the first instance, of items which depict the foreigners themselves (mostly Portuguese) or motifs connected with them, such as guns, playing-cards, tobacco pipes, etc., and, secondly, those items which were commissioned by foreigners and, therefore, often made in an alien, non-Japanese style.[14] The latter include, in particular, objects used by missionaries and Japanese Christians; their decoration tends to show links with Christianity. Also in this category are the articles commissioned by foreign merchants from Japanese lacquermasters chiefly for export use. Lastly, these wares also influenced the decoration of lacquer objects that neither represented foreigners nor served their purposes but which, on stylistic grounds, must be included among the Namban lacquers.

With the exception of the last group, Namban lacquers were made neither in the classic traditional techniques nor in the new simple style of the Kōdai-ji lacquers. Rather, the lacquermasters tried to cope with these foreign themes by using foreign means: Korean mother-of-pearl techniques, Chinese scroll motifs, and geometric patterns supplied by the Europeans combine with the new subjects and forms to produce a truly 'exotic' mixture that has its own, very individual peculiarities even for present-day Japanese. Frequently the motif of autumn grasses, so typcial of the Kōdai-ji lacquers, also occurs in the composition of Namban lacquers, though generally in a much more compact form and often in combination with animals and birds.

Namban lacquers are difficult to date: the earliest might antedate the Kōdai-ji lacquers, because Portuguese missionaries and merchants, later followed by the Spanish, the Dutch and the English, had been coming to Japan since the middle of the sixteenth century; the latest Namban lacquers continued to be made for export well into the seventeenth century. [15] Of course, these late pieces hardly belong within the framework of a history of Japanese lacquerwork. They were for export, and as such, their decoration was no longer determined by the style of the Momoyama period – and scarcely by that of the Edo period; in accordance with the wishes of the customer it now assumed forms which it would be more accurate to describe as 'in the Japanese manner' rather than as Japanese art. The painted Japanese screens with representations of foreigners are generally dated somewhere around 1590 to 1614 – particularly if they show Christian motifs – and it would probably be safe to assume a similar date of origin for most Namban lacquers.

A folding chair now in the temple of Zuikō-ji in Kyōto (Pl. 123: *Namban-jin makie-kōisu*) is a model of decoration depicting the Portuguese. Not only does the back splat show the foreigners with their characteristic clothes and their strange profiles, but what with the dog, the vine branch and the 'Namban scrolls' framing the splat, it presents an additional number of motifs typical of this group of lacquer works. The Namban scrolls, several variants of which occur in the Momoyama and early Edo periods, constitute a stylistic element as yet completely alien to Japanese art. It derives from the Chinese scrolls which were found chiefly on procelain. [16]

This chair is also a good example from the point of view of technique since, as in numerous other Namban lacquers, gold hiramakie and e-nashiji are used in combination with silver hiramakie. This point is worth mentioning because sprinkled silver dust is never used in Kōdai-ji lacquerwork.

Similar representations of foreigners on lacquer objects of the most varied kinds occur up to the early Edo period: on saddles, stirrups, a powder flask, writing- and other boxes. [17]

Among objects with a religious function, particularly worth noting are five cylindrical pyxes, decorated on the lids with the letters IHS (Jesus Hominum Salvator)[18] in combination with the three nails of the Crucifixion and a cross of flowers. Since later, at the time of the merciless persecution of Christians beginning in 1614, the possession of items serving the Christian cult could be life-endangering, the survival of these pyxes is extremely fortunate. Conversely, it is understandable that the tell-tale letters IHS were later scraped off one of the boxes. Like all Christian utensils, the pyxes were certainly made before 1614.

Plates 124 and 125 show one of the boxes now in the possession of the temple of Tōkei-ji in Kamakura (*Budō makie-seiheibako*). The central design on the lid, the monogram IHS, is surrounded by a halo in gold lacquer and mother-of-pearl with a Namban scroll border. In the other boxes sawtooth patterns take the place of the scrolls. This pattern, for which mother-of-pearl inlay was particularly favoured, and which was constantly used in Namban lacquers, originally derived from the formal repertoire of Korean lacquerwork of the Li period (1392-1910). In fact, as a result of numerous trade links, Korean lacquerwork was already known in Japan during the Muromachi period; unlike Chinese mother-of-pearl lacquers it appears to have had no influence on contemporary Japanese lacquermasters. In both lacquerwork and ceramics the Korean influence only began to be strongly

Plate 123 Folding chair showing a Portuguese. Early 17th c. Ht 1.05m. Kyōto, Zuikō-ji

felt following Hideyoshi's two Korean wars (1592-1593 and 1597-1598), in the course of which many Korean craftsmen, as well as objects in the form of booty, found their way to Japan. In lacquerwork this influence reveals

Plate 124 Pyx. Before 1614. Ht 9cm. Tōkei-ji, Kanagawa province

Plate 125 Pyx. From above

itself in different ways: in a preference for awabi shells, with their delight-ful colouring rather than for the yakugai shells so far more commonly used; in formal elements such as the sawtooth and beaded border line patterns; in the new forms of scrolls (see p. 177); in the preference for unshaped (rather than pre-cut) bits of mother-of-pearl for inlays and in 'warigai,' inlays of pieces of mother-of-pearl deliberately cracked. [19]

The pyxes show both the sawtooth pattern and the inlay of unshaped mother-of-pearl bits which so emphasized the 'exotic' character. The latter are easily discernible on the side of the Tōkei-ji box (Pl. 124).

Many lacquer works in the Momoyama and early Edo periods were commissioned by European merchants, even at a time when Christians were already being persecuted. Considering that they were intended for export, it is not just coincidence that most of these objects, particularly chests and cabinet-cupboards, are now in European collections.

A small chest of drawers in the Kunsthistorisches Museum in Vienna (Pl. 126) is possibly one of the earliest pieces of this kind to have reached Europe. It is recorded as early as 1596 in the inventory of the collection at Ambras, owned by Archduke Ferdinand of Tyrol. [20]

Surviving letters and diaries indicate that there was great activity in the

Plate 126 Small chest-of-drawers. Before 1596. 31:42.5:29cm. Kunsthistorisches Museum, Vienna

early seventeenth century between European merchants and the lacquer-masters in Kyōto; it is even quite likely that all the Namban export lacquers were made in a small number of workshops in Kyōto. In 1617 in one of these workshops supplying the European market, fifty lacquerers were working on day and night shifts,[21] an indication of how numerous the commissions were even after the interdict on Christianity.

The lacquermasters lacquered and otherwise decorated for foreigners a variety of objects unknown in Japan itself, which consequently lacked suitable names. Thus, for example, small chests with domed lids (an unusual shape in Japan) were and are described as 'boxes in fish sausage shape' (kamabokogata), since the Japanese language, using 'hitsu' only for flat-lidded chests, has no term for round-lidded ones.

A particularly beautiful and well-preserved small chest in this kamaboko shape (Pl. 127) has been in a private collection in Germany for some years. The decoration is unmistakably in the fresh, lively style of the Momoyama period. The autumn plants are designed less with an eye for the rhythm-and-line beauty of the Kōdai-ji lacquers, but rather to decorate a given area as densely and fully as possible. A very un-Japanese *horror vacui* apparent in many Namban lacquers is most likely the result of the customer's specific wishes. The makie sections provide a lively contrast to the mother-of-pearl which is used either in unshaped pieces scattered within the decoration, or arranged in sawtooth and diamond bands which clearly emphasize and subdivide the shape of the chest.

Three other kamaboko chests of this kind are so closely related to the one illustrated in size, motif, technique and overall style, that they can be attributed to the same workshop or indeed to a single master. One of them

Plate 127 Small chest in the Namban style. Early 17th c. 14.4:19.8:11cm.
Wuppertal, Dr Kurt Herberts

in the Itsuō Museum in Ikeda-shi near Osaka, has an outer case bearing the name 'Doña Aña Aarz [=Alvarez] Giron' and the coat of arms of the Spanish family of Giron. Even if it never reached its destination and remained in Japan, it was nevertheless clearly made for Spanish clients. [22]

Geometric devices such as stripes, triangles and diamonds now appear frequently, and, as typical and integral parts of Momoyama and early Edo lacquerware, they are evidence of the eagerness with which foreign motifs were adopted for more than depicting the human figure. Beginning with the Heian period, the motifs used in lacquerwork had derived almost exclusively from nature (with the exception of the 'textile' circular patterns of the Kamakura period; cf. p.77); so these geometric patterns represent a real innovation in the art of lacquerwork. In the Momoyama and early Edo periods they are often used to frame the design. In this context – so essentially alien to far-Eastern art – geometric elements also appear in the famous

Plate 128 Gaming board. Exterior. Early 17th c. 4.4:31.5:53cm. Tōkyō National Museum

gaming board in the National Museum in Tōkyō (Pl. 128: *Kiyomizu-
Sumiyoshi makie-raden-sugorokuban*) and in a Namban secretaire in the Staatliches Museum für Völkerkunde in Munich (Pl. 129).

Just how much these 'Western' elements were in vogue in the
Momoyama and early Edo periods is further demonstrated by the fact that
they were not restricted to articles made for foreigners but also occur in
purely Japanese lacquer objects: for example, two matched sword cases
(Pl. 130: *Makie ni-shū tantōbako*), which according to tradition Hideyoshi
gave to Date Masamune, Daimyō of Sendai. While the inner case shows, on
a black-lacquer ground, serried ranks of the kiri devices favoured by
Hideyoshi, and its interior is decorated with silver chrysanthemums on
nashiji, the outer case is covered with a very unusual diaper pattern. In the
ungilded bands between the diamonds, the wood grain is clearly visible
under a kind of Shunkei-nuri. The projecting ledge of the inner box, which
holds the lid in place, is also decorated with Namban scrolls – all in all two
very odd boxes, the very unusualness and eccentricity of which seems
deliberately recherché.

Also linked with the name of Hideyoshi is a small cabinet with drawers
(Pl. 131: *Nashiji makie-tansu*) which Hideyoshi was allegedly very fond of
and gave to Tokugawa Ieyasu. The inside and outside present a lively

Plate 129 Namban secretaire. 17th c. 32:45:30cm. Munich, Staatliches Museum für
Völkerkunde

contrast: the exterior shows an emphatically geometric pattern, the interior a design of stylized plum blossom scrolls closely covering the drawer fronts with elegant curves. This small cabinet is another example of the use of foreign and Japanese elements resulting in an odd combination.[23]

But the wealth of Momoyama lacquers is by no means exhausted by the three categories so far mentioned: the traditional works, the Kōdai-ji lacquers, and articles in the Namban style (together with those influenced by the Namban style).

In 1602, as an inscription on the inside of the lid informs us, a chest was made in the classical karabitsu shape, the clean-cut form of which is splendidly enhanced and made truly festive by an ivy tendril decoration in gold makie (Pl. 132: *Tsuta makie-karabitsu*). The technique is simple but the design quite remarkable. This decoration shows the skill with which the Japanese artists of the time were able to combine their love of nature and gift for precise observation with comprehensive stylization and two-dimensional effects; it shows how they restored object and decoration to a single entity. In this context, we should refer to the nagi tebako of the Muromachi period (Pl.83) in which this typically Japanese gift for decoratively stylized naturalism had first revealed itself.

The ivy-tendril chest belongs to the Itsukushima shrine on the island of Miyajima. It was donated in 1602, to serve as an outer storage chest for the shrine's most treasured possession, the sutra scrolls, which date from around 1165. In that same year, 1602, Sōtatsu spent some time on Miyajima restoring the sutra scrolls. It is quite conceivable that this painter of genius designed, or at least influenced, the decoration of the chest, for similar ivy tendrils are to be found in his early works.[24]

More forcibly even than many Kōdai-ji lacquers, this chest illustrates a characteristic typical of Momoyama and early Edo lacquerwork: the extraordinary degree of harmony between the decoration and the shape of the object. Gone is the pictorial isolation which marked the decoration of Muromachi work; the dominant influence of painting is broken, and the

Plate 130 Inner and outer sword case. Late 16th c. 8.4:44.9:8.8cm and 13.3:47.6:11.7cm

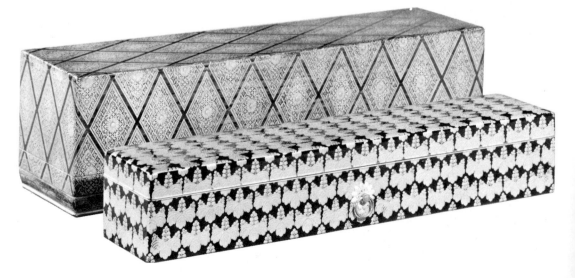

result is an art object which seems almost modern in its close linking of form and ornamentation. In an article well worth reading, Okada argues that the Momomaya period was developing a new understanding for the very essence of arts and crafts, a sense for the relationship between the function of an object and its decorative form.[25] In the field of lacquerwork, ceramics and even textiles it is now possible to refer to their 'functional beauty' – a concept that was previously unknown. During the Muromachi period, the striving after pictorial effect and literary reference had determined the nature of the lacquer design; the shape of the object was of minor importance. True, the Kamakura and Heian periods had adapted the designs to the basic shape but rather from an unfailing artistic instinct than from deliberate attention to an object's function.

According to Okada, the new awareness of the form and essence of an object was rooted in the great passion for collecting that pervaded the Muromachi period. Constant judicious contact with the items being collected, and perhaps with Chinese ceramics in particular, meant that collectors and connoisseurs developed a fine appreciation of functional beauty. An appreciation which blended perfectly with the new artistic impulses of the Momoyama period.

Momoyama period

Plate 131 Tansu decorated with plum scrolls. Late 16th c. 71.5:103:56.1cm. Nagoya, Tokugawa Museum

The result was not only decorative lacquerwork on the very highest level, but also the production of many new, practical lacquer items for everyday use. To this category belong, above all, the portable boxes with handles and the small cabinets of various kinds, for instance the 'bentōbako' (tiered breakfast boxes) and the 'sagedansu' (small portable cabinet-cupboards with doors and drawers for writing implements etc.); there are also the eating utensils comprising three, four or five bowls in the same or different shapes, and a small table, linked by a common decorative motif to form sets. Particularly common are the 'mitsu-wan' (three bowls) which always consist of a bowl on a high foot, another on a lower one and a third, flat, plate-like bowl. Mitsu-wan include for example the so-called 'Hidehira-wan' (Pl.133; named after a northern Japanese prince), which were produced from the end of the Muromachi period, chiefly in the provinces of Iwate and Miyagi. They are lacquered red on the inside and black on the outside. The border on the exterior is decorated with a curved cloud motif in gold lacquer onto which gold foil has been applied in a diaper pattern. The lower parts of the bowls show plant or blossom motifs.

The very fact that these food bowls were used at every meal for soup, rice and vegetables, meant their shape was necessarily determined by their function. The shape and size of the foot ensured that the bowl stood firmly; the height and curvature of the body of the bowl were made to fit the hand; the slight inversion of the rim was designed to facilitate the act of drinking.

Lacquered bowls for food had of course existed in mediaeval Japan, but it is typical of the Momoyama period that not only did the decoration change (in both design and technique), but that the shapes of the utensils were also redesigned and modified; the reason was that in the Momoyama

Plate 132 Chest with ivy decoration. 1602. 44.2:57:46.7cm. Miyajima, Itsukushima-jinja

period lacquerwork broke a class barrier. Henceforth, beautifully decorated lacquer objects were no longer primarily votive offerings to temples or
status symbols for the nobility, but became utensils for everyday use in the
middle classes as well. The very fact that they were in normal daily use had
a revitalizing effect and led to different, or new, convenient shapes. This
development, which was to continue well into the Edo period, began in the
Momoyama period in Hideyoshi's time.

Among the lacquer objects which, from the Momoyama period onward,
were created in a multitude of shapes, are tea-caddies for the 'usu-cha' (a
variety of the tea ceremony), collectively known as 'natsume.'[26] Just as the
tea ceremony witnessed the lowering of social barriers during the
Momoyama period – in 1588 Hideyoshi expressly included devotees of the
tea cult from the lower classes among the guests he invited to the famous
ten-day tea festival of Kitano – so, too, scenes from everyday life were now
often depicted on the lacquer tea-caddies. For example, a black-lacquer tea
caddy in the so-called 'kinrinji' shape (Pl. 134) shows, in gold makie, a scene
of tea leaves being sorted – an obvious reference to the function of the
container. The tea harvest and sorting of tea leaves, often linked with the
motif of the bridge at Uji (even today the best tea still grows around Uji),
were favourite subjects in the Momoyama and early Edo periods. The most
famous example of this is the 'Ujibashi-byōbu' (folding screen) by the
painter Morikage (active until around 1680).

Some of these tea-caddies are signed, but apart from the names of masters such as Hidetsugi, Seiami, Kisan, etc., little or nothing is known of
their makers. Much the same is the case with lacquered sake bowls
(sakazuki) which, beginning with the Momoyama period, show a similar
abundance of decorative motifs.[27] Here too there is a host of names, but
their owners should be regarded more as skilled craftsmen rather than
artists.

Finally, the Momoyama period also sees the origin of the 'inrō,' those
small, multi-cased medicine containers worn by men on their girdles,
which were to be at their best in the eighteenth and early nineteenth centuries (see p. 211).[28] But, although inrō appear in Momoyama paintings, not
one of the surviving pieces can with any certainty be ascribed to this period.
Inrō of even the early Edo are rare today.

Many different types of lacquerwork prove that, starting with the
Momoyama period, such items were prized and used by the nobility as
well as the middle classes. But in one area, apparently, there was no
popularization: carved lacquers. When carved lacquerworks were first
made in Japan and whether and how they can be distinguished from
Chinese work is still an open question today. Japanese written sources

Plate 133 Hidehira-wan. Early 17th c. Japan, private collection

clearly indicate that the manufacture of carved lacquer in Japan dates from the Momoyama period at the latest, and that the masters of the so-called Tsuishu school (see below) worked for the shōgunate from the early seventeenth century up to the end of the Edo period.

The true origins remain very much in the dark. Reference has already been made (see p.97) to the lacquermaster Monnyū, who is said to have produced carved lacquerwork in the Chinese style as early as the time of Yoshimasa. The apocryphal genealogical tree of a family of lacquermasters with the surname 'Tsuishu' (carved lacquer) goes back still further, to the fourteenth century in fact. (For the family tree of the Tsuishu masters see note. [29]) Of the first seven masters of this school nothing but their names and approximate dates of their work is known. The eighth, however, a man by the name of Tsuishu Heijirō, is somewhat less ephemeral not because his works have survived but because he is mentioned in the literature of the

Plate 134 Tea caddy with Uji decoration. Early 17th c. Japan, private collection

period. Indeed, up to 1868, successive generations of Tsuishu masters refer to him as the founder of their school.

Tsuishu Heijirō, also known as Chōshū (Nagamune), worked in Edo for the shōgun Tokugawa Ieyasu (died 1614), surviving the latter by several decades. He is said to have died in 1654. Proof that he did actually produce carved lacquerwork is provided by, among other things, his artist's name. He made up the composite name Yōsei, by taking one syllable from the names of the famous Chinese masters of carved lacquer, Yang Mao (pronounced Yōmo in Japanese) and Chang Ch'eng (Chōsei in Japanese). This allusion to the names of late fourteenth-century masters might also be seen as expressing the artist's credo – a preference for early Chinese carved lacquers rather than for contemporary Wan-li wares.

All the subsequent masters of the Tsuishu school, who served the shōgunate until 1868, called themselves Tsuishu Yōsei after him; the twentieth master of this name died in 1952.

Although there is a complete list of the names of all Tsuishu masters, very little is known about their work. In 1687, the tenth master, who had been employed by the Shōgun Tsunayoshi since 1683, is said to have made a carved-lacquer table which earned him particular praise. In 1927 there were still two lacquer articles, signed 'Tsuishu Yōsei' and dated 1707[30] and 1714[31], in a Japanese private collection. Unfortunately, both pieces, which might have added to what is known about old Japanese carved lacquer, have disappeared and there is not even a pictorial record. In 1796 the fifteenth master was commissioned to make a round carved-lacquer table and finally, in 1861, the eighteenth master carried out repairs on the Tōshōgū in Nikkō.

Despite all this information, which proves beyond doubt the existence of carved lacquer in Japan, at least beginning with the Momoyama period, the term carved lacquer is almost automatically associated with China. Japanese research has so far not sufficiently probed the subject of Japanese carved lacquer; so far, the available source material has not even been systematically assembled. (Nor can this problem be tackled from Europe or America.) Considering the great interest in lacquerwork in Japan, this 'forgetting,' this identification of carved lacquer with China, is amazing. This might partly be explained by the fact that initially Japanese carved lacquerwork was quite deliberately modelled after Chinese prototypes, and accordingly, up to the nineteenth century, there was no noticeable Japanization in either technique or style. On the other hand, it seems that from the time of Tsuishu Yōsei up to the end of the Edo period, Japanese carved lacquer works were almost exclusively made for the Tokugawa family, in which case they were perhaps never very numerous.

Even today, it is difficult to identify as Japanese, with any certainty, any carved-lacquer objects made before the middle of the nineteenth century for the very reason that in carved lacquerwork, in direct contrast to Kamakurabori, no typically Japanese style evolved. One argument against the Japanization and popularization of carved lacquerwork may have been that these works did not appear sumptuous enough for the *nouveaux riches* of the seventeenth century, greedy for gold decoration; moreover, ordinary people could not afford them, since they were long in the making and therefore expensive. Only starting with the mid-nineteenth and the beginning of the twentieth centuries a Japanization of carved lacquer came about, that is, a new native style was developed (see p.222). Looking back from this

Momoyama period

point, it seems safe to assume that two things appear to be typical of Japanese carved lacquers: a realistic design – in plants often combined with very elegant draughtsmanship – and a preference for a uniform level in relief work, in other words, designs within the same plane. While the Chinese artist, when cutting, treated the lacquer as a plastic material which could be modelled in depth and rounded, his Japanese counterpart appears to have been more concerned with constant levels, even if in different relief planes. These 'levels' are often more apparent to the sense of touch than to the eye, which is deceived by the effect of shadows and surface gloss.

Until definitely authenticated and preferably dated pieces of Japanese carved lacquer come to light, such theories must of necessity remain hypothetical. At this writing, we have only a vague idea of what early Japanese carved lacquers could have looked like, but we must acknowledge that they were made for the shōguns at the latest from the Momoyama period on. A black carved-lacquer box (Pl. 135: *Tsuikoku-kōgō*), which by general consensus – but without concrete evidence – is regarded as Japanese and could date from the Momoyama period is shown here.

Plate 135 Black carved-lacquer kōgō. Early 17th c. Ht 5.1cm, diam. 19.8cm. Kamakura, Enkaku-ji

The early Edo period 8

THE TRANSITION FROM THE MOMOYAMA STYLE TO THAT OF THE EARLY EDO period was gradual; several decades were also needed for the Tokugawa shōgunate to establish itself politically. Nevertheless, if it were necessary to set accents and pick out specific dates for the better understanding of the evolution, the year 1635 would be worth mentioning. Two important events are linked with this date: the abrupt isolation of Japan from the rest of the world, and the stipulation that the daimyōs must spend alternate years in Edo and on their estates. This arrangement was one of the most skilful moves of the Tokugawa shōguns to keep the daimyōs under control and to restrict their economic power by imposing a costly standard of living.

Not much later, in 1637, the death of Kōetsu represents a milestone in the history of art. Up to this time, the art of lacquerwork, especially in Kyōto, may justly be considered a continuation of the Momoyama style. Here, particularly influenced by the Kōdai-ji lacquers, numerous works of great beauty were made. The preference for startling contrast waned; instead, with the same simple and vivid technique, the composition was even more carefully thought out and balanced, and many additional types of lacquer articles were developed.

Plate 136 Food box with vine tendrils and squirrel. 1st third 17th c. Ht 26cm, diam. 27.2cm. Tōkyō National Museum

A tiered food box (Pl. 136: *Budō-risu makie-jikirō*) is one such example of early Edo lacquerwork in a refined version of the Kōdai-ji style. Its shape may have been inspired by Chinese lacquer boxes; the motif of the quirrels in the vine scroll design certainly derives from China. By using two different shades of gold, e-nashiji, and in places, a particularly thin sprinkling of gold dust, the decoration achieves the effect of four shades of colour which blend very well with the glossy black ground. In all, this is a very appealing and elegant work. *Early Edo period*

Other motifs frequently used in the early Edo period are arrowroot leaves, melons and gourds, ivy, clematis, bindweed, morning glories and tendrils. The shell and seaweed motif has been mentioned before (p. 145) and is shown here on a small box (Pl. 137: *Kai to kaisō makie-kobako*) the stepped shape of which lends it a particular charm. The combination of makie and e-nashiji clearly derives from the Kōdai-ji lacquers; the sawtooth pattern in gold lacquer on the upper edge of the box proper is borrowed from the Momoyama period's wealth of forms. The refined shape of the box, though, already belongs to the Edo period.

The 'tabikushige' (comb case for travel) is as practical in its make-up as it is witty in its decoration of long-eared hares over waves (Pl. 138: *Nami ni usagi makie-tabikushige*). [1] This box – the top of which shows signs of considerable wear over the centuries – merits special attention as a particularly good example of early Edo lacquerwork. On the one hand, the addition of two drawers (for small items and an inkstone) to the basic tebako shape is an innovation which demonstrates the extent to which lacquer objects were now intended for actual use and therefore required redesigning. On the other hand, the love for rhythm and movement, so typical of the Momoyama period, has been translated here most vividly and elegantly in the decoration. The scene depicted, equally amusing from every angle, covers all four sides in a continuous design, underscoring in this manner the

Plate 137 Small box and cover decorated with shell and seaweed. 1st third 17th c. Japan, private collection

shape of the box as a complete entity.

Generally speaking, it is characteristic of this period to continue the decoration around the corners of a box even though it does not show the same dramatic motion as in the hare box. It occurs, for example, in almost all 'kakesuzuri' (Pl. 139),[2] small portable chests, usually with three drawers (for inkstone, writing-paper and documents) which were much favoured by merchants in the Edo period. This manner of linking all sides of a box by a single composition is new. This deliberate continuing of the design, and thus of the observer's attention to it, did not exist in earlier tebako. The way each side remains a display side in its own right and yet is linked with the others, demonstrates the great talent for composition of the lacquermasters or the painters who made the preliminary drawings.

A further characteristic of the design of the period – as the tea caddy in Plate 134 presages – is a preference for scenes from everyday life: motifs, therefore, devoid of literary association, and recognizable at a glance. For centuries, Japanese painters had been creating an 'illustrated cultural history' scarcely duplicate by any other nation in the world; now the lacquermasters in their turn took up these subjects. For example, during this period, the transportation of large stones to be used in the building of castles is frequently depicted (Pl. 140);[3] boats being towed is another new motif in lacquerwork which was applied up to the middle of the Edo period. The scene is frequently so skilfully composed that the boat and the men on the shore hauling it are represented either on different sides or on the lid and the

Plate 138 Comb box for travel. 1st half 17th c. 23.7:21.5:27.8cm. Tōkyō National Museum

sides of the box, with the rope – automatically followed by the eye – providing the link.

Everyday items like cosmetic brushes, hair ribbons, tobacco pipes, etc. are now also considered worth depicting, and prove that the middle class, and in particular the increasingly affluent merchants, were now taking their place among the connoisseurs of lacquerwork and imposing their tastes.

In addition to those articles which continue the tradition of Kōdai-ji lacquerwork, another group of lacquerwork stands out in the Momoyama and early Edo periods: the coloured lacquers,[4] which soon were well liked by the daimyōs and city-dwellers (Pl. 141). For the first time since the Nara period, that is, more than eight hundred years ago, gold dust, silver dust and mother-of-pearl were no longer the exclusive medium of expression combined with the classical black or red lacquers: in addition, yellow, green and brown lacquers for painted decoration were used. The coloured lacquers were obtained by additions of mineral and vegetable dye stuffs. Other pigments cannot be mixed with lacquer since they easily change colour and become unattractive. Accordingly, in genuine lacquer painting the palette is restricted to five hues: black, red, yellow, green and brown.

Plate 139 Kakesuzuri with roe deer on Mikasayama. 1st half 17th c. 28.1:28:42.8cm. Tōkyō National Museum

This enforced renunciation of the full range of colours is, nevertheless, balanced by the unifying effect of these warm, harmonizing colours.

Yet if a more vivid colouring was desired particularly with respect to white and blue, the lacquerer went back to the old technique of mitsuda-e (see p. 15) and he frequently applied lacquer painting and oil painting on the same article.

The origins of these coloured lacquers might have been inspired by the bright-coloured Momoyama paintings, but the painted Chinese lacquerwares of the late Ming period probably also served as models. In the Edo period this sprightly lacquer technique, so expressive of *joie de vivre*, was particularly favoured for articles in daily use, in other words, for articles that made no attempt to impress or look expensive. Accordingly, items connected with eating, in particular, include numerous pieces decorated with coloured lacquer painting; we see it on 'bon' (trays), 'wan' (bowls), 'jūbako' (food containers consisting of several boxes placed on top of each other) and 'sagejū' (a jūbako in a light carrying frame with a handle). Incidentally, the sagejū was a new utensil, which also appears for the first time in the early Edo period.

Also loosely connected with these coloured lacquers are the 'sumi-aka' (Pl. 142),[5] the earliest examples of which go back to the late Muromachi period, but which now appeared with greater frequency. All these lacquer works are relatively simple in technique and not too expensive to produce. With their practical, appealing shapes, decorative colour effects and high quality, they constituted a lively popular substratum which delighted city

Plate 140 Tray depicting the hauling of large stone. 1st half 17th c. 52:32.7cm. Tōkyō National Museum

Plate 141 Plate with painted decoration of vine tendrils. 17th c. Ht 7.8cm, diam. 39.6cm. Tōkyō National Museum

Early
Edo period

Plate 142 Sumiaka with kiri devices and chrysanthemums. 1619. Sugau Ishibe-jinja, Ishikawa province

people and daimyōs alike. They are distinctly different from the sumptuous, glittering, gold showpieces made by the official lacquermasters for the shōgunate and from the ceremonial display pieces for the daimyōs. These simple makie and coloured-lacquer articles of the early Edo period formed the basis for the many specialized kinds of lacquerwork which were developed in the various provinces (kawari-nuri), and which, up to the present day, have kept the art of making lacquerware alive among the people (see p. 196).

It has already been pointed out that in Namban lacquerwork the saw-tooth and the beaded border line motifs derived from Korean lacquers of the Li period. But the Korean influence was not restricted to the deliberately alien Namban lacquers, some of which were intended for export; it can also be seen – albeit differently expressed stylistically – in the world of the Japanese teamasters.

The unadorned Korean tea bowls which so well answered the aesthetic requirement for natural simplicity, were held in the highest esteem by Japanese devotees of the tea cult. So it is not surprising that the teamasters also should have turned their attention to other Korean arts and that in their sphere lacquerwork should also show the influence of Korean pieces.

The best known example of this are the so-called *Meigetsu-wan*, a set of four red-lacquer bowls of different sizes with mother-of-pearl inlay (Pl. 143).[6] Their original design is attributed to the teamaster Oda Urakusai, a younger brother of Oda Nobunaga, and pupil of Rikyū (1545-1621); he became a Buddhist priest in 1585, when he assumed the name Urakusai. In the bowls he designed, the way in which the mother-of-pearl is handled, in particular, points to Korea; he uses the 'warigai' technique, that is, mother-of-pearl to which cracks and fissures are pur-

Plate 143 Meigetsu-wan. Early 17th c. Ht 7cm, diam. 11.2cm. Kamakura, Meigetsu-in

Plate 144 Meigetsu-zen. Early 17th c. 8:32:32cm. Tōkyō National Museum

posely added after it has been cut to shape. The warigai technique was much favoured in Korean Li lacquerwork, and reached Japan via this intermediary. Warigai also makes it possible to apply mother-of-pearl decoration to curved surfaces, a possibility which in the *Meigetsu-wan* was realized with the greatest skill. Cherry blossoms in thin, varicoloured, iridescent mother-of-pearl are inlaid not only on the curvature of the bowls but even right in the obtuse-angled corners where the curved and vertical zones meet. The blossoms present a charming contrast to the red-lacquer ground and their crazed surface adds an interesting touch.

In the temple of Meigetsu-in at Kamakura there is a small votive table with a raised border, known as *Meigetsu-zen*, but unrelated to the bowls; an exact counterpart, but with the lacquer in a better state of preservation, is owned by the National Museum in Tōkyō (Pl. 144). The border area is in red lacquer; the black-lacquer centre, with its narrow mother-of-pearl edge carries the main mother-of-pearl decoration. As in Korean lacquers, this is worked in the iridescent, blue-green-pink shell of the awabi, not in warigai, and is closely linked stylistically to the decoration of Korean works. The carefully arranged, rather dense decoration of early Korean lacquerwork had, in the fifteenth century, resolved itself into slender, harmoniously designed scrolls which – with a preference for the diagonal – now cover the lacquer surface. Their rhythmic pattern is accentuated by peony blossoms, small, lambently curved leaves and round dew drops. The main effect of these articles is achieved by the peaceful, harmonious movement of the very thin scroll designs which, in Li lacquers, are always made up of short pieces of mother-of-pearl. The small Meigetsu table is very closely related to works of this kind. The composition of this Japanese piece is indeed a little more restrained than in comparable Korean works, but even so, the pleasure in elegantly traced lines is unmistakable. Certainly the Kōdai-ji lacquers of the Momoyama period also show a fine instinct for rhythmic beauty of line, but the particular form of scroll on the

Early
Edo period

Plate 145 Box for paper. Early 17th c. 11.5:23:24.5cm. Atami Museum

Meigetsu-zen derives directly from Korea.

The small table has great quality: the way the mother-of-pearl edge framing the black lacquer field echoes the inverted corners is in very good taste, and the fluidity in the scroll composition is both offset and contained by the small leaf motifs in the corners. The very handsome colour harmony of red, black and iridescent mother-of-pearl – unknown in Korean lacquers – very definitely expresses the spirit of the Momoyama period.

A box for paper in the museum at Atami (Pl.145: *Karakusa raden-ryōshibako*) also shows strong Korean influence, yet in this case it is combined with typical Namban elements like the floral crosses and the wave-shaped tapering of the scrolls. The emphatic double framing of the scroll design field should probably also be attributed to European rather than Korean influence. Despite the great charm and interest of the box, a sense of tensions unsolved prevails among the heterogeneous components of the design. The scroll motif nevertheless relates it to the Meigetsu-zen. [7]

The Meigetsu-wan, the small table and the box for paper very likely still belong in the Momoyama period. A sutra box in the temple of Hompō-ji (Kyōto) shows a greater degree of adaptation in its Korean motifs (Pl.146), which does not necessarily imply a later date of origin. The box was donated to the temple by Honami Kōetsu (1558-1637). The deed of gift, written by Kōetsu himself, has survived, and the mother-of-pearl characters on the lid are cut in his style of writing.

Kōetsu, the most versatile and important artist of the Momoyama and early Edo periods, perhaps himself never actually made a single lacquer article. [8] Nevertheless, he strongly influenced the art, because after he re-

Plate 146 Sutra box with scroll decoration. ca 1605. 12.5:28.5:38.2cm. Kyōto, Hompō-ji

ceived a gift of land from Ieyasu at Takagamine near Kyōto in 1615 he gathered around him artists and artisans in all fields. It is possible that several masters worked from his designs, and according to Okada's research, it is likely that they included members of two branches of the Igarashi school in Kyōto.[9] (There was indeed a family connection, since Kōetsu's granddaughter married the lacquermaster Igarashi Tarōbei.) The common link of the so-called Kōetsu lacquers is Kōetsu's basic concept, which almost certainly included both the design and the materials to be used. Individual differences should be attributed to the lacquermasters adapting themselves with varying degrees of success to Kōetsu's ideas.

The Hompō-ji sutra box is not one of the 'typical' Kōetsu lacquers. The relationship of the decoration to Korean lacquerwork is unmistakable. This would indicate one of two things: either the design was the work of Oda Urakusai, who was clearly influenced by articles of Korean origin (see p. 176), and whom Kōetsu knew well; or Kōetsu, before his own style had fully developed and because of his connections with various teamasters (also with Furuta Oribe), had very thoroughly studied Korean mother-of-pearl lacquers. There is no proof of this, but it is certain that the scrolls of this sutra box are linked with the scroll designs of Korean mother-of-pearl lacquers. Yet they are not imitations, as is the case with the Meigetsu-zen and the Atami paper box. In the sutra box, the degree of modulation and enrichment is unparalleled, and for that very reason the sutra box might be attributed to an important artist like Kōetsu. The scrolls spread all over the surface like calligraphy – Kōetsu was one of the three most famous calligraphers of his time – and instead of one single kind of blossom there are three different varieties.

The characters 'hokkekyō,' which include the name of the sutra kept in the box, are contained in a rectangular field – a treatment similar to that used on the inscription on the manuscript box of the year 919 (see Pl. 14). Perhaps Kōetsu, whose works often attest to his preference for the Heian period, deliberately chose this form as a reminder of the old sasshibako, which had been in the possession of the Ninna-ji since 1186 – that is, also in Kyōto – and which he had certainly known. The most recent research puts the date of the Hompō-ji box around 1605.[10]

The writing-box with the representation of a boat bridge, the so-called *Funabashi makie-suzuribako* (Pl. 147), is rightly regarded as the prototype of the Kōetsu lacquers.[11] The initial striking impression made by this writing-box is caused by the completely new, dramatically ballooning domed lid, rising mountainlike above the almost square box. This shape is unprecedented. Also typical of Kōetsu writing-boxes is the planning of the interior. Up to this time, the inkstone had usually been in the centre of the box, flanked on either side by small brush trays, but now Kōetsu divides the interior of the box into two halves and puts inkstone and water container in the left half. The change meets a very real need and is characteristic of the functionalism of so many seventeenth-century articles. The box is positioned to the right of the paper during writing; Kōetsu's arrangement therefore shortens the distance between the ink-loaded brush and the paper. Only a few earlier examples have survived, but after Kōetsu this arrangement occurs frequently.

Both the pictorial representation and the written characters of the design refer to a tenth-century poem about the boat bridge at Sano.[12] Boats and waves form the gold-lacquer ground which is spanned in magnificent simplicity by the lead-band arch of the bridge. The twenty-five characters carved out of solid silver quote the poem but, by the most ingenious omission of the characters for 'ship' and 'bridge' closely integrate the pictorial and written decoration.

Yet the relationship between the written characters and picture is no longer the same as in the boxes of the Muromachi period, nor is their relationship to the box itself the same. In the Muromachi lacquers the literary element was often stronger and ultimately more decisive than the visual aspect. As in a pictorial riddle, the characters were woven into the design – but not as structural elements – and pictorial representation and written characters alike primarily expressed the poetic content; and in no sense were they closely related to the shape of the box. Here, in Kōetsu's box, the characters, ornamental details and the very materials used (lead, gold lacquer, silver) are equal in terms of decorative value and are directly related to the shape of the writing-box.

The way the intersecting diagonal lines of the boats and the bridge lend visual emphasis to the dome of the lid; the way the vertical lines of the characters impose, as it were, a framework for these diagonals; the way the overlapping band of lead fuses the lid with the shallow body of the box into a single unit: this is applied art in the best sense of the term. The shape of the box, the decoration and the intellectual content form a balanced, indivisible entity.

The writing has been superimposed on the background in much the same way as were Kōetsu's lines of poetry on the famous scrolls painted with 'shita-e' (background pictures) by Sōtatsu. But whereas in the latter

Plate 147 Funabashi writing-box. Before 1637. 11.8:22.8:24.2cm. Tōkyō National Museum

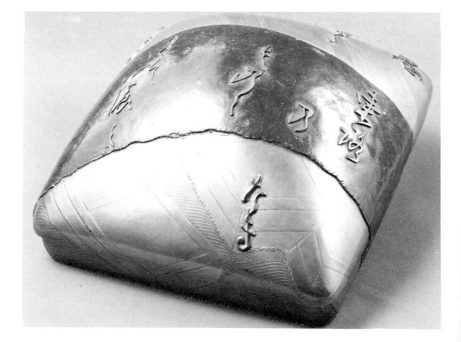

the picture and the text are unrelated in content, here they are inseparably linked; they complement each other in both inner meaning and outer form.

Among other lacquerwork directly based on Kōetsu's designs and possibly made under his supervision, are a flute case with roe deer,[13] and a writing-box with a man carrying brushwood (Pl.148: *Kikori makie-suzuribako*). In this writing-box, too, the steep, imposingly domed lid gives an impression of strength, dignity and supreme skill; here, too, the curve is further emphasized by the fact that the composition is based on large diagonals which brace the corners against each other across the top of the lid. Also, every other line of the decoration, every variation in the materials used (black lacquer, gold lacquer, lead and mother-of-pearl) bear witness to the highest degree of artistic economy. To get some idea of the sheer genius required for a design of this kind, one need only consider some of the details of the brushwood carrier-box: how the diagonals of the bundle of brushwood and the position of the head are balanced by the opposing diagonals of the ground, the feet, arms and the straps holding the bundle; and how this precarious balance – somewhat assisted by the materials used – is firmly linked to the shape of the box by two verticals and a single horizontal (the staff in the man's hands).[14] These works, with their monu-

Plate 148 Kōetsu: writing box with man carrying brushwood. Before 1637. 10.3:22.7:24.4cm. Atami Museum

mental firmness and clarity, are definitely stamped with a completely individual style[15] and far surpass the general generosity of spirit of the Momoyama period.

Nor is the funabashi writing-box the only example of Kōetsu's strong identification with the Heian period; we also see it in other lacquers attributed to his designs. For instance, a writing-box in the National Museum Tōkyō (Pl.149: *Roshū makie-suzuribako*) takes its subject, a boat in a reed bank, from a famous scene in the Heian anthology *Sanjūroku-nin-kashū* (see p.43). Another writing-box, the lid of which is covered with a dense mass of fern called 'shinobu' (polypodia) in makie,[16] also has superimposed, in heavily raised lead characters, several words from a poem in the *Kokin-shū* anthology, in which the poet mentions shinobu.

Is this then a renaissance, a revival of the golden age of mediaeval Japan? Yes, but not an imitation: rather a new, independent interpretation of the old themes. In the case of the writing-box with the boat in the reed bank, Kōetsu makes the boat project obliquely from the lower left to the upper right of the design, in a manner very reminiscent of the Heian period. But unlike the 'model' (Pl.150), he does not design the reed stalks in the same

Plate 149 Kōetsu: writing-box with boat in reeds. Before 1637. 4.5:22.5:24.6cm. Tōkyō National Museum

direction, but he depicts them, from lower right to upper left, by emphasizing the opposing diagonals, almost vertical to the boat. The elegance and airy lightness of the Heian representation here gains a greater strength and also relates it to the shape of the writing-box. Kōetsu avoids dividing the surface area of the lid into exactly symmetrical diagonal fields, but creates a balanced distribution of weight within the composition, and an aesthetically satisfying unity of shape and decoration. At that, the overall composition, rounded out at the top by a flock of chidori, seems so simple and casual that only closer inspection reveals its artistic significance.

Technically, Kōetsu lacquerwork is marked by the new, idiosyncratic combination of makie and mother-of-pearl with lead, and the liberally stylized inlays raised in emphatic relief above the lacquer ground. The Kōetsu lacquers are not 'elegant,' but in form, technique and composition alike they express the magic power of genius. The element of this new style most easily imitated – the technique – was being copied as early as the first half of the seventeenth century: lead inlays can be seen in works which are certainly not based on Kōetsu's designs – proof of the powerful effect of his style. To what extent it is possible, in individual cases, to speak either of 'Kōetsu lacquers' or simply of works in the manner of the Kōetsu school, can best be judged not by the technique but rather by the quality of the composition.

A bookshelf, known as *Nenohi-dana* (Pl. 151), is a relatively early work; although it shows the influence of the Kōetsu style, it also still owes much to the traditions of the Muromachi period. The motifs on the horizontal shelves derive from the Genji-monogatari, another reference back to the Heian period.[17] The vertical walls and the interior of the small, built-in cupboard are radiant with falling leaves and pine needles, worked in makie, mother-of-pearl and pewter inlay. The decoration was probably not designed by Kōetsu himself; according to Okada (in Hayashiya, *Kōetsu*,

Plate 150 Page from the Sanjūrokunin-shū anthology. ca 1112. Kyōto, Nishihongan-ji. Reproduced from *Sanjūrokunin-shū*

p. 136), it may be the result of a collaboration between the teamaster Furuta Oribe and the lacquermaster Kōami Chōgen, who died in 1607.

A small chest (sagedansu; Pl. 152) for Nō books, decorated in hiramakie, mother-of-pearl and lead inlay, bears witness to the influence of the Kōetsu style in a different way. It does not possess the forcefulness of the lacquers definitely designed by Kōetsu; rather it evokes the horizontal scrolls painted by Sōtatsu with calligraphy by Kōetsu. There is nothing comparable in the art of lacquerwork – though there is in painting. This small chest gives credence to an otherwise hard to prove tradition: that Sōtatsu played a significant part in the development of the so-called Kōetsu style.

Beginning with the Nara period, stylistic links with lacquerwork can be seen occasionally in textiles as well as in metalwork and ceramics. After the middle of the seventeenth century, however, something quite unique occurs. Not only are there general similarities, in the style of the period or in the use of certain ornamental forms, but, in addition, the most important

Plate 151 Nenohi bookshelf. Early 17th c. 65.1:72.4:33cm. Japan, private collection

master potter of the period, Nonomura Ninsei (active in Kyōto around 1670), was very definitely influenced by the very nature of the material as such: by the gloss of the black-lacquer grounds, the contrasting gold lacquers and – a technical detail – the use of kirigane, those small, three- or four-sided inlays cut out of sheet gold. Ninsei's tea jar (Pl. 153), with its cherry blossom motif, most skilfully transmutes these typical characteristics of Japanese lacquerwork and places them at the service of ceramic decoration. The connection is unmistakable and just as evident in other Ninsei work. This influence is all the more remarkable because after the Momoyama period lacquer art was no longer leading in Japanese applied arts as it did in mediaeval Japan; new, future-oriented developments now evolved more strongly in the fields of ceramics and textiles which, unencumbered by old traditions, experienced a great flowering in the seventeenth century. But the general atmosphere of the period and of the city of Kyōto, was especially conducive to a lively interchange between the arts: as in the instance of Kōetsu, who – himself active in so many spheres – inspired painters, calligraphers, potters and lacquermasters equally. In Ninsei's work this meeting of the arts is made manifest.

When Kōetsu died in Kyōto in 1637, Yamamoto Shunshō, who lived in the same town, was twenty-seven years old. After first studying poetry and Chinese literature, Shunshō dedicated himself to lacquerwork and became a well-known and esteemed master. His chief contribution seems to have been in bringing about a new flowering of togidashi, which, for a long time, had yielded to hiramakie and takamakie. Not many of his works have survived, but a writing-box (Pl. 154), decorated with loosely arranged

Plate 152 Small chest for Nō books. 1st half 17th c. Tōkyō, Seikadō collection

'nadeshiko' flowers (a species of pink) in togidashi and hiramkie on a ground sprinkled to produce a cloud effect, gives some idea of his style. As in so many lacquers of the early Edo period, here too the new elegance is combined with the heritage of the Momoyama period.

As the seat of the imperial court and – except during the Kamakura period – of the government, the town of Kyōto had until and into the early Edo period played the leading role in Japanese lacquerwork. Understandably, the Kōdai-ji and the Kōetsu styles also were most influential among the Kyōto lacquermasters, who could see these inspiring works right in their own town. Kōetsu's death in 1637 can be seen as marking the end of Kyōto's undisputed primacy in lacquerwork. For some time previously, provincial lacquer centres had been growing up here and there; Edo in particular, as the seat of the Tokugawa shōgunate, had been increasing in importance since 1603.

Written sources indicate that Tokugawa Ieyasu and his successors, above all his grandson Iemitsu (shōgun from 1623 to 1651), summoned numerous lacquer artists to their court in Edo and provided them with commissions. Some of these artists founded schools which produced many

Plate 153 Ninsei: tea jar. ca 1670. Tōkyō, Seikadō collection.

generations of lacquermasters active in the service of the Tokugawa.

Evidently the commissions granted by the shōgunate did not so much involve those practical items for everyday use mentioned earlier which gave the lacquerwork of the seventeenth century so much of its fresh, creative impetus; rather, the chief concern of the official lacquermasters in Edo was to satisfy the needs of the shōgunate, and of the daimyōs living in the capital, for ceremonial showpieces. Not functionalism but sumptuous, intricate effect was the prime purpose of such objects; consequently, the bulk of the output in Edo primarily consisted of the traditional type of lacquerwork of the Muromachi period, which involved the use of richly differentiated techniques. Echoes of the simple but extremely vivid Momoyama style, based in Kyōto, are rare in Edo.

Of the artists summoned to Edo, mention has already been made of the master of carved lacquer, Tsuishu Yōsei (see p. 167). Other founders of important families of lacquermasters were Kajiwaka Hikobei who, in the Kan-ei era (1624-1643) is said to have specialized primarily in making inrō for the Tokugawa family; and Koma Kyūi (died 1663), who in 1636 was officially honoured by Iemitsu for his makie work. Although there is insufficient knowledge about the work of the first Kajikawa masters, there is a good writing-box by Koma Kyūi in the National Museum in Tōkyō (Pl. 155). It has a pleasant shape with rounded-off corners, a slightly bowed

Plate 154 Shunshō: writing-box with pinks. Mid 17th c. 4.5:15.7:20.3cm. Tōkyō National Museum

outline and an almost flat lid. The decoration consists of a brushwood fence with climbing ivy (*Shibagaki ni tsuta makie-suzuribako*). The technical details are particularly interesting inasmuch as Kyūi produced a kind of coloured makie, even though the colours are somewhat muted and reticent. The hedge is rendered in quite shallow brown relief with traces of sprinkled gold on the small branches in the background. Before being sprinkled with gold, the leaves and tendrils received a coat of red paint which, in places, is visible through the gold. Inside the lid there is a design in silver makie, of herons in a shower of rain.[18] The delicate, sensitive realism and the well-balanced colour harmony which later, in the eighteenth century, were to distinguish many works by the Koma family, apparently were characteristic even of the founder of the Koma school.

More easily accessible than either the Koma or the Kajikawa school is the Kōami school of the early Edo era, in the works of Nagashige, tenth Kōami master. The only known works of his predecessors are the Sakura-sanjaku writing-box (Pl. 106), made by Kōami Sōhaku, and Kōami Matazaemon's shrine doors in the ancestor hall of the Kōdai-ji (Pl. 121). A rather injudiciously perpetuated Japanese legend, which survives even in the most recent publications, claims that Nagashige as a very young man collaborated on

Plate 155 Koma Kyūi: writing-box with brushwood fence. 1st half 17th c. 5.5:18.2:24.2cm. Tōkyō National Museum

these Kōdai-ji doors; yet he was not born until three years after their completion. He lived from 1599 to 1651 and finished his master work in 1639: a set of three cabinets (tana) with numerous boxes for writing implements (Pl. 156), paper, and clothes; a mirror stand and further accessories. This whole set formed part of the dowry of Tokugawa Iemitsu's eldest daughter. She married Mitsumoto, Prince of Bishū (Owari), who was also descended from the Tokugawa family and whose family crest appears on all pieces in the dowry.

This set of lacquer furniture and utensils comprises more than fifty items in all. They are ceremonial showpieces of the first order, and their overwhelming sumptuousness flaunts the enormous wealth of the firmly established Tokugawa shōgunate. The painter Iwasa Matabei (1578-1650) was commissioned to carry out the overall design of this luxurious trousseau; the metalwork was by Kenjō, a member of the famous Gotō family. Nagashige is said to have spent three years, from 1637 to 1639, on the lacquer decoration.

Again, the theme of all the representations derives from the tale of Prince Genji (more specifically, from the Hatsune chapter), which, in the

Early
Edo period

Plate 156 Kōami Nagashige: Hatsune writing-box. 1639. 2.7:22.7:25cm. Nagoya, Tokugawa Museum

Edo period, was considered symbolic of a happy life. This is why the cabinets and all their companion pieces are described as *Hatsune makie-sandana*.[19]

These princely lacquers are rightly regarded as the standard work among the Edo lacquers of their time. With minutest attention to detail, they are executed with very complicated techniques: in richly modelled takamakie combined with togidashi (so-called shishiai-makie) on a nashiji ground; in hiramakie and with inlays of kanagai, kirigane, coral and chased metal. (Almost all the plum blossoms in the illustration are examples of metalwork by Gotō Kenjō.) The overall effect is overwhelmingly lavish and colourful. Considered in terms of craftsmanship alone, these works are highly significant; but they do not rely for their effect merely on dazzling

Plate 157 Kōami Nagashige: picnic box. 32:32.6:19cm. Hamburg, Museum für Kunst und Gewerbe

skill and very obvious costliness: the artistic achievement as a whole, manifest in conception, form and style, is also on a very high level.

An inscription on a picnic box with a carrying handle (sagejū; Pl. 157) in the Hamburg Museum für Kunst und Gewerbe states that it was also made by Kōami Nagashige, based on pictures by Kanō Sanraku (1559-1635). The picnic box does not show the glowing magnificence of the Hatsune lacquers, nor does it have any coral or chased silver inlay. The various gold-lacquer techniques, though, are applied with great care and in great variety, and the composition is superb. Whether the box really was made by Nagashige will be possible to determine only after this master's *œuvre* as a whole has become more accessible.

It is interesting to see how the longing for rich colours so obviously displayed in seventeenth-century textiles, ceramics and metalwork – also, since 1634 so triumphantly expressed in the adornment of the lacquer

Plate 158 Detail of a lacquer door. 2nd quarter 17th c. Overall dimensions 181:104.5cm. Nikkō, Tōshōgū

decoration in the Tōshōgū shrine at Nikkō–invades the emphatically traditional art of gold lacquers in Nagashige's work (Pl.158). Even kanagai is used as a means of colour contrast, but this longing for colours is really fully expressed by the use of coral and chased-metal inlays.

The effect is very different from that of lacquer works in the Kōetsu style, despite the fact that the latter are equally 'colourful' with their gold and black, their mother-of-pearl and lead colours. But while in Kōetsu lacquers the contrasts remain within a relatively subdued colour scale, while colour effect and material are balanced and the dull, heavy lead very effectively offsets the gleam and glitter of the lacquer and mother-of-pearl, the style initiated by Nagashige and continued by later Kōami masters in the mid and late Edo periods often leads to a one-sided emphasis on glittering splendour. Particularly so, if everything is covered by gold and nashiji and no dark black-lacquer ground remains visible. Nagashige has very skilfully avoided the dangers of too much glitter. He very cleverly achieved certain differentiated effects by applying maki-bokashi and other techniques even when using gold on gold.

The beautifully executed *Gosho-kuruma suzuribako* (Pl.159), by an unknown master, is at much the same level of stylistic achievement as

Plate 159 Writing-box with court carriage. Mid 17th c. 3.9:20.9:21.4cm. Tōkyō National Museum

Nagashige's work. This writing-box, too, belongs among those conserva- *Early* tive seventeenth-century Edo lacquers which continue the Higashiyama *Edo period* tradition and seek to achieve a rich, imposing effect.

A *kōgō* with a lime branch (Pl.160: *Bodaiju makie-kōgō*) is quite different from these works. It was donated by Tokugawa Mitsumoto (1625-1700) to the Ampuku-ji temple in Osaka, and consequently could hardly have been made before the middle of the seventeenth century. Nevertheless, it still echoes something of the unfettered, flowing style of the Momoyama period; the ease with which the twigs and seed pods fit the six-lobed shape of the box is reminiscent of the draughtsmanship of the Kōdai-ji lacquers. But from the technical point of view, the execution in takamakie on a nashiji ground is definitely related to the 'traditional' Edo lacquers. The donor, Tokugawa Mitsumoto, was ruler of Bishū and resided in Nagoya, which is somewhere halfway between Kyōto and Edo. On the evidence of this kōgō, would it be safe to conclude that in Nagoya an Edo technique was handled in the Kyōto style? In any case, the difference is unmistakable between this bodaiju kōgō donated by Mitsumoto and the Hatsune dowry made for his wife (see p.189) in Edo.

The conservative attitude of the Edo lacquermasters is also evident in the work of Tatsuke Chōbei (active around 1667). The writing-box in the illustration (Pl.161: *Sumidagawa makie-suzuribako*), which has a writing-table to match, is indeed very close to the work of the Higashiyama period.[20]

Plate 160 Kōgō with lime branch. Mid 17th c. Osaka, Ampuku-ji

Next to the Kōami, Koma and Kajikawa masters, Yamada Jōka in particular gained a reputation as an outstanding lacquermaster in contemporary Edo. He was active around 1681; his name was also used by his pupils.

Up to the mid-Edo period, into the early eighteenth century, the growth of luxury and the increased demand for lacquers richly decorated with gold and silver were general and uninterrupted. But after the country had lapsed into total isolation and there ceased to be any external or internal stimulus to creative thought, the traditional tendencies of Edo lacquers did not permit any true evolution, even though the standard so far attained was more polished and refined.

Next to Kyōto and Edo, there was a third major centre of lacquerwork in the early Tokugawa period: Kanazawa in Kaga, the present-day province of Ishikawa. Around the middle of the seventeenth century, Maeda Toshitsune, the third Daimyō of Kaga, summoned the lacquermaster Igarashi Dōho I from Kyōto where he had been living to his seat of government at Kanazawa.[21] With him came his adopted son Dōho II and his pupil Shimizu Kyūbei, both equally important artists. A few years later, Toshitsune also summoned Shiihara Ichidayu from Edo; he was a pupil of

Plate 161 Tatsuke Chōbei: Sumidagawa writing-box. ca 1660. 5.2:22.7:25.2cm.
Tōkyō National Museum

Kyūbei's brother Shimizu Genjirō, who is said to have specialized in making inrō. The creations of these artists were the basis for the great fame the Kaga-makie (lacquers made at Kaga) enjoyed.

Igarashi Dōho 1 (died 1678) is the first great master of Kaga-makie. He was descended from Igarashi Shinsai, who had worked for Ashikaga Yoshimasa (see p. 119) in the Higashiyama period. One of the best known works attributed to Dōho 1 – they are unsigned and cannot be distinguished with absolute certainty from those of his son – is a comparatively narrow rectangular box for song books with a decoration of autumn plants beside a fence. [22] The stalks, leaves and grasses are raised only slightly in gold relief above the black-lacquer ground; in the chrysanthemum and kikyō blossoms mother-of-pearl inlays alternate with gold and tin kanagai, and coral is used for the buds. Like almost all seventeenth-century lacquers, the workmanship of this box is superb and particularly apparent in the way, for instance, in which the panicles of the susuki grasses are set with kirigane.

The great care lavished on technical details is apparently as much a sign of the times as the fondness for colour repeatedly referred to above. Thus, for example, in a writing-box also attributed to Igarashi Dōho 1 (Pl. 162), mother-of-pearl blossoms are glued on alternately with white rice paste and black lacquer, because the adhesive agent showing through the mother-of-pearl, makes the blossoms appear to be of different colours. But in spite of their fondness for new colour effects, which is typical of the period, and in spite of their customary precision and technical versatility, the Igarashi lacquers are clearly distinct from the works of other lacquermasters, particularly those of the Kōami school. They are characterized by greater simplicity and clarity, the result primarily of keeping the composition uncluttered and leaving much empty space. The empty background, the 'air,' often consists of black lacquer, which has a mellower and deeper glow than the nashiji grounds preferred by the Kōami masters. The interiors and exteriors of Igarashi lacquers are often in striking contrast in both style and technique, yet they are always vivid and imaginative in design.

Shimizu Kyūbei, the pupil of Dōho 1, included two 'shishi' (lions) among the peony plants decorating one of his writing-boxes. Both animals are inlaid in solid metal chased by the metalmaster Gōto Teijō. [23] In a general sense this inlay of solid metal in the lacquer decoration resembles the technique used for Kōami Nagashige's Hatsune lacquers (cf. p. 189). But in contrast to Nagashige, Kyūbei leaves more than half of the surface in unadorned black lacquer which offsets the animals and the golden takamakie decoration, yet avoids their looking too ostentatious, glittering and important.

It is astonishing how with such complicated means the Igarashi masters were able to attain an apparently simple, easy and elegant end; how they managed to avoid the dangers of undue emphasis on manual dexterity and lavish pomp. The Kaga-makie of the second half of the seventeenth century is the absolute equal in quality of lacquerwork produced in either Kyōto or Edo.

Of course, there were also lacquermasters working in Kanazawa at the time who did not belong to the Igarashi school. In 1656 one of them, the otherwise unknown master Kitagawa, decorated a saddle and matching stirrups with a long-tailed bird and a cherry tree in blossom, [24] using a considerable amount of kanagai and kirigane on a black-lacquer ground sprinkled with gold in a cloud pattern. This saddle is not especially out-standing, yet with its decoration – lavish and beautiful without being either cold or glittering – and its exact date, is a welcome indication of the high standard of Kanazawa lacquerware in the early Edo period. Right up to modern times Kanazawa has had its share of able lacquermasters. [25]

The output of some of the provincial schools of lacquerwork, which were now gradually forming under the protection of the daimyōs, was simpler and less ambitious.

Information about the earliest of these local centres of lacquer art refers to Aizu-Wakamatsu in the province of Fukushima. When Hideyoshi sent Daimyō Gamō Ujisato, a man of genius and a Christian, to Aizu-Wakamatsu in 1590, Gamō Ujisato found lacquermasters already working in the town. For the most part they copied Hidehira-wan (see p.164), proof that these wares were also known and admired to the south of their initial place of origin. Gamō Ujisato did his best to encourage this local, unpreten-tious form of lacquerware because it sold well outside the province, and thus contributed to both its prestige and the stabilizing of its economy.

Plate 162 Igarashi Dōho I: writing-box with autumn-field decoration. Before 1679. 4:22:24cm. Japan, private collection

Later, Aizu-Wakamatsu at first produced mostly plates and trays decorated with coloured-lacquer painting, the so-called 'Aizu-bon'.' Then,
these coloured lacquers gave way to chinkinbori and simple makie work
(the latter preferably decorated in 'keshi-makie,' which involves only a thin
sprinkling of fine gold dust). By the end of the Edo period these articles
were also exported. These late Aizu-nuri articles, however, were made
exclusively either for everyday use or as cheap souvenirs, without any
pretensions to artistic merit.

'Jogahana-nuri,' which takes its name from a place in the present-day
province of Toyama, allegedly goes back to the Momoyama period.[26]
Jogahana-nuri is a form of decorative painting on a lacquer ground using oil
paints – or at least oil mixed with lacquer – rather than real coloured lacquer. The technique is said to have been devised by a lacquermaster named
Jigoemon who went to Kyūshū, learnt the mitsuda-e process there from the
Chinese in Nagasaki, and established its use when he returned home. His
work must have brought him considerable fame, since he is alleged to have
received an invitation from Tsunanori Shōunkō (1643-1724), the fifth
Maeda-Daimyō, who surrounded himself in Kaga with many artists, scholars and teamasters.[27] Tsunanori was particularly interested in every kind
of arts and crafts. In his reign the *Hyakkō-hishō* was compiled: a kind of
specimen collection of techniques used by various artists, which has survived to this day. It contains a whole set of lacquerwork samples and
detailed descriptions of the various different types of coloured-lacquer,
gold dust and sprinkling techniques.[28]

Apparently no examples of Jigoemon's work survive: accordingly, nothing is known about the appearance of early Jogahana lacquers or their
relationship – if any – to Chinese coloured lacquers of the period. As it is,
the term Jogahana-nuri has almost become a 'brand name' in Japan for
painting in red, green, brown and white – the latter is only possible with oil
paint – on a lacquer ground.

Via Nagasaki – its port remained open to the Chinese even after Japan
had shut itself off from the rest of the world – Chinese lacquers of the late
Ming period appear to have had some influence on the art of Japanese
lacquerwork. For example, various sources indicate that lacquer objects
with very thin, blue-green, iridescent mother-of-pearl inlays 'in the
Chinese manner' were made in Nagasaki during the early Edo period. They
were known as 'aogai-nuri,' which, literally translated, means 'blue mussel
lacquer.' (Chinese works of this type are famous in Europe as '*laque
burgautée*.') A certain lacquermaster, Chōbei, who later used the name
Aogai Chōbei, is said to have learnt this technique from the Chinese in
Nagasaki in about 1620, but once again there is not a single example of work
from his hand. Early seventeenth-century aogai lacquers can no longer be
identified today.

Nevertheless, this technique of inlaying extremely thin mother-of-pearl
in lacquer seems to have become something of a tradition on Nagasaki, for a
hundred years later, in about 1720, a lacquermaster called Somada learnt
the same process there. Somada Kiyosuke originally came from Toyama,
and thus introduced a second wave of Chinese influence to this northern
coastal province, after Jigoemon's earlier introduction of Jogahana-nuri.

It is remarkable that in Japan both these techniques should have remained restricted to more or less provincial works: they never caught on

either in Kyōto or indeed with the 'official' lacquermasters in Edo.²⁹ The influence of Chinese lacquerwork does continue to the present day, however, in the province of Toyama where mother-of-pearl lacquers in the Chinese style are still being copied, if only in very stereotyped versions and for the most part using thick white mother-of-pearl rather than aogai for the inlays.

Other provincial lacquer centres which, in the course of the seventeenth century, developed their own techniques are Wakasa in the present-day province of Fukui, and Tsugaru in the province of Aomori. In the 'Wakasa-nuri,' which is still being produced today in the south of the province, layers of different coloured lacquers are applied to a ground deliberately rendered uneven by the addition of small pieces of egg shell, rice chaff, etc. Very thin gold or silver foil is then pressed so firmly into this 'relief' that it fits every unevenness like a skin. Then a coating of transparent lacquer is applied and, after it has hardened, everything is polished down to form a smooth surface. As a result, the layers of coloured lacquer under the gold foil reappear in places to produce rather unusual patterns. The precursors of this technique allegedly go back to the Momoyama period, but only around 1660 did it at all become known as Wakasa-nuri – a name given it by the ruling daimyō of the Sakai family.

'Tsugaru-nuri' is made along similar lines, but without the gold foil and with many more layers of coloured lacquer. Green, red, yellow and brown are the colours most commonly used to produce the requisite spotted-marbled effect. The technique is said to have been used first in 1685 by Ikeda Gentarō, the son of a lacquermaster by the name of Ikeda Gembei, and it is still a specialty of the town of Hirosaki (in the provine of Aomori), where every shop stocks all kinds of small, useful boxes decorated with Tsugaru-nuri in a thoroughly solid, workmanlike manner.

The latest – but, from the artistic point of view, the most important – 'provincial technique' to be developed was the chinkinbori of Wajima, in the province of Ishikawa. The chinkin technique as such had, of course, been known since the Muromachi period (see p.110). But when, in the Kambun era (1661-1672), a loamy yellow clay (known as keisodō) was discovered near Wajima, chinkinbori soon became a speciality of this remote little town, because the soil, when burnt, pulverized and mixed with the lacquer, provided the particularly firm, crack-proof ground so essential for any engraving technique. The fame of Wajima-nuri has survived to the present day (in more recent times the town has been producing makie work as well as chinkinbori) and Mae Taihō, one of the best-known lacquermasters today who has been honoured wth the rare title of a 'jūyō-mukei-bunkazai hojisha,'³⁰ makes his modern chinkinbori lacquers there (see p.245).

In summing up the early Edo period, we can see that the lacquers of the seventeenth century have proved to be extraordinarily varied. While at first – particularly in Kyōto – the sparkling, vivid ideas of the Momoyama period continue to have some influence, the emphasis gradually shifts. The demand increases, especially in Edo, for showpieces, sumptuously embellished with gold lacquer in the ever richer and more complex techniques employed. To this end, the lacquermasters refer back to the Higashiyama tradition, making it the basis for additional embellishment and complexity. Though in articles of this kind the decorative motifs often still derive from poetry, especially from the Genji-monogatari, on the whole the poetic content is no longer quite so important.

By purely technical standards, almost all seventeenth-century lacquers are quite superb. But although the artist's mastery of design and composition remains the decisive factor, there are the first indications of the tendency – predominant in later work – to allow difficult techniques to become an end in themselves and to degenerate into a mere show of virtuosity.

The early Edo period was the first in the history of lacquerwork to make possible the evaluation of a number of artists of school-founding stature, foremost, of course, the genius Kōetsu. Peace and prosperity now made lacquerwork an art form available also to the rich middle classes; even more to the point, their needs led to the creation of a whole series of new, functional lacquer utensils which are both practical and aesthetically pleasing. Lacquermasters are at work in numerous localities throughout the land, and even though all the provincial centres did not attain as high a standard as Kaga, where the powerful and art loving Maeda daimyōs encouraged not only lacquerwork but also painting, metalwork and pottery – 'kutani' porcelain in particular – the simple wares in the folk art tradition from Aizu-Wakamatsu, Jogahana, Toyama, Wakasa, Tsugaru and Wajima also contribute to the vitality and versatility of early Edo lacquer art.

THE MID-EDO PERIOD COVERS THE DECADES BETWEEN APPROXIMATELY
1681 and 1764 – the dates vary slightly according to whether the period is
being considered from the political or the art-historical point of view; there
is no perceptible break between it and the early Edo period. The high point
of the era is in its early stages, in the first, glittering fifteen years of the
hedonistic, elegant, luxury-loving Genroku period (1688-1703).

Certain key words are enough to evoke the artistic achievement of this
period: the Genroku era witnessed the beginnings of the exuberantly decorative Imari porcelain, and a new high in the development of Kakiemon
porcelain under Shibuemon; it was the time when Yokoya Sōmin made his
famous sword furniture; and thanks to Miyazaki Yūzensai and his dye
technique, known as 'Yūzenzome,' the textile arts in Kyōto made imposing
progress. In this Genroku era, Basho, Ihara Saikaku and Chikamatsu wrote
poetry, and the Kabuki and Bunraku theatres vied for the favour of the
masses.

The strict legislation of the Tokugawa shōgunate continued to prevent
the newly rich but despised merchants from climbing the social ladder, and
from taking an active and responsible part in politics; the middle-class
'jeunesse dorée' tried to compensate for any burgeoning social tensions with
insatiable hedonism.

The most famous exponent of the high-living Genroku era and its newly
rich middle class was Ogata Kōrin (1658-1716), painter and lacquer artist,
and one of Japan's great geniuses in the realm of decorative painting. He
was born into a family of Kyōto silk merchants who had enjoyed the favour
of those in power since Hideyoshi's time, and had become wealthy in the
process. He was a great-grand-nephew of Kōetsu, whose artistry continued
to be reflected in generation after generation of his family: Kōrin's grand-
father Sōhaku had lived for a time in the artist's village of Takagamine, and
his father Sōken, the prosperous owner of the Karigane-ya silk shop, was an
art lover and a well-known calligrapher in the manner of Kōetsu. Wealth
and love of art determined Kōrin's style of life, which was extravagant and
unconventional. By 1694 Kōrin had already sold his entire inheritance after
his father's death, so he could enjoy life in his own way. His artistic activity
appears to have taken place mainly in his last fifteen years: more than half
his pictures are signed with the title hokkyō – originally a Buddhist title, but
often bestowed on painters – which he received in 1701. He spent two short
periods in Edo (1701 and 1707-8); his final years in Kyōto were apparently
spent in unfavourable circumstances, after the fall of his influential patron
Nakamura Kuranosuke.

Kōrin occupies an eminent position in the art of lacquerwork. The
esteem accorded him has, at times, even threatened to eclipse Kōetsu;
'Kōrin lacquer' became a household word, an omnibus term used to denote,
without any foundation in fact, both older pieces influenced by Kōetsu and
much later imitations.

In present-day Japan, however, great caution is exercised before an item
of lacquerwork is attributed to the hand of Kōrin. We do know from his
legacy – which in due course went to the Konishi family, who adopted
Kōrin's son – that Kōrin had made many designs and preliminary drawings
for lacquer works, but very few objects are definitively recognized as having
been made by Kōrin himself. Nothing can be proved, since the best pieces
are unsigned, while – apart from deliberate fakes – many works by his

latter-day successors were signed with his signature to mean 'in the manner of Kōrin.'

Three writing-boxes are said to be copies by Kōrin of lacquers by Kōetsu: the *Sakuragai*, the *Minowa* and the *Sumino-e suzuribakos* (Pl. 163).[1] On the original box in which the last of these belonged, there is an inscription, allegedly written by Kōrin himself, to the effect that the writing-box is a copy of one by Kōetsu. Since the Kōetsu box has not survived, a comparison is unfeasible.

Both externally and internally the sumino-e writing-box is obviously related in form to Kōetsu's funabashi box (Pl. 147), but the highly domed lid is not quite so imposing. The design consists of lead-inlay rocks in gold-lacquer waves with superimposed, silver-written characters, which makes it definitely comparable to the boat-bridge box. But in the sumino-e box the motif has been transformed into an almost abstract design, the waves ares stylized and the rocks – scarcely recognizable as such – seem to be there rather more for reasons of breaking down the surface into rhythmic patterns than for the creation of a realistic design. The second edition of Kōrin's drawings,[2] published in Kyōto in 1890, contains a fan design which also depicts wave-dashed rocks, in which the more or less amorphous mass of the rocks is similarly contrasted with the stylized waves; and the foaming crest of the wave on the sumino-e box is akin to a wave in the fan drawing.

As interesting as a comparison between the Kōetsu original and the Kōrin copy might have been were it not impossible, Kōrin's individuality and his stature as an artist are certainly more clearly revealed in the lacquers which were entirely his own creations. His most famous work is the *Yatsuhashi* writing-box in the National Museum Tōkyō (Pl. 164). The box is unsigned and there are no early references to it in literature, yet no one in Japan questions its attribution to Kōrin. Again the centuries-old shape of the suzuribako has been reinterpreted and modified.[3] Kōetsu having moved the inkstone to the left, Kōrin now combined the usually separate paper- and writing-boxes in one single unit. His yatsuhashi box is on two levels:

Plate 163 Kōrin: Sumino-e writing-box. 10:23:24.5cm. Tōkyō, Seikadō collection

the lower is for paper, while the upper holds inkstone, water-dropper and brushes in the usual way. The longer sides of the flat, overlapping lid are scallop-edged vertically, making it easier to grip when removing the lid, a very pleasing solution both aesthetically and practically, which, combined with the rounded-off corners, lends the high box a certain lightness and elegance.

But the decisive factor is the decoration, which takes up a motif derived from the *Ise-monogatari*: the eight-fold bridge ('yatsuhashi' means eight bridges) across the iris swamp. This theme was a particular favourite of Kōrin's: with or without the three characters, which, in the *Ise-monogatari*, are connected with the story; with or without even the bridge. (The famous pair of six-panel folding screens in the Nezu Museum shows only the iris plants). Here on the writing-box, both major elements, the bridge and the iris plants, are shown, if only in quite simple, stylized forms, but with great skill in composition and in the use of materials. The planks of the bridge are rendered in lead; the supporting posts in silver; the iris blossoms in bluish, greenish, and reddish iridescent aogai mother-of-pearl without any interior engraving or gold-lacquer painting; the leaves and stalks are in gold makie. The water of the swamp is not actually depicted on the exterior but merely implied by the black-lacquer ground. It is characteristic of Kōrin's extraordinary instinct for materials that for the black lacquer he should employ a

Plate 164 Kōrin: Yatsuhashi writing-box. 14.4:19.9:27.3cm. Tōkyō National Museum

technique which produces a non-reflecting, mat surface (tsuyakeshi). This deep tranquil shade suggests the dark water of the swamp; the interior of the lower box, on the other hand, shows imaginatively stylized 'Kōrin waves' in gold-lacquer on a black ground, thereby emphasizing the association with 'water.' (The lid and upper part of the box are covered inside with plain gold lacquer in the ikakeji technique.)

This writing-box is an outstanding piece of work, which one never tires of looking at. Kōrin's mastery is expressed in the skilful arrangement of the lead bridges which link the side walls and the lid, and at the same time, impel the observer's eye to move in a prescribed direction. It is expressed also in the allocation of the iris plants, some in clumps, some single; in the variations in length, direction and degree of movement of the identically shaped leaves, and particularly in the vivid overall effect created by the use of such perfectly matched materials.

The yatsuhashi writing-box does not have the grandness of the Kōetsu lacquers, or their severity and weightiness, or even the almost architectural solidity of composition achieved by opposing diagonals. It is flatter, not merely because of the shape of the lid, but also because of the design which, by omitting descriptive detail, transforms the motifs into large, simplified areas, resulting in a decorative pattern. There is no attempt to deny the iris plants their actual appearance; on the contrary, their very quintessence is shown. It is in this decorative, two-dimensional stylization of nature that Kōrin reveals himself as the Japanese artist par excellence; it is this self-same ornamental effect (one can also see it in the recessed hand-grip on the lid) which, compared with the Kōetsu lacquers, lends an airier elegance to this writing-box and should be clearly recognized as Kōrin's own personal style.

Kōrin was of course continuing in the spirit of the Kōetsu lacquers, if only in the emphatic use of lead inlays and in the generous spirit expressed in the overall design, which is in such obvious contrast to the rather crowded style of other lacquers of the Genroku period. But Kōrin seems to enrich the Sōtatsu-Kōetsu tradition with his own new stylistic characteristics of suppleness, fluidity and elegance. The ready wit, sometimes expressed in his pictures, in no sense contradicts the spirit of the yatsuhashi writing-box while it could never be reconciled with the severity of Kōetsu lacquers.

There is one further writing-box which is not definitely attributed to Kōrin, but is nevertheless referred to time and again when the question of works from his hand arises: the so-called *Narihira-suzuribako* (Pl. 165). [4] (Narihira was the poet whose experiences are recounted in the *Ise-monogatari* and whose poem immortalized the eight-fold bridge over the iris swamp.) The very large and flat box has an 'okibuta,' that is, a lid consisting of a simple board with slanted edges, but without vertical walls, which sits on top of the box and is held in place by just two strips of beading on its underside. The broad expanse of the lid is boldly decorated with a single fan, bearing a head-and-shoulder protrait of Narihira. Fans had been used as decorative motifs in lacquerwork since the Kamakura period, and references back to classical themes of this kind are typical of Sōtatsu, Kōetsu and Kōrin. [5] But the idea of spreading one single fan in a great sweep across the entire box is certainly quite new.

The spread of the fan is sprinkled with fine reddish gold dust partially worn away by now, with the details of the poet's face and the outline of his ceremonial hat left free; the hair is painted on in black lacquer; the garment is inlaid in pewter and the ribs of the fan in silver. The uncluttered, old technique admirably suits the composition. This writing-box is far removed indeed from the luxury and intricate detail of decoration so fashionable with other lacquermasters of the period.

Whether Kōrin actually carved out the decoration of this box with his own hands is something that cannot be proved. But among his surviving drawings[6] there is a design for a writing-box (Pl. 166) which, although it was intended to have an overlapping lid, as far as the decoration itself (the fan motif with the portrait of Narihira) is concerned, exactly matches the suzuribako in the Nezu Museum. At least the design of the box can, therefore, safely be attributed to Kōrin.[7] The Narihira suzuribako has certainly always been highly esteemed by lacquermasters. At one time it belonged to

Plate 165 Kōrin: Narihira writing-box. Detail. Overall dimensions 4.8:19.9:27.4cm. Tōkyō, Nezu Museum

Koma Kansai II, who in turn gave it to his pupil Zeshin, the most important lacquer artist of the nineteenth century. An inscription by Zeshin on its outer box mentions these facts.

If, on the basis of the few lacquers attributed to him today, one were to come to any conclusion at all about Kōrin's style as a lacquer artist, it would be justifiable to say that he adopted the Kōetsu style but that, in accordance with the overall trend in art, he transformed the bold splendour of the Momoyama period into a more flexible, more appealing kind of elegance. The severe, constructional aspect of Kōetsu's compositions gave way to Kōrin's lighter, more freely flowing ideas, which reveal a real gift both for rhythm in the way he apportioned the decorative surface and for ornamental effect. The technical execution illustrates time and again the sureness of Kōrin's feeling for the essential natures of the various materials he employed; even when used sparingly, he elicited from them an amazingly varied expressive potential. It is this artistic economy that also raises his work above the, at times, all too glamorous lacquers of his later imitators.

Tsuchida Sōetsu, a lacquermaster working in Kyōto, was strongly influenced by both Kōetsu and Kōrin. He was a contemporary of the latter and also copied his work.[8] He had a particular penchant for the combination of lead and mother-of-pearl inlays and handled these materials with great skill. Inrō by Sōetsu and his successors, who worked in the same style (and used the same name), are also quite common in Western collections.

Nagata Yūji was another Kyōto lacquermaster who frequently produced work in the Kōetsu-Kōrin manner. His exact dates are unknown, but the second and third decades of the eighteenth century are traditionally regarded as his main period of creativity, a dating with which the most recent

Plate 166 Kōrin: design for the Narihira writing-box. Reproduced from *Kōrin shin-sen hyaku-ga*

Japanese publications also concur.[9] Other accounts, however, put it a century later; but although there are stylistic and technical grounds which make this seem likely, there is as yet no concrete proof.[10] He too adopted the combination of lead and mother-of-pearl inlays, sometimes on a natural wood ground, but in his work one looks in vain for the spontaneity of Kōrin's composition. Nagata Yūji's chief claim to fame lay in his use, in takamakie, of tin powder for the lower layers, a technique which was named 'Yūji-age' after him.

Although Kōrin was often imitated, one cannot speak of a Kōrin school in the sense of an uninterrupted tradition. Apparently not until around 1800 was there a Kōrin 'renaissance' of any importance; it was initiated by the painter Sakai Hōitsu (1761-1828). Apart from closely identifying with the Sōtatsu-Kōrin style, Hōitsu also collected Kōrin's drawings and had them printed to commemorate the one hundredth anniversary of his death.[11] In the last decades of the Edo period, the Edo master Hara Yōyūsai is said to have produced lacquer works after Hōitsu's drawings in the Kōrin style (see p.222). And towards the end of the Meiji era, Kōrin seems to have become 'worthy of copying' again. He was the last great master of the Edo period actually to break new ground in Japanese lacquerwork even if he was continuing in the spirit of Kōetsu's lacquers. Nor, apart from deliberate copies, did he simply imitate Kōetsu lacquers: on the contrary, he developed stylization which, in his paintings too, enabled him to produce work with a particularly 'Japanese' feeling.

A contemporary of Kōrin, of Tsuchida Sōetsu and possibly also of Nagata Yūji in Kyōto, was Shiomi Masanari (otherwise known as Seisei or Masazane), a lacquermaster of an altogether different style.[12] He is thought to have been a pupil of Shunshō (see p.185), and like him, he especially favoured the technique of togidashi. In this medium he produced carefully executed lacquers of such exquisite finesse that the term 'Shiomi-makie' later was to become a synonym for good quality togidashi lacquers. His best-known work is the *Hirasan* writing-box (Pl.167),[13] which shows the landscape around Lake Biwa near Kyōto. It is not worked exclusively in togidashi: the boat and the mountains in the background are in relief. But the vivid, minute detailing of the waves clearly illustrates Masanari's artistry in togidashi. An inrō by him, dated 1710, which used to belong to the Berlin State Museums but vanished after 1945, was an especially attractive specimen of Shiomi's mastery of coloured togidashi.[14] Whereas togidashi had been the principal technique in the Heian period, hiramakie and takamakie subsequently gained importance. Following on from Shunshō and Shimoi Masanari, several eighteenth-century lacquermasters turned their attention once again to togidashi, and particularly toward the end of the century, some extraordinarily beautiful coloured togidashi lacquers were made (see also p.217).

This period sees the first, occasional, use of powdered gold, so extremely fine it resembles dust – a technique much favoured during the Meiji period. The individual particles are so minute that in the sprinkled decoration they are no longer recognizable as such but form a unified, homogeneous gold surface. The velvety texture of older gold lacquers in which, at least through a magnifying glass, the individual particles of gold can still be made out, is thereby lost, and with it, occasionally, one especially attractive effect of all sprinkling techniques. But on the other hand, this incredibly fine gold dust made it possible to obtain particularly delicate nuances of the different shades of red, yellow and green gold. To the late eighteenth-century lacquermasters, as they strove for miniature-like effects on inrō and all kinds of other small containers and boxes, the new material was most welcome. (See, for example, the toy-like lacquer objects from Marie Antoinette's collection, now in the Musée Guimet in Paris.)

Shiomi Masanari himself or his pupils allegedly later went to live at Edo, which was gradually becoming the very centre of the art of lacquerwork. The prevalent tendency there toward excessively lavish gold lacquerwork has been referred to earlier: the shōgunate and the daimyōs, pledged to temporary residence in Edo, vied with each other in a display of splendour and wealth. The love of luxury was taken to its ultimate extreme by Tokugawa Tsunayoshi, shōgun from 1680 to 1709; the makie works of these years, characterized by their superabundance of gold, are known as 'Jōken-in-jidai-mono,' that is, objects from the time of Jōken-in, after his posthumous name, Jōken-in. A typical specimen is a cabinet with landscape decoration (Pl. 168: *Sansui makie-dana*) which Tsunayoshi himself gave to Prince Yanagisawa of Mino. The cabinet is subdivided in a number of ways

Plate 167 Shiomi Masanari: writing-box with Mount Hira. ca 1700. 4.8:22.9:24.8cm. Tōkyō National Museum

into small cupboards, sliding-doors and drawers; all surfaces are densely sprinkled in nashiji. In very rich gold-lacquer techniques (takamakie and shishiai-makie) the display sides show landscapes in which pines, bamboo and plum trees frequently recur as symbols of good fortune. Kirigane, kanagai and even solid silver inlays are freely employed. The name of the lacquermaster responsible for this little cabinet is unknown, but its almost excessively rich gold decoration makes it a standard work of the Genroku period and gives a good idea of the type of work turned out not only by the 'court lacquerers' of the Kōami, Koma and Kajikawa families, but also by the other lacquermasters active in Edo at that time.

In comparison with contemporary Kyōto lacquers, such pieces can eas-

Plate 168 Cabinet with landscape decoration. ca 1700. 86.4:86.4:35.5cm. Tōkyō, Ōkura Shūkokan

ily give the impression of being a bit awkward and lacking in vividness. What was expected of the lacquermasters in Edo was not so much lively ideas and compositions of their own – they often had to work from preliminary drawings by painters of the Kanō school – but rather, the most obvious splendour. Inheritors as they were of the Muromachi tradition, albeit by now in a more schematic, less original manner, they tried to do justice to the claims made upon them through excessive technical virtuosity and the use of gold in a manner so profligate as to verge on pointlessness. If ever there was a time in the history of Japanese lacquerwork when the terms 'arts and crafts' had to be compared in a negative sense to the word 'art,' these would-be traditional Edo lacquers of around 1700 would be the first in line.

Up to thirty coats were used for the ground alone – for makie works at that, not for carved lacquers – and what with the gold dust sprinkled into the subsequent layers, and the gold foil and kirigane so generously applied, it seemed as if the material value, not the artistic creation, were the main concern. Thus, on the one hand, the conventionalization of forms and formulae are the norm for many Edo lacquers of the Genroku period. If one compares these too-rich, too-complex luxury pieces overloaded with wearysome detail with their models, the Higashiyama lacquers, which, after all, are themselves so richly decorated with gold lacquer, the Edo lacquers look hollow and cold. Conversely, the high artistic level of the earlier works, the overall design and content of which exclude any evaluation on purely materialistic grounds, becomes even more apparent.

Perhaps most suitable to escape such luxuriant excess were the inrō for which the real high point was the eighteenth century. Their very smallness may have acted to counterbalance, to a certain extent, any ostentatious intentions. Thus, two inrō masters were among the best known lacquermasters in Edo at that time: Kajikawa Kyūirō (died 1682?), who was famed as the best inrō master of his time, and Yamada Jōka, who worked for the

Plate 169 Saddle and stirrups with wisteria decoration. 1734. Tōkyō National Museum

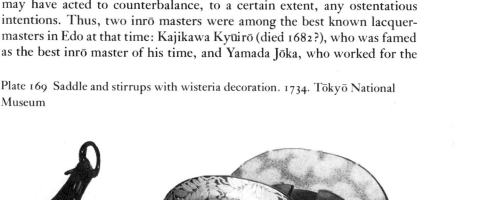

shōgun and, apart from inrō, specialized in the gold-lacquer decoration of small boxes for incense and the like.

Other masters whose names at least deserve a mention are: Kōami Nagafusa (1628-1682), Kōami Nagasuku (1661-1723), Koma Kyūhaku (died 1715) and his son Kyūhaku II, who is also known under the name Yasuaki or Anshō. [15] In 1689, Nagasuku and Kyūhaku jointly supervised the makie work, when necessary repairs were being carried out on the Tōshōgu shrine in Nikkō.

All these Edo masters produced richly decorated, technically competent pieces of lacquerwork often using coral, ivory, metalwork or mother-of-pearl inlays; but they all kept within certain bounds, apparently fixed by convention. None of them managed to break out and engender the creativity and innovation that Kōrin brought about in Kyōto. Works like the saddle and matching stirrups (Pl. 169: *Fuji makie-gura-abumi*), dated 1734, in which all the surfaces are decorated with a wisteria motif in two-coloured gold makie, kirigane and kanagai, repesent a continuation of the traditional school. Around this time the excessive luxury of the Genroku period was replaced by a simpler and more attractive manner of decoration, but still there is not the least sign of either a really new style or of forward-looking

Plate 170 Ritsuō: writing-box with Chinese ink decoration. 1720. 5.2:21.2:23.3cm. Tōkyō National Museum

Plate 171 Tanida Chūbei: box and cover decorated with lacquer painting. ca 1760.
Ht 12cm, diam. 21.5cm. Tōkyō National Museum

ideas. A certain lassitude was spreading through the art of lacquerwork.

The lacquermaster who in Edo did break out of the conventional mould and create something really new was Ogawa Haritsu, better known under his artist's name of Ritsuō (1663-1747). Like Kōrin, whose contemporary he was, but whom he outlived by three full decades, Ritsuō too appears to have been a versatile, gifted eccentric, prone to bewilder those around him.[16] Born in Ise, he went to Edo to study haikai poetry under Bashō; Hanabusa Itchō also taught him to paint, and in addition, he was active as a potter. His main interest, however, was to be lacquerwork. In certain respects Ritsuō also has links with Kōetsu, since, in contrast to the prodigality with which the lacquermasters working for the shōgunate employed gold foil and gold dust, he preferred to inlay contrasting materials, generally in a black-lacquer ground. But he did not restrict himself to the use of mother-of-pearl and lead; on the contrary, he liked to combine materials that were as strange and distinctive as possible to offset the lacquer: ivory, coloured ceramics, small pieces of carved red lacquer etc. Kōetsu and Kōrin, unmistakably limiting themselves to gold or black lacquer, lustrous mother-of-pearl and heavy, dull lead, combined harmonizing, because complementary, values that enhanced one another and never jeopardized an object's unity of material and shape. But Ritsuō's work often contains an element of bizarre playfulness, and the multiplicity and arbitrary choice of his materials sometimes interferes with the essential nature of the lacquer itself.

In comparison with the pure Japanese work of Kōetsu and Kōrin, Ritsuō's lacquers seem quite strange; indeed, he was clearly influenced by Chinese arts and crafts of the Ming and Ch'ing periods. In fact, what perhaps comes closest to his lacquers are possibly those Chinese screens in which numerous inlays of different materials are used to complement the basic lacquer.

This penchant for Chinese taste reflected a similar preoccupation among the educated Japanese with Chinese philosophy and poetry, an inclination which had been encouraged by the shōguns from the time of Ieyasu onwards, and reached its peak under Tokugawa Yoshimune, shōgun from 1716 to 1745. Ritsuō took his love of everything Chinese to such extremes that, in a writing-box dated 1720 (Pl. 170: *Kohoku makie-suzuribako*), he even inlaid a piece of real Chinese ink in the lid; next to it he imitated another piece of Chinese ink in lacquer relief inlaid with a two-colour porcelain plaque with a dragon design. The rather mat black-lacquer ground is sprinkled with finely powdered mother-of-pearl.[17]

Kümmel has described Ritsuō as 'one of the most unpleasant virtuosos of all time and of any nationality,'[18] and, in fact, his works lack the distinction generally characteristic of Japanese lacquerwork. But he was highly esteemed by his contemporaries, probably because his pieces were such a change from the usual gold lacquers of the Edo masters; they met the need for colour and reflected the contemporary vogue for things Chinese.

His most important pupil was Mochizuki Hanzan, active in Edo around the middle of the eighteenth century. The style of inlay, involving carved lacquer, ceramics, coloured glass, ivory etc., and known as 'Haritsu-zaiku' after Ritsuō, was still being practised there at the beginning of the nineteenth century by Shibayama Yasumasa and other masters.

The joy in new materials, observed in lacquerwork starting with Kōetsu, is not the prerogative of lacquermasters alone. In metalwork the origins of a similar development can be traced back to the Momoyama and early Edo periods. There is a noticeable propensity for new combinations of iron or bronze with gold, silver and shakudō (a copper alloy) and also, from at the latest the eighteenth century onward, *cloisonné*.[19]

Tanida Chūbei,[20] another lacquermaster whose work also shows strong Chinese influence, worked in Edo at about the same time as Ritsuō's pupil Hanzan. (It would seem that the Chinese influence was stronger in Edo, the seat of government of the shōgunate, than in Kyōto.) Painting on a red lacquer ground was Tanida Chūbei's speciality (Pl. 171); he was particularly fond of painting flowers both in gold and coloured lacquer, and in mitsuda-e. At some stage, probably around 1760, he entered the service of Prince Hachisuka of Awa and settled in the latter's domain on the island of Shikoku. He is said to have been expressly commissioned by the prince to carry out lacquerwork in the Chinese style, but not many of his works are known today. The elegance of his lacquer painting, especially those of

Plate 172 Iizuka Tōyō: Ujigawa writing-box. 1775. 5.5:23.7:26.1 cm. Kyōto, Gosho

flowers, so clearly distinguished them from the generally rather provincial coloured-lacquer paintings of his time that the name 'Tanida-nuri' was coined specifically to describe his and other similar works.

Another famous lacquer artist of the second half of the century was Iizuka Tōyō;[21] he too served the same Prince Hachisuka, but he worked in Edo. The dates of both his birth and his death are unknown, but his *chef-d'œuvre*, a paper box and companion writing-box (Pl. 172: *Uji-gawa-hotaru makie-ryōshibako-suzuribako*), bears the date 'An-ei 4th year' (1775). Both boxes, which have belonged to the Japanese imperial house-hold since the beginning of the Meiji period, are richly decorated and superbly executed works which surely were perfect reflections of the prince's desire for showpieces. The fine colour gradation, even within the gold shades proper, and the skilful contrast between the forceful decoration of the exteriors and the more elegant, finer ornamentation of the interiors are evidence of both the traditional skilful craftsmanship of the Japanese lacquermasters, and a very discerning personal taste. Almost more beauti-

Plate 172a Iizuka Tōyō: Ujigawa paper box. 1775. 16.5 : 33.8 : 41 cm. Kyōto, Gosho

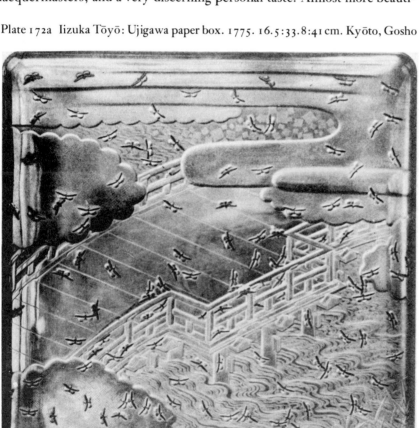

ful than these large boxes, and more indicative of Tōyō's standing as an artist, are his inrō, in which the colour harmony, in particular, is a never-ending delight. His pupils and successors were active as inrō-makers up to the middle of the nineteenth century, but they seldom produced anything to equal his work.

Koma Kyoryū, who was also active in Edo somewhere between 1771 and 1788, likewise specialized in the manufacture of inrō (Pl. 173). He was a pupil of the fifth Koma master, Kyūhaku, and produced some very fine togidashi lacquers. Several members of the Koma school at that time distinguished themselves by the beauty of their togidashi work; one of these, Koma Yasutada, merits specific mention.[22]

The end of the eighteenth century can be described as the golden age of togidashi in general, and of coloured togidashi in particular. It is not that geniuses of the calibre of Kōetsu or Kōrin, or even merely self-willed talents like Ritsuō, were now creating outstanding and innovating works; it is simply that, after a long period of domination of hiramakie and takamakie, the general standard of top-quality togidashi was now very high. Every

Plate 173 Koma Kyoryū: inrō. 2nd half 18th c. Tōkyō National Museum

conceivable variation of this technique is found, principally on inrō, but sometimes also on incense boxes, etc. The comparative rarity of pure gold togidashi is explained by the marked preference for coloured togidashi, in which the decoration was painted on in different shades of red, green, yellow etc., and then sprinkled over with fine gold dust in varying densities. Sometimes, instead of underpainting, coloured lacquer dust was sprinkled in. Occasionally the colour effect was further enhanced by a particularly glossy black-lacquer ground (rōiro-nuri).

An especially distinguished and elegant effect was produced by the so-called 'sumie-togidahsi' technique, in which powdered charcoal was spinkled into a silvery-grey ground, causing the finished design to resemble an ink painting (sumi-e).

It may have been economic reasons – a general period of depression, with the concomitant decrees banning luxuries – which forced the lacquermasters in these years to use the expensive gold more sparingly, which they could do all the more easily since very handsome effects could be achieved with coloured togidashi. Also, strong colours were much favoured at the end of the eighteenth century, since this was the golden age of coloured woodcuts; the middle class, which loved the woodcuts, could only have welcomed coloured inrō.

The vast fund of motifs on which the inrō-masters could draw for their subjects was almost unlimited. There were Buddhist and Taosit themes, scenes from old Japanese and Chinese sagas and fairy tales, written characters and maps, flowers and birds, good luck symbols of various kinds, as well as designs which refer to annual festivals and the world of the theatre. Ukiyo-e sometimes exercised a direct influence too, since there are inrō which are clearly based on preliminary drawings by masters of the woodcut and occasionally even show their signatures.

Of course making inrōs for an ever greater public was not practised by all lacquermasters to the same degree. The conservative Kajikawa masters for example, to take but one group, stood rather aloof and adhered more to the style of court-approved Kanō painters (Pl. 174). Following their models, they decorated their inrō in a somewhat stereotyped manner with landscapes, waterfalls, pavillions under trees, chrysanthemums by the East Fence, etc.

In the eighties and nineties, various masters of the Koma school specialized in flower and bird designs. Their accuracy in depicting nature is quite impressive, and generally, lacquer designs from the end of the eighteenth century to the end of the Meiji era (in 1912) developed an ever increasing propensity toward naturalism. This evolution did not take place in lacquerwork independently: it corresponds to the realistic painting of the time.

In addition to the signatures of the lacquermasters, the inrō of the late Edo period frequently refer to the painters who designed the lacquer decoration, or whose preliminary drawings were used. These preliminary drawings were handed down from generation to generation by the families of the lacquermasters. By this time, there were also printed books of sample decorations from which the required motifs could be chosen. This accounts for favourite subjects appearing in almost identical form in the works of quite different lacquermasters.

The influence of painting on lacquer decoration was unmistakable as early as the Muromachi period, and since the Momoyama period, it can often be proved that the lacquermaster was responsible only for carrying out the work, not for its design. This was all right as long as the painters and lacquermasters worked exclusively for the sophisticated court circles and the aristocracy. But when the art of lacquerwork became less exclusive and more articles decorated with lacquer became objects for everyday use in middle-class households as well, less care was devoted to their design everywhere. Towards the end of the Edo period, almost the entire art of lacquerwork showed signs of compositions growing slack, stereotyped and devoid of vitality.

Besides inrō, in which the skill of the Edo lacquermasters manifested itself for the last time, considerable attention was also paid to lacquered sword scabbards. Since the Edo era was an age of peace, interest shifted from the sword itself to decoration, especially that of the scabbard. In this instance, there was, of course, rather less ornament or decorative design

Plate 174 Kajikawa master: inrō. Early 19th c. Tōkyō National Museum

than a variety of structured lacquer ground. A plain, smooth coat of lacquer could not in the long run satisfy the perpetual desire for novelty; so literally about three hundred types of 'saya-nuri' (sword-scabbard- lacquering) were developed. New styles were constantly being created, involving the use of pulverized mother-of-pearl, egg shells, fish skin, grains of cereals, alternate layers of red and black lacquer, string or even the texture of cloth showing through the lacquer. These varied techniques may have been of interest to the owners of the sword scabbards, but they are not to the art historian. The various types of saya-nuri are generally included under the heading of 'kawari-nuri' (=changed lacquer techniques), which describes all non-classical techniques, such as, among others, Tsugaru-nuri.

Still, the chinkinbori revival did have artistic significance. Ninomiya Tōtei, a doctor active in Edo at the end of the eighteenth century, was the first to specialize in this technique, which until then had mainly been used at Wajima. A story linked with his name has it that, instead of a burin or a knife, he used a pointed rat's tooth to engrave the lacquer ground. Tōtei copied Chinese chinkinbori works and is said to have been particularly skilled in depicting peacocks. But the fame of his works seems to have outlived them, for not one is known today.

A few years later, at the beginning of the nineteenth century, Tachi Gasui, a chinkinbori master, lived in Wajima. In the vicinity of this small town, on the Noto peninsula, at the end of the seventeenth century, a clayey earth was discovered, which provided the means for making an unusually hard, chip-proof lacquer ground (see p. 198). With his very attractive work, Tachi Gasui, who studied painting in Kyōto and probably used the artist name Tate Junsuke, was the first to spread the fame of the Wajima chinkinbori beyond the peninsula – a fame that lasts to this day. A five-tiered jūbako (Pl. 175),[23] dated 1817, which is still in a private collection in Wajima, is a beautiful example of his art. All the vertical sides carry an engraved decoration of pine needles rubbed with gold on an olive-green-lacquer ground, while the lid shows a broom and rake design. The pine needles, broom and rake, in this witty abbreviation, allude to the famous Japanese tale of the old married couple Jō and Uba who lived in harmony and contentment under the pines of Takasago. The few motifs alluding to the story are distributed on the surface with much decorative skill, and the colour effect of the golden lines on the greenish ground is most attractive and harmonious.

Generally speaking, lacquer art presents a multi-faceted aspect during this Bunka-Bunsei era (1804-1829), when Japan's economic situation had improved, owing to reforms undertaken by Matsudaira Sadanobu, and the Tokugawa period was witnessing a last cultural flowering. For the last time good examples of gold-lacquer work in hiramakie and takamakie were produced in Edo for the shōgunate and the princes. The trousseau made around 1816 for Toyohime, the daughter of Tokugawa Harutomi of Kii is a good example (Pl. 176). In the provinces, however, and for middle-class use, gold lacquer was largely replaced by coloured-lacquer grounds, by coloured-lacquer painting in partial relief, and by inlays of various kinds.

Several reasons can be put forward for this decline in the use of gold lacquer in the late Edo period. In the first instance, the unfavourable economic situation at the end of the eighteenth century which led to re-peated banning of luxury articles – restricting, among other things, the use of gold dust and gold foil. Probably more important, though, was the ever-increasing tendency to naturalism, of which mention has already been made. Not content with the colour abstraction necessarily inherent in pure gold-lacquer decoration, what the public wanted were representations which were also true in colour. Besides coloured lacquer, which had become ever more important since the Momoyama period, coloured inlays and overlays of ivory (sometimes dyed), coloured glass flux, semi-precious stones, egg shells and pieces of cut lacquer became more and more popular in the late Edo period. This trend had started with Ritsuō, but it only became predominant in the last decades of the Edo period. It is not surprising that a kind of Ritsuō renaissance should be discernible at this very time, and that able lacquermasters like Koma Kansai and Shibata Zeshin (see below) should specifically sign their work 'in the Ritsuō manner.' But the more colourful and the 'truer to nature' the decoration became, often the less it was due to the inherent nature of lacquer art. Not only were the inlays made of uncongenial materials, but even the lacquer ground itself was now frequently abandoned in favour of grounds of unlacquered wood, bamboo, raffia veneers and basketwork. Obviously the traditional lacquer techniques had been very thoroughly exploited and new effects were sought.

Ōki Toyosuke (died 1858), for example, tried to widen the scope of

Plate 175 Tachi Gasui: chinkinbori-jūbako. Lid from above. 1817. 33.5:19.6cm. Japan, private collection

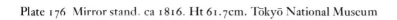

Plate 176 Mirror stand. ca 1816. Ht 61.7cm. Tōkyō National Museum

*Mid- and late
Edo period*

lacquerwork by applying lacquer decoration to colour-glazed pottery and porcelain; he was not very successful, however. Of greater significance and more enduring effect was the work of Tamakaji Zōkoku (1806-1869) who lived in Takamatsu (Shikoku) (Pl. 177). He used the painting and engraving techniques of Kimma- and Zonsei-nuri which originated in Thailand and Burma,[24] and he worked principally in carved lacquer, that is to say he employed processes other than the old traditional sprinkling techniques. Zōkoku was the most famous carved-lacquermaster of his time,[25] and it is in his work that, for the first time, a certain Japanization of the technique is noticeable. Significantly, he used not only the traditional carved-lacquer subjects originally derived from China, but also purely Japanese themes. Other contemporary carved-lacquermasters, who lacked his independence, however, were Gamō Morimasa,[26] who was renowned for his guni work, and various members of the school of Tsuishu Yōsei (cf. p.167).

Towards the end of the Edo period the old makie techniques were very obviously exhausted, and only a few masters remained untouched by the general decline. Even so, they created nothing really new but tended to continue the old traditions in technique and style. Among these are Koma Kansai and Hara Yōyūsai (1772-1845) in Edo, and Sano Chōkan (1791-1863) in Kyōto. But the names signify little since hardly anything is

Plate 177 Zōkoku: carved lacquer kōgō with Sumiyoshi dance. Mid 19th c. Ht 3cm, diam. 8.6cm. Japan, private collection

known about these masters. Japanese experts either simply end the art of lacquerwork with Kōrin, or, at best, have not very systematically re-searched the late and minor masters of the eighteenth and nineteenth centuries. In the West, although their inrō have been collected by the hundreds, the number of comprehensive studies of individual masters or schools remains negligible. These omissions are understandable since earlier lacquerwork, because of its greater artistic merit, has a prior claim to critical attention. But as a result, a number of things may be said, or even copied from earlier sources, about the masters of the late Edo period, but very little can be proved. How significant, for instance, is a mention of Koma Kansai? There were three successive generations of lacquermasters of this name: Kansai I, who died in 1792; his son (1766-1835), said to have been one of the best pupils of Koma Kyoryū; and his son, who adopted both the name and the profession in 1824 when his father became a priest (Pl. 178).[27] Whether and how their works differ from one another, or which

Plate 178 Koma Kansai: inrō. 1st half 19th c. Tōkyō National Museum

works bearing the signature Koma Kansai should be attributed to whom, are problems that remain to be studied, although Koma Kansai II is generally regarded as the most important of the three. Even a brief glance at the Kansai-signed lacquers – for the most part – reveals such significant differences in technique and style that very likely in fact, they spread across three generations, in other words, the period from around 1780 up to the middle of the nineteenth century. Nor can any praise of Koma Kansai conceivably extend to every item that bears that name.

Rokkaku Shisui claims, and more recent Japanese publications agree, that Yōyūsai worked in the manner of Kōrin after preliminary drawings by Hōitsu (Pl. 179). But the most that can be said of his surviving works is that their draughtsmanship is an approximation of the Kōrin style of painting; but there is no direct link with the Kōrin lacquers. Yōyūsai does not appear to have used lead or mother-of-pearl, although he was adept in the old makie techniques.

Plate 179 Hara Yōyūsai: inrō. 1st half 19th c. Tōkyō National Museum

From the Meiji period to the present day

IN 1867 THE LAST TOKUGAWA SHOGUN RESIGNED HIS POWER, AND AFTER centuries of domination by the shōgunate, the rulership reverted to the Japanese Emperor. The Meiji restoration of 1868 brought about fundamental changes in the power structure of the state; in 1871 the old fiefs were abolished and Japan's long period of isolation from the rest of the world came to an end.

The abolition of feudal tenures meant that the daimyōs lost their existing sources of revenue and, with them, their capacity for patronage, and the ability to attract artists to their feudal seats and to finance them. The lacquermasters, with their means of financial support gone – up to that time they had, for the most part, been employed by the shōgunate or the provincial princes – now had to adapt to living off the sales of their work. That was difficult enough in itself because, in certain cases, a good piece of lacquer art can take years to complete. But much more serious was the fact that, ever since the country had been opened up again, the demand for traditional native lacquerwork had dropped alarmingly: after 1868 large sections of the wealthy upper class tried to adapt their way of life and consequently their houses and implements, to European or American models.

Accordingly, the lacquermasters were suddenly confronted with the problem that both old-style patronage and suitable markets no longer existed. The situation became so critical that the government tried to help, initially, as in other arts and crafts by encouraging export. Export, however, primarily means mass-production, and whereas ceramics and textiles were successfully adapted to it by alteration in their manufacturing process, the lacquermasters found this change almost impossible for technical reasons.[1] Yet, at first, working for export seemed the only possible means of helping the lacquermasters to overcome the serious crisis.

Japanese lacquers, both old and contemporary, together with other forms of applied art had been greatly admired at the World Exhibition of 1873 in Vienna. As a result, English and Australian art dealers asked the competent authorities in Japan for export consignments of Japanese lacquerwork. To meet the demand, production had to be increased, and quality, which had deteriorated considerably in the last decades of the Edo era, had to be restored. With these twin objectives in mind, the Kiritsu Kōshō Kaisha company of Tōkyō set up workshops and expanded the export trade. The company, soon to be followed by a few smaller, less important ones, remained in existence from 1874 to 1891.

It employed good lacquermasters, ceramic- and metalworkers, and the company workshops became centres for both the training and the higher education of the young craftsmen; the important lacquermaster, Shirayama Shōsai, for instance, worked in one of them. Incidentally, the success of Japanese lacquerwork abroad caused it to be shown in industrial and art and craft exhibitions in Japan itself, beginning with the year 1877.

Initially, the demand for quality was aimed exclusively at improving the craftsmanship rather than the creation of a new style. To this end, a conscious attempt was made to link up with the better work of the past, and for the time being, the formal resources of the Edo period served once more. The old technical tradition, which, in this instance, served as a link, was still being continued by two lacquermasters in particular: Nakayama Komin and Kawanobe Itchō, both of whom had already been working during the late Edo era.

Komin (1808-1870) as a pupil of Hara Yōyūsai (see p.224) was well versed in the traditional gold-lacquer techniques of togidashi, hiramakie and takamakie; his fine and meticulously executed work – which had made him famous even before the Meiji period – could now serve as a guideline to others. A small octagonal box for sweetmeats imitating an insect cage in shape and decoration (Pl. 180: *Mushikago makie-kashibako*), is regarded as his masterpiece. In it, Komin very skilfully combined different shades of gold with mother-of-pearl inlays.

From Meiji period to present

Apart from works of this type, he also made copies of Heian lacquers, which makes him one of the earliest among the 'classicist' lacquermasters of the Meiji era who turned to the past. His pupil Ogawa Shōmin (1847-1891) copied several of the most famous lacquer works of the Nara, Heian and Kamakura periods. [2] Such copies were primarily made in order to study and revive the old techniques; still, they also reflect a certain backward-looking attitude of mind, which set in around 1880. In reaction to the totally uncritical imitation of everything foreign during the early years of the Meiji era, there was at that time a recollection of the past flowering of Japanese culture in the Middle Ages, and a fondness for copying the masterpieces of that period.

A little later, yet a third reason boosted the manufacture of such copies and imitations, one that often had most unpleasant ramifications: the collecting craze of European and American art lovers, which set in towards the

Plate 180 Nakayama Komin: small box for sweetmeats. Mid 19th c. 10.6:9.7:12.1cm. Tōkyō National Museum

end of the nineteenth century. 'Thanks' to these collectors, downright fakes were produced in the period from 1895 to 1915. There are interesting examples of well-known works of the early thirteenth century, for instance, being 'newly created' for this purpose. Frequently, the fakers had no qualms about taking their motifs from surviving old lacquers, but they paid little attention to the shapes of the objects or to their proportions. In spite of the old motifs and the deliberately induced crazing of the lacquer, such fakes often betray their much later date of origin to the expert because they contain an extremely fine gold dust which was unknown at the time they were allegedly made. For sale abroad – only a relatively small number of authentic old pieces have so far found their way out of Japan – the lacquermasters apparently did not trouble to specially manufacture the old, coarser type of gold dust. But this trouble they were quite willing to go to for a few reproductions of famous works, expressly designated as such, in other words, not as fakes in bad faith.

There seems to have been a preference for copying old masterpieces up to, and perhaps including, the Kamakura period. Occasionally, but without intent to fake, motifs of the Momoyama period were also used.

Foreign interest in Japanese handicrafts of course did more than just inspire copyists and fakers; it was important also in making Japan reconsider its own native values and native style instead of – as in the first years of the Meiji period – merely copying anything that came from the West. The names of the American, Ernest F. Fenollosa,[3] and the German, Gottfried Wagner,[4] both of whom considerably furthered the cause of Japanese arts and crafts in the Meiji period, are still revered in Japan today.

The second lacquermaster to continue the old makie traditions well into the Meiji period was Kawanobe Itchō (1830-1910). As a boy of twelve he entered the official lacquer workshop of the Tokugawa shōgunate at Edo, which was run by the Kōamis and was appointed court lacquermaster ten years later. Even then he showed particular interest in the study of the old traditional techniques, and in the Meiji period as well, he applied his artistry to the continuation of the old Kōami tradition – as the small lacquer tablet in the illustration (Pl. 181), with its landscape design, clearly indicates. When Itchō showed greater stylistic independence, the effect was sometimes weakened.[5]

Shibata Zeshin, the greatest lacquer artist of the nineteenth century (1807-1891), was a great deal less dependent on the old technical and stylistic traditions. He, too, lived in Edo. (In 1869 the imperial residence was transferred from Kyōto to Edo which was renamed Tōkyō.) Even before the shōgunate ended, Zeshin was well known and respected.

In 1818, when he was only eleven years old, he had been apprenticed to Koma Kansai II in order to learn the art of lacquerwork. Five years later, however, he took up painting instead, studying under various masters. He worked in the realistic style of the Shijō school and generally painted plant and animal subjects. Just when he again applied his considerable talent to lacquerwork is not known precisely, probably not until the last years of the Edo period. Zeshin used coloured lacquers more frequently than gold or silver. Yet with true artistic instinct, he avoided applying an overabundance of realistic colour to his lacquerwork. Instead he conjured up from the lacquer medium itself the utmost subtlety of expression by varying its texture, juxtaposing, perhaps, the same colour shade polished to a high gloss on a dull, patina-like surface. Thus, without using a particularly wide range of colour, he achieved contrasts within the individual colours themselves and between the decoration and the glossy ground as well. A lacquer picture, dated 1881, showing a lotus pool[6] – interesting, because under the influence of Western painting it was made to be framed – and also the writing-box, dated 1886, with a sake bottle among spring flowers (Pl. 182: *Tanpopo makie-suzuribako*), are both good examples of this very effective technique.

Zeshin's unfailing eye for composition combined with his careful observation of nature are particularly apparent in his most famous work, the *Karasu-sagi makiebako* (Pl. 183), which dates from the beginning of the Meiji period. On this box two flocks of birds in flight are contrasted with each other; both are depicted in relief: black crows on the lid and on two of the side walls, silver herons on the remaining two sides. The different flight patterns of the two bird species are admirable in the way they are observed and depicted; and the way the vivid design remains subordinate to the distinctive, very modern-looking shape of the box is superb. Although the old sprinkling techniques are also used here, this box clearly proves Zeshin's independence from the traditions of classical lacquerwork.

After a long interval, lacquerwork had again, in the person of Zeshin, found an outstanding creative talent. That he should have been the undisputed leading lacquermaster even during his own lifetime may actually

Plate 181 Kawanobe Itchō: lacquer tablet. 2nd half 19th c. 13.3:12.7cm. Tōkyō Geijutsu Daigaku

have been due not only to the high quality of his work, but also to the fact that his style of decoration provided such a good answer to the contemporary demand for realistic representation.

In his old age, Zeshin did lacquer paintings on paper in which his gifts as a painter blended perfectly with his mastery of lacquer techniques.[7] In the long history of lacquerwork, Zeshin's work was the first to achieve complete independence for lacquer decoration: that is, it no longer served to adorn an object but became part of the art of painting. The Japanese art of lacquer did not then pursue this path, but even after Zeshin it continued to exercise its function of decorating objects. Not until our own century did lacquer paintings on canvas or murals in coloured lacquer appear with any frequency; but both are closer to painting than to actual lacquerwork as such. Foremost among Zeshin's pupils was Ikeda Taishin (1825-1903),[8] who also created lacquers distinguished by a sophisticated restraint in design.

Zeshin, Komin and Itchō were already well-known artists when, at the beginning of the Meiji period, lacquerwork was confronted by problems

Plate 182 Shibata Zeshin: writing-box with sake bottle. 1886. 3.3:19.4:22.6cm. New York, The Metropolitan Museum of Art, Rogers Fund, 1936

that threatened its very existence. It goes without saying that these masters, particularly Zeshin and Itchō, participated in large measure in the efforts to renew and change lacquer art. In this they were joined by Ogawa Shōmin, Komin's pupil, and Shirayama Shōsai (1853-1923). Since there was no longer any princely patronage to provide the secure framework within which they and other lacquermasters could function, attempts were made, from around 1888, to support lacquerwork through new official or semi-official institutions.

The most important in this respect was to be the Tōkyō Art School (Tōkyō Bijutsu Gakkō), founded in 1888. In 1890, Ogawa Shōmin was appointed to take charge of its lacquer department; he was followed later by Kawanobe Itchō and Shirayama Shōsai. (Shōmin had been one of the founder-members of the lacquer artists' association, Nihon Shikkō-kai, in 1889.) The Art School, which in 1949 was merged into the present-day Tōkyō University of Art (Tōkyō Geijutsu Daigaku), became a new and important centre of the arts; art schools and specialized technical schools which were later established in the provinces were modelled after it. Whereas previously the new generation had received its training in the workshops of the lacquermaster families, the schools took over at the end of

Plate 183 Shibata Zeshin: box with crows and herons. ca 1880. 12.4:18.5:13cm. Tōkyō National Museum

the nineteenth century and made possible the development of a new tradition.

In 1890 the Emperor Meiji convened the Imperial Academy of Art, a kind of art advisory council originally consisting of ten members, including Zeshin as the representative for lacquerwork.[9] At long last, because of this Academy, the traditional arts won official support from Japan's most exalted personage. In 1896, Itchō and Ikeda Taishin and, in 1906, finally also Shirayama Shōsai became members of this highly regarded institution.

Zeshin, Itchō and Shōsai assisted in the lacquer decoration of the newly built Imperial Palace in Tōkyō from 1886 to 1889. The imperial court was one of the period's main sources of commissions for lacquerwork and for arts and crafts in general. Of course, this meant that the lacquermasters accommodated themselves to the taste prevailing at court. The resulting works are distinguished chiefly by the utmost care for minute detail and the skilled use of various different gold-lacquer techniques rather than by new or individualistic ideas. A writing-box (Pl. 184) which, together with the matching paper-box, was given by the Emperor to Erwin von Bälz, the German court physician, is a good example of such work.

Plate 184 Writing-box. Interior of lid. ca 1900. Overall dimensions 4.5:22.3:24.4cm. Berlin State Museums, Museum of Far Eastern Art

Finally, the creation of the National Museums in Tōkyō, Kyōto, and Nara also helped foster public interest in the native arts of Japan, including that of lacquerwork.[10] The nucleus of the present outstanding lacquer collections in the Tōkyō National Museum consists of the items sent to Vienna for the World Exhibition of 1873. On the way back, the ship carrying some of the exhibits sank; it created a sensation throughout the world a year and a half later when it was salvaged from the bottom of the sea: these works of art made of wood were found in perfect condition despite their long immersion in salt water, thanks to their protective coat of lacquer.

To organizational efforts to create a place for lacquerwork in a changed world, and the linking to earlier artistic traditions to improve its quality, were added the findings of what for Japan at the end of the nineteenth century were the new natural sciences. In the recently established chemical research centres lacquer was closely analysed and studied to find possible new uses for it. The lacquermasters themselves had been seeking new coloured lacquers since 1885, and gradually these efforts met with success; the colour range – so far restricted to black, yellow, green and brown – was broadened to include shades of white, blue, orange and violet. Outstanding work was done in this connection by Rokkaku Shisui (1867-1950). In contrast to the old coloured lacquers, the new ones no longer needed to be applied impasto but could be painted on thick or thin as required; furthermore, they permitted colour transitions as well as particularly delicate shades of colour. These numerous and useful potentialities made the new coloured lacquers superior not only to the old but even to the paintings in oil colours on a lacquer ground (mitsuda-e).

The quest for new bases onto which to apply the lacquer met with similar success. Experience had proved that Japanese lacquer objects made of wood tended to split and crack rather easily in countries with a drier climate. Accordingly, after considerable research, for objects intended for export the wooden substructure was now often replaced by a light metal, aluminum being particularly favoured. This substructure was completely covered with layers of lacquer before receiving its lacquer decoration. Works of this kind found a ready sale abroad around the turn of the century.

As has already been stated, thanks to tradition-bound artists like Komin, Itchō and Shōmin, the link with the old gold-lacquer techniques was never completely severed. Shirayama Shōsai (1853-1923), who proudly described himself as an independent artist, now tried to infuse these old decorative processes with new life. He had mastered makie, carved-lacquer and raden techniques, and had shown great aptitude for successfully experimenting with many more techniques. (The extremely fine gold dust of the Meiji period provided a scope for technical innovations). His particular strength lay in the fields of togidashi and unusually small-scale decoration. Typical of his work is a small octagonal box (Pl. 185: *Hakkakukei-kashiki*) made at the beginning of the twentieth century. It combines the most minutely detailed gold lacquerwork with coloured-lacquer grounds and aogai inlays of various kinds to create a lavish overall effect. The eleven horizontal zones which make up the decoration of the small container virtually represent a catalogue of Shōsai's versatile technical repertoire.

Yet this box also shows that up to the end of the Meiji period there was no new style in the art of lacquerwork. Primarily, every effort up to that point had been concentrated on initiating technical colleges, artists' associations and exhibitions, and on improving quality. Only in the following decades were there signs of combining the venerable art of lacquerwork with the modern way of thinking, to determine shape and composition on the basis of a new individual style. This will be discussed at a later point.

What about Meiji lacquerwork outside Tōkyō? Although lacquer articles continued to be produced at Kyōto, only Kimura Hyōsai (1817-1885) was an outstandingly able master. At Kanazawa the long-established fame of Kaga-makie was further enhanced by excellent works. The most important artists there were Sawada Jisaku, Shimizu Kamon, Asano Sōsaburō and Igarashi Tajirō, whose works were every bit as good as those of the Tōkyō masters. At Wajima, the reorganization in 1878 of a lacquer guild (Kafuku-sha), established some forty years previously, greatly improved the technical proficiency of its members. The emphasis continued to be on chinkinbori and makie works which, as 'Wajima-nuri,' were increasingly

Plate 185 Shirayama Shōsai: box for pastries. Early 20th c. Ht 13cm, diam. 10.3cm. Tōkyō National Museum

prized throughout Japan. Fujiwaka Shunzō (Bunkidō), Zōkoku's (see p. 222) younger brother, worked at Takamatsu on Shikoku, and at Hiroshima, Ikeda Ikkokusai III distinguished himself by his multicoloured lacquers in relief. [11] For the rest, local varieties of the art of lacquerwork which had prospered since the early Edo period (see p. 196ff.) continued to do so. Unpretentious items for daily use – perhaps made in Tsugaru-nuri, Shunkei-nuri, or painted with coloured lacquers – suited the taste of the people. The tradition of these simple, pleasing, everyday utensils extends to the present day.

Of the various provincial wares, Kamakurabori is outstanding. From the beginning of the Meiji period, it was produced in great quantity, not only in Kamakura proper. Its uncluttered beauty was much favoured for eating and writing utensils as well as implements used in the tea ceremony. Kamakurabori has remained viable up to the present day; indeed, in modern post-war Japan, Kamakurabori and Negoro-nuri – which is similar in effect – are particularly valued. Today, Kamakurabori, being a form of art comparatively simple to make, is also produced by non-professionals; many of the old motifs like camellias, peonies, and birds are almost identical to those used a hundred years ago.

But this type of Kamakurabori, as has been pointed out, no longer attempts to simulate Chinese carved lacquers. Almost invariably, a large part of the ground is not decorated, and although the wooden substructure is not visible, the way it is carved serves to emphasize rather than disguise it. Because of the Japanese preference for 'sabi' and 'shibui,' the very simplicity and unaffectedness of such work makes it a special favourite among connoisseurs.

Still, in the Meiji era provincial lacquers like these were ignored by the officialdom of art. Only in the twenties of our own century did Yanagi Sōetsu make the general public aware once more of the beauty and import of this true folk art.

On the whole, by the end of the Meiji period, the lacquermasters had generally succeeded in adapting to the new social conditions; the princely patrons of former times were now replaced by art schools, artists' associations, museums and research centres which provided a certain measure of support. The official backing for lacquerwork, initiated at the end of the nineteenth century, increased considerably, and the export trade grew rapidly. The artistic significance of export lacquers was, admittedly, rather minimal. At the World Exhibition held in Paris in 1900, praise was voiced for individual pieces but, at the same time, Japanese lacquerwork was criticized for a lack of original design and for insufficient effort to overcome the influence of the conventional Edo patterns and shapes. Such criticism could not be very effective at the time because there just happened to be no new, independent style in Japan then. But for all that, contact with the outside world did introduce new ideas into Japan, and a few lacquermasters did try to find a new style by improving the shapes of their articles and by showing more restraint in the decoration.

Generally speaking though, despite the regeneration of the various techniques that resulted from the close study and copying of famous old lacquerware, there was a complete dearth of work of real artistic merit at the beginning of the twentieth century. This dilemma remained, in a sense, the dominant factor in the Taishō era (1912-1926), and right up to the Second

World War. Characteristic of this period is a not very happy attempt to combine the revived tradition with the new, contemporary spirit of the times. But the old-fashioned masters, who often created technically sound work, lacked the ability to come to terms with the new spirit of a changed world. Their creations, reminiscent or even imitative of work of the Edo-Meiji eras, are often sterile and lack individual vitality. Still, younger or more modern artists who were also influenced now by modern Western painting, were uncertain how to adapt their ideas to the medium of lacquer. Likewise, they only rarely achieved a really individual mode of expression, since they were all too willing to imitate foreign forms.

The most pleasing products of this period come from Akatsuka Jitoku (1871-1936) and Tsuishu Yōsei xx (1880-1952), both of whom were highly regarded in their time. Indeed, both were appointed to the Imperial (or, after the war, Japanese) Academy. While Akatsuka Jitoku with his makie work still belongs more in the old tradition, some of Tsuishu Yōsei's carved lacquers are entirely modern.

Plate 186 Tsuishu Yōsei xx: writing-box with pumpkin motif. Detail. ca 1915. Japan, private collection

Yōsei liked to work with individually applied layers of differently coloured lacquers which were exposed again in the process of carving (Pl. 186). He did not strive for gentle modulation but rather for a stratified surface of contrasting colours. His carved lacquers are much more concerned with flat surfaces rather than with relief; they are reminiscent of modern European sgraffito work, which, in spite of various layers of colour, very definitely emphasize that same quality of flatness. By this new approach to exploit all the possibilities inherent in carved-lacquer techniques, Yōsei xx very decisively put an end to the prevailing standards of using Chinese carved lacquers as models.

From Meiji period to present

In the decades immediately following the Meiji period when the foundations were being laid for modern, present-day lacquerwork, Rokkaku Shisui (1867-1950) played an important part. A native of the province of Hiroshima, he passed his final examination in 1893 and became one of the first graduates of the lacquer department of the Tōkyō Art School. He then went abroad with Okakura Kakuzo (Tenshin) and worked at the museum in Boston. On returning to Tōkyō, he was appointed Professor at the Art School. Deeply impressed by the Chinese lacquers of the Han period excavated in Lolang in Korea (for a while Shisui himself took part in the dig), he made the history of lacquerwork his special subject. While a young man, he was influenced by the classicist style of his teacher Shōmin and, on his return from Boston, he began by making copies of a number of the Shōsōin lacquers; from the 1920s on, his work shows the influence of Han lacquers. More important, however, than Shisui's artistic achievement is his work as a scientist. His significant contribution to the discovery of new coloured lacquers has been referred to before (see p. 233); but particular credit is due him for his book *Tōyō-shikkō-shi* (published 1932; second edition 1960), the first reliable history of Far Eastern lacquerwork by a Japanese. Shisui was lacquer artist, research scientist and teacher all in one. Much the same can be said of Mizoguchi Saburō (1896-1973), who together with Rokkaku Shisui, Akatsuka Jitoku, Uematsu Hōbi (1872-1933) and Matsuda Gonroku (born 1896), when the present emperor was crowned in 1928, made the lacquer articles presented by the emperor to mark the occasion. Mizoguchi later concentrated more on research, teaching and museum work; and was one of the foremost experts on Japanese lacquerwork until his death in 1973. Matsuda Gonroku, who is the same age, has, since the end of the Taisho period, been considered the leading exponent of makie. Plate 187 shows one of his earliest works. [12]

In the mid-1920s the revival of interest in Japanese folk art sparked a quest for new modes of expression appropriate to the age. In contrast to the excessively ornamental style of the past hundred years, the beauty of simple, uncluttered shapes with a minimum of decoration once more received due recognition. In 1927, lacquerwork was included for the first time in the annual government-sponsored art exhibition ('Teiten,' continued after the war by 'Nitten'). Examples of lacquerwork had previously been shown at art exhibitions arranged by artists' associations and at industrial and commercial exhibitions, but this new mark of recognition by the highest official ranks had an extremely invigorating effect; it also evoked a spirit of competition among the artists.

In 1928 the Industrial Arts Institute (Sangyō Kōgei Shiken-jo), a kind of technological research institute, was founded. In its three branches in

Tōkyō, Kurume (Kyūshū), and Sendai, research into the materials, techniques and uses of modern applied art is carried out; lacquer techniques are the special province of the institute at Sendai. By its research and experiments, the Sangyō Kōgei Shiken-jo has encouraged and stimulated the art of lacquerwork to the present day.

Besides those already named, other lacquermasters active in the Taishō and early Shōwa periods who also deserve mention are: Takano Shōzan (1899-) and Komo Tōzan (1882-) both of whom, like Matsuda Gonroku, chiefly favour classical makie; Yoshida Genjūro (1896-) and Yamazaki Katsutarō (1899-), who are more interested in modern decoration using coloured lacquers. Outside Tōkyō there is Mae Taihō (1899-) in Wajima, famous for his chinkinbori, and Isoi Joshin (1883-1964) in Takamatsu; his speciality was kimma-nuri (Pl. 188).

The war, the complete devastation of Tōkyō, and the shortage of raw lacquer (which before the war was imported in vast quantities because home production was insufficient for the requirements of export lacquers) dealt Japanese lacquerwork a series of heavy blows. After the immediate postwar years, however, in about 1950, there was an amazing revival and a complete breakthrough resulting in a lacquer art no longer hemmed in by earlier styles. A contributing factor was that international taste suddenly recognized the aesthetic preëminence of Japanese structures and Japanese styles of decoration. Accordingly, in order to be 'modern', Japanese lacquermasters no longer attempted to strike a balance between the East and the West but could confidently rely on their own instinct as artists.

Furthermore, in an age of industry and mechanization, the Japanese government took effective measures to protect the old arts and crafts so rich

Plate 187 Matsuda Gonroku: covered box with animal motifs. 1919.
16.1:25.1:21.8cm. Tōkyō Geijutsu Daigaku

in tradition. Under the provisions of a law of 1951, the National Commission for the Protection of Cultural Properties (Bunkazai Hogo Iinkai) was set up in 1954. It fulfills a number of important functions including, for instance, the selection of 'Kokuhō,' that is National Treasures. Works of art designated as Kokuhō, which include numerous lacquer items, receive special protection and may not be sold abroad. The latter stipulation was very important after the war, to check the export of Japanese art objects.

But not only works of art are protected by this body; there are also the so-called 'intangible cultural properties' (mukei bunkazai), which, among other things, include the traditional techniques of applied art. The Commission appoints as 'custodians' artists who have complete mastery of such techniques and are able to pass them on. In the field of lacquerwork, five masters and four techniques were initially selected: Matsuda Gonroku and Takano Shōzan for makie, Otomaru Kōdō (born 1898) for carved lacquer (Pl. 189), and Mae Taihō for chinkinbori (Pl. 190).

In addition, the Nihon Kōgei-kai (Japanese Arts and Crafts Association) was established, of which almost all lacquermasters are members. (Only a few ultra-modern artists are not; they belong to the Gendai Kōgei Bijutsu-ka Kyōkai, founded in 1961.) In conjunction with the National Commission for the Protection of Cultural Properties, the Japanese Arts and Crafts Association has, since 1954, put on the now famous annual exhibitions of traditional Japanese arts and crafts (Nihon Dentō- Kōgei-ten). The lacquer

Plate 188 Isoi Joshin: pastry box. ca 1960. Ht 8.5cm, diam 23cm. Wuppertal, Dr Kurt Herberts

exhibits are of a gratifyingly high standard, and clearly indicate in which particular branch of lacquerwork the finest results are achieved today.

The two most striking characteristics of this modern lacquer art are without doubt the diminishing importance of the decoration in favour of the very subtle shaping of the object proper. The two are linked because the lacquer surface with its gloss and smoothness underscores the purity of proportion to even greater effect when there is no decoration at all. And conversely, the nobler the shape of a box, small container, bowl, etc. the more beautifully it sets off the gently mirroring lacquer skin. It is no coincidence that there are a great many undecorated pieces which merely have a coating of black or red (or black *and* red) lacquer, and that even in those items which do have a decoration, it is generally restrained nowadays.

This new preference for the mutual offsetting of a beautiful shape by an undecorated lacquer surface, and vice-versa, is best expressed in modern dry-lacquers. The kanshitsu technique, which permits extremely precise shaping and very thin, delicate walls in an object, and which had been relegated to the background after the Heian period, plays a major role in contemporary lacquerwork.

Plate 189 Otomaru Kōdō: tea caddy. ca 1960. Japan, private collection

The most important exponents of this technique are Masumura Mashiki (born 1910; Pl. 192), Tadokoro Hōsai (born 1912; Pl. 191), Matsunami Hoshin (1881-1954), Yamanaga Kōho (born 1889), and Okude Jusen (born 1916). The first three are or were active in Tōkyō; Yamanaga Kōho lives in the province of Gifu and Okude Jusen in the province of Ishikawa.[13] In the work of these masters lightness, simplicity and elegance of form combine with the deep shimmering glow of the red and black lacquer to produce most attractive results. Moreover, both Masumura Mashiki and Tadokoro Hōsai work not only with lacquered cloth (kanshitsu) but also with lacquered paper (harinuki) and with lacquered leather (shippi).

Although for dry-lacquer no master has as yet been nominated 'jūyō mukei bunkazai-hojisha' (Living Cultural Asset), the leading exponents of two other techniques – the quality of which is notably high today – have been rewarded with this honorary title: Otomaru Kōdō for carved lacquer and Isoi Joshin for kimma work. Both these techniques are at present used

From Meiji period to present

Plate 190 Mae Taihō: tea caddy

almost exclusively in Tōkyō and Takamatsu. The latter town had already been the centre in the Edo era – particularly while Tamakaji Zōkoku had been alive – of the kimma and carved-lacquermasters; today, together with Tōkyō and Wajima, Takamatsu is a leader in the art of lacquerwork.

Modern carved lacquers tend to show the typically Japanese striving for a flat surface effect which has been referred to in the context of some of Tsuishu Yōsei xx's work. Two or three coats of lacquer, each consisting of layers of a different colour, are superimposed, to be partially uncovered later by the carving of the design. The juxtaposition of these coats tends to lie almost flat over a different coloured ground: each individual layer contributing its part to the overall design. As a result, the surface of the object as such remains intact although the carving does subdivide the surface into a pattern of planes.

The most important carved-lacquermasters are Otomaru Kōdō (born 1898) and his sons Otomaru Kaoru (born 1922), Otomaru Hiroshi (born 1927) and Otomaru Jun (born 1929); in addition there are Yoshida Baidō (born 1896), who lives in Kanazawa, and Okabe Keishō (born 1912), living near Takamatsu (Pl. 193).

In kimma work, which lately is being produced by quite a number of lacquermasters, a modern process of Japanization appears to have been underway during the past five or six years. The decorations used by the

Plate 191 Tadokoro Hōsai: tea caddy. ca 1960. Tōkyō, Bunkazai Hogo Iinkai

Plate 192 Masumura Mashiki: dry-lacquer fruit bowl. 1963. Ht 7.8cm, max. diam.
48.2cm. Berlin State Museums, Museum of Far Eastern Art.

venerable master Isoi Joshin (cf. Pl. 188) – usually blossoms or birds and almost geometrical edges and borders – were peculiarly rigid and devitalized, and even today the work of many kimma artists reflects this style. (It might derive from Thai models because the technique originally came to Japan from Thailand.) In the last few years especially, Namba Jinsai (born 1903) has developed a much freer style which he himself calls 'drawn kimma' (egaki kimma; Pl. 194). His work shows archetypically Japanese motifs such as waves, bamboo swaying in the wind, or autumn grasses done in light, flowing lines more evocative of painting than engraving. Namba Jinsai's work has lent a very peculiarly Japanese gracefulness to the rather stiff kimma technique. It may or may not be a coincidence that this particular master lives in Ashimori-shi (province of Okayama), in other words, he is not in direct touch with the Takamatsu tradition.

Plate 193 Okabe Keishō: incense box. 1964. 2:6:6cm

Plate 194 Namba Jinsai: table in egaki-kimma. 1962. 12:60:36cm

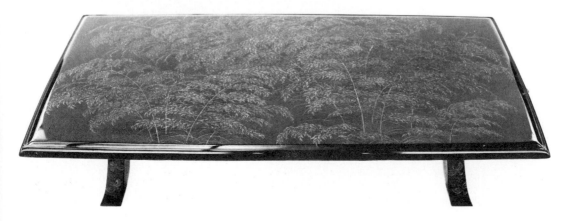

Plate 195 Ōba Shōgyo: box with hyōmon inlay. 1964. 18:28:15.5cm

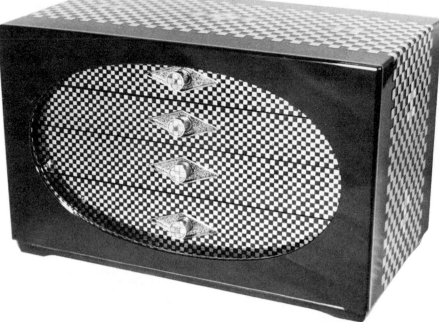

Plate 196 Fujii Kambun: writing-box. 1963. Ht 7cm, diam. 36cm

Plate 197 Terai Naoji: small screen. 1963. 38:176cm

The kimma lacquers of Asata Shinsui (born 1901) and Noda Minoru (born 1934) sometimes approximate his style, whereas Kawakubo Kazu (born 1932) and Ōta Kazuko (born 1920) are, on the whole, more directly in the lineage of Isoi Joshin. Tsuji Hokuyōsai (born 1909), with his very restrained, almost geometrical decorations, is an exception among the kimma masters.

Good work is also being done in the field of hyōmon inlays in lacquer, although this technique seems less appealing to modern taste than either dry lacquer or carved lacquer. The leading master is Ōba Shōgyō in Kanazawa (born 1916; Pl. 195); but there are also Miura Meihō (born 1900) and Taguchi Yoshikuni (born 1923) in Tōkyō.

The technique of chinkinbori has been mastered by only a few present-day lacquer artists, and it is just as well that Mae Taihō (born 1899) has been appointed its 'custodian.' He now lives at Wajima, the source, for two hundred years, of the best chinkinbori. But Fujii Kambun of Tōkyō (born 1888 in Wajima) has also produced some very charming pieces using this technique (Pl. 196).

Modern makie work looks strangely insignificant. Its carefully detailed, elegant and lavish gold effect somehow does not seem to answer the present-day mood, which prefers bolder designs on larger surfaces. Besides Matsuda Gonroku in Tōkyō, only Terai Naoji in Kanazawa (born 1912; Pl. 197) and Inami Kirokusai in Wajima (born 1902) are worth naming.

The quality of modern lacquers inlaid with mother-of-pearl is not very

Plate 198 Kuroda Tatsuaki: tea caddy. ca 1963. Ht 8.8cm, diam. 8.5cm. Japan, private collection

good. Only rarely do any of today's works in this technique meet with critical approval. Kuroda Tatsuaki of Kyōto (born 1904; Pl. 198), however, is an important exception. In his work the entire lacquer ground is sometimes tightly paved with pieces of broken and cracked mother-of-pearl of various sizes; the black lacquer is visible only where they meet at the joints. His small tea caddies and boxes rely for their effect on their shape and the texture and colour of the mother-of-pearl only; there is no additional decoration. Indeed, this new way of using mother-of-pearl – which is vaguely reminiscent of the warigai technique of the Momoyama period – is very attractive.

In conclusion, mention must be made of Akaji Yūsai of Yokohama (born 1906; Pl. 199), whose work is highly prized in Japan. He makes bowls and containers of superimposed concentric rings of different diameters, which means that these items always have ribbed walls. He decorates these plain, well-proportioned objects with simple bold-coloured lacquers. Black, red, green, yellow, and occasionally gold are the only colours Akaji Yūsai uses; even so, they are used solely to emphasize the structure – not as a decoration. The harmonious results attained by this artist, with such simple means, are striking.

The work of today's leading lacquermasters shows that the art of Japanese lacquerware has survived both its decline during the late Edo period and the acute crisis it faced in the Meiji era. Old techniques rich in tradition, good craftsmanship, unfailing instinct for form and modern styling have been combined in what is at present a very viable art. There is, of course, the danger that lacquer objects, which are painstakingly made by hand, will in the future be replaced in many areas of domestic use by synthetics. But mass-produced goods can never attain the quality of good lacquers. The standard of present-day lacquerware fully justifies the hope for the future of this oldest and most typical Japanese art.

Plate 199 Akaji Yūsai: bowl. ca 1960. Ht 10.2cm, diam. 42cm. Tōkyō, Bunkazai Hogo Iinkai

Notes

(Full details of the publications referred to in the notes can be found in the bibliography)

CHAPTER I

1 Summaries of lacquer finds up to the end of the tumulus period are published in *Pageant of Japanese Art*, vol. 5; in *Nihon Bijutsu Zenshū*, vol. 1, and in *Nihon Bijutsu Taikei*, vol. 7. These surveys written by J. Okada date the finds comparatively early.

2 The articles excavated in Korekawa are looked after by the Bunkazai Hogo Iinkai (Commission for the Protection of Cultural Properties of Japan) in Tōkyō.

3 The research is being carried out by the Bunkazai Hogo Iinkai.

4 Cf. 'Exhibition of Japanese Old Art Treasures' in *Tokyo Olympic Games* (catalogue), nos 59-63.

5 Some scholars believe that the lacquer tree, *rhus vernificera*, was imported from China to Japan in about the fourth century AD. If so, prehistoric Japanese lacquer objects must have been made with the sap of the native lacquer tree, *rhus succedanea*; but this indigenous sap was never used in the later, highly developed Japanese lacquer art (cf. Sir Harry Garner, *Chinese and Associated Lacquer*, p. 7).

6 According to traditional Japanese legend, this Emperor reigned from 392 to 291 BC; factual dates are unknown.

7 Buddhism in Japan is generally taken to date from when the Korean King of Paekche (Kudara) sent the Japanese Emperor Kimmei a standing Buddha figure in gilt bronze. Previously, on the evidence of the 'Nihonshoki,' this was thought to have occurred in 552 AD. More recent Japanese research, however, considers 538 to be more likely, that being the year mentioned in the *Jōgū Shōtoku hooteisetsu*, the earliest biography of Shōtoku Taishi, which dates from the seventh-eighth centuries. Cf. *Nihon-shi jiten*, p. 195, under 'Bukkyō-koden'; G. Kobayashi and T. Fujita, *Nihon bijutsu-shi-nempyō*, p. 2.

8 Further illustrations of the shrine in, among others, Y. Yashiro, *Art Treasures of Japan*, vol. 1, pls 40-2. Tests with ultraviolet rays have revealed that, despite theories to the contrary, the reds, yellows and greens on the Tamamushi shrine are, in fact, examples of genuine lacquer painting, while the flesh tones of the bodies are painted in mitsuda-e.

9 Cf. T. Akiyama, *Japanische Malerei*, p. 22, and also M. Sullivan, *The Birth of Landscape Painting in China*, pp. 131 and 135. For the links between the Tamamushi shrine and Korea cf. T. Kayamoto, 'Tamamushi-zushi no baai. Nihon bijutsu no oyoboshita Chōsen no eikyō,' *Museum*, no 23 (February 1953).

10 The reference is to palmetto-like elements resembling woollen tassels. They occur in a very similar form on a box in the Shōsōin. The box, in

turn, shows close links with Korean wall-paintings in old Koguryō graves. Illustration of the box in *Treasures of the Shōsōin, the Middle Section*, pls 60 and 61.

11 A clear summary, with numerous literary references, of the influx of Koreans into Japan since the end of the fourth century can be found in the introduction to B. Lewin, *Aya and Hata*. For Korean influence on the art of the Asuka period cf. R.T. Paine and A. Soper, *The Art and Architecture of Japan*, pp. 14-15; for the influence of Korean ceramics on Japanese Sueki wares see R.A. Miller, *Japanese Ceramics*, p.25.

12 Cf. H. Arakawa, *Makie*, p.74; and J. Okada in *Nihon Bijutsu Taikei*, vol.7, p.160.

13 T. Hasumi, in his book *Japanische Plastik*, throws a clear light on this Japanese desire to learn. On p.153 he writes that, during the reign of the Empress Genshō (715-724) alone, more than 550 Japanese came back from China after acquainting themselves with all aspects of T'ang culture, and that their knowledge and experience were of inestimable value in the Nara period.

14 N. Ueno and M. Sakamoto, *Nihon chōkoku zuroku*, pp. 31ff. and pls 64-73, 76-9; *Pageant of Japanese Art*, vol.3, pp.21-2; Paine and Soper, *The Art and Architecture of Japan*, pp.26-7 and pls 16ff.

15 The earliest dry-lacquer sculptures in Japan mentioned in literary sources were two statues of Buddha, votive gifts from the Emperor Tenchi (662-671); cf. O. Kümmel, 'Beiträge zur Künstlergeschichte,' *Ostasiatische Zeitschrift*, vol.13 (1926), p.57, n.1.

16 This variant of dry-lacquer is known in Japanese as 'kokuso.' For Far Eastern lacquer techniques and their history see K. Herberts, *Das Buch der ostasiatischen Lackkunst*; also B. von Ragué, 'Zur Technik ostasiatischer

Lackarbeiten,' *Nachrichten der Gesellschaft für Natur- und Völkerkunde Ostasiens*, no 92 (1962).

17 In the *Tōdai-ji kemmotsu-chō*.

18 An identical but undated quiver appears as illustration no 36 in the catalogue of the exhibition 'Treasures from the Shōsōin' put on by the National Museum in Tōkyō in 1959.

19 For shippi boxes of the Nara period cf. J. Okada's article in 'Shippibako,' *Museum*, no 161 (1964); also S. Mizoguchi, 'Kingin-dei-e shippibako,' *Museum*, no 96 (1959).

20 Shunkei-nuri is a technique whereby the wooden substructure remains visible under a layer of transparent yellowish or reddish lacquer. It was popular in the seventeenth century and is alleged to have been invented by a lacquermaster by the name of Shunkei, said to have been active at the end of the fourteenth century.

21 'Heidatsu' is the Japanese pronunciation of the Chinese term 'p'ing-t'o.' Heidatsu was later replaced by the Japanese word 'hyōmon.'

22 Cf. Okada in *Nihon Bijutsu Zenshi*, vol.1, p.155. Okada, however, neither illustrates nor describes the objects.

23 An inscription, dated 735, on a 'koto' (a zither-like musical instrument) with heidatsu decoration in the Shōsōin, clearly proves the instrument to be of Chinese origin. Here, too, the rich silver inlays are engraved in the finest detail. There is a good close-up illustration in *Sekai Bijutsu Zenshū*, vol.15, p.94.

24 Cf. the circular phoenix pattern in no 8 of the catalogue of the exhibition 'Treasures from the Shōsōin' put on by the National Museum in Tōkyō in 1959.

25 J. Harada, *English Catalogue of Treasures in the Imperial Repository Shōsōin*, p.161, 'Kōrai-raden'

26 H. Arakawa, 'Raden,' *Museum*, no 96

(March 1959) and no 105 (December 1959).

27 Probably written by Fang Shao in 1118. Cf. J. Okada, 'Bunken-jō yori mita Kōrai-raden'

28 Although mirrors decorated with mother-of-pearl are mentioned in Chinese writings of the Sung period, not a single one of these works is known to us. Recently S.Y. Lee attributed a number of Chinese mother-of-pearl lacquers to the Sung period, but as yet his case does not seem to be fully proven.

29 In the Shōsōin there is a group of seventeen plates of almost uniform size, all of which are made of keyaki wood and painted. Generally, they are described as mitsuda-e; in fact, however, in only four plates is the colouring agent bound with oil; the rest have a coating of oil in the manner of yushoku.

30 Cf. the box no 63 in the exhibition 'Treasures from the Shōsōin' put on by the National Museum in 1959.

31 Sources of the Nara period do not give a name for this process. Nowadays it is identified with 'chirimaki,' a technique which is first mentioned by name in writings of the Heian period.

32 Cf. Okada in Nihon Bijutsu Zenshi, vol.1, p.157. According to Okada it is apparently just the ground, and not any pattern as such, that has been sprinkled in; in other words, the process is similar to that used on the arrows in the National Museum in Tōkyō.

33 H. Arakawa in his book Makie, published in 1962, supports the claim that it was a Japanese invention.

34 A cloisonné mirror in the Shōsōin (colour plate 7 in Nihon Bijutsu Taikai, vol.9) is an outstanding instance not only of the intricate circular pattern but also of the delight in colour. Its authenticity, however, is questioned by Sir Harry Garner (Chinese and Japanese Cloisonné Enamels). The previously cited catalogue of the exhibition 'Treasures from the Shōsōin' gives good examples of textiles (nos 8, 88, 126), ivory (no 2) and mother-of-pearl inlays in a wood ground (nos 13 and 27), all of which show the complicated structure of the round patterns which can be enlarged at will.

35 R.A. Miller, Japanese Ceramics, p.28ff; S. Umehara, 'Nihon ni okeru tasaiyū no yōki,' Bijutsu Kenkyū, no 226 (1963).

36 See Nihon Bijutsu Zenshi, vol.1, p.151.

CHAPTER 2

1 The latest research on the subject of mandara, shrine and hall is published in Kokuhō tsurenzure-ori Taima-mandara, and in Taima mandara zushi zufu.

2 A wooden box with hyōmon inlays is entered in the Ninna-ji go-shitsu gomotsu jitsuroku for the year 950. Cf. also Nihon Bijutsu Taikei, vol.7, p.164.

3 A detail of one of the rare hyōmon works from the end of the Heian period is illustrated in Nihon Bijutsu Taikei, vol.7, pl.48.

4 H. Arakawa lists these written sources in his article 'Shoki makie-hin ni tsuite.'

5 In togidashi works of the Heian period, the top lacquer layer is not given a final polish. As a result they are not as glossy as later togidashi articles in which this last burnishing stage was standard practice.

6 967-984, written in twenty rolls.

7 Makura no sōshi, written around 1020.

8 Written by Murasaki Shikibu at the beginning of the eleventh century.

9 Illustrated in Nihon Bijutsu Taikei, vol.7, figs 37 and 38.

10 Though nowadays the temple is generally referred to as the 'Tō-ji,' its old name 'Kyōōgokoku-ji' is also

occasionally used.

11 In connection with the exhibition 'Nihon kokuhō-ten,' put on by the National Museum Tōkyō in 1960, H. Arakawa published the first study of this group of works (including an analysis of the order in which they were made) under the title 'Shoki makie-hin ni tsuite.' A comb, said to have belonged to Sugawara Michizane (845-903), also shows very early, but, in this case, non-representational makie decoration ('Taimai sōge kushi' in the Dōmyō-ji Temman-gū in Osaka; for illustration see no 160 in the 'Nihon kokuhō-ten' exhibition catalogue). On it tortoiseshell inlays alternate with spots of sprinkled gold dust which apparently have not been given a final coating of lacquer.

12 H. Arakawa, 'Shoki makie-hin ni tsuite,' p.13.

13 Kukai, 774-835; posthumous name: Kōbō Daishi.

14 Judging by the entry in the *Engi-gyoki*, it would appear that it was Fujiwara no Tadahiro who commissioned the box; during the Engi era (901-923) he was the keeper of these booklets which had been brought to Japan in 806. Of the original set of thirty-eight booklets, eight disappeared; the rest became famous as the 'thirty booklets' (Sanjūjō sasshi). Since 1185, the books and box have been in the possession of the temple of Ninna-ji near Kyōto, as an entry in the 'Tōhō-ki' shows. Cf. S. Mizoguchi in *Sekai Bijutsu Zenshū*, vol.4, p.188.

15 For colour illustration of the sasshibako see K. Herberts, *Das Buch der ostasiatischen Lackkunst*, p.47.

16 Close study not only of the manner of sprinkling but also of the coarseness or fineness, regularity or irregularity of the gold dust is always important when it comes to deciding the date of origin of a makie object. In general it holds true that irregu-

larly shaped, relatively large particles of gold, which do not show sharply defined outlines, are characteristic of the early period. In order to achieve more precise outlines, the gold dust had to be graded according to shape and size, and particular care had to be exercised in the actual process of sprinkling. Significant progress in this direction is evident in lacquers of the Kamakura period, cf. ch.iv. As time went on, the lacquermasters used finer and finer gold dust, finally achieving the extremely fine powder of the Meiji period. Studies of this nature can only be carried out on the originals themselves, since in standard illustrations such details are lost.

17 These comparisons can be made only with the objects themselves, since photographs, according to lighting conditions, can be very deceptive.

18 See *Nihon Bijutsu Taikei*, vol.7, pp.164-5. Apart from the makkinru sword scabbard in the Shōsōin, the arm-rest is the oldest surviving work with representational sprinkled decoration.

19 *Pageant of Japanese Art*, vol.5, p.40.

20 For the history of the different forms of scrolls, cf. K. Morita, *Nihon no monyō*, pp.132ff. Very close still to the lotus scrolls on the sutra box in Pl.18 are four lotus scrolls in gold and silver togidashi on the black-lacquered upper face of an altar base (possibly dating from around 1110) in the Chūson-ji (pl.179 in *Chūson-ji*).

21 The idea of using, within the decoration, a sprinkling technique which, strictly speaking, is intended for the lacquer ground, cropped up again later in the Momoyama period when the so-called 'e-nashiji' was extensively used.

22 The way the mountains are depicted has points in common with a Hōraisan scene in the lid of a stole box which could well date from

around 1100. The box is now in the Hōryū-ji-kan of the National Museum in Tōkyō and is illustrated in T. Maeda, *Japanese Decorative Design*, fig. 29.

23 For example an eight-lobed mirror of 988 illustrated in *Nihon Bijutsu Zenshi*, vol. 1, p. 321.

24 Illustrated in *Nihon Bijutsu Taikei*, vol. 9, no 61.

25 *Hōsōge-mon kondō kyōbako*, published in *Kokubō-jiten*, p. 171.

26 Around the middle of the eleventh century it became a custom to copy sutras and bury them in metal containers.

27 Cf. B. von Ragué, 'Zur Quellenkunde koreanischer Lacke mit Perlmutt-Einlagen,' p. 250.

28 An excellent survey of this gradual process of Japanization and a clear analysis of the essentially Japanese elements in the art of the period are given by A. Soper's 'The Rise of Yamato-e.'

29 G. Samson, *A History of Japan to 1334*.

CHAPTER 3

1 O. Kümmel, *Die Kunst Chinas, Japans und Koreas*, p. 141.

2 Besides Kiyohira, Fujiwara Motohira and Fujiwara Hidehira are also entombed there. It is not known for certain whether the Konjiki-dō was built exclusively as a burial place or whether the idea of an Amida hall may not have been considered at the same time. It could be that a combination of the two was intended. Cf. *Chūson-ji*.

3 The current programme of restoration is planned to continue over a period of several years. The protective hall (Saya-dō; built in 1288) formerly surrounding the Konjikidō has been moved to another spot. In its place a larger structure is being erected which also enables one to look at the outside walls of the Konjiki-dō including the roof.

4 The pillars of the Konjiki-dō are among the earliest examples of ikakeji.

5 This process is described as 'kakiwari,' a term dating from the Edo period.

6 In cross-section the pillars resemble the cross-section of an orange.

7 Called 'haritsuke-hō' or 'fuchakuhō.' For an accurate description of the different raden techniques see H. Arakawa, 'Raden.'

8 In the Phoenix Hall the so-called 'kannyū-hō' process was used, which involved carving out of the wood the exact shape of the piece of motherof-pearl to be inlaid; in the 'daitaibori' method of the Konjiki-dō, on the other hand, only the rough outline was gouged out.

9 According to the inscription on a temple bell, the Chūson-ji was founded in 1105. The sutra hall was built in 1109, the Konjiki-dō in 1124.

10 Numerous editions, including those by N. Kusogami (1944) and Sh. Tanaka (1960).

11 An inscription in Chinese ink on the base of the board supporting the arrows mentions that the quiver was used in 1131 during a visit by the Emperor Sutoku to his father, the ex-Emperor Toba. In 1136, Fujiwara Yorinaga presented it, along with a gold-lacquered bow and some arrows, to the Wakamiya shrine (a subsidiary shrine of the Kasuga-taisha) as a gift from the imperial household. Cf. T. Inoue, 'Kasuga-taisha hirayanagui ni tsuite.'

12 The box has been designated a National Treasure and is in the possession of the Commission for the Protection of Cultural Properties of Japan (Bunkazai Hogo Iinkai). An inscription on the underside of the box states that it was donated to the Hōryū-ji in 726; this inscription, however, only dates from the Edo

or Meiji period and does not make sense. Cf. M. Yoshioka, 'Katawaguruma makie-raden-tebako.'

13 The interior of the lid of the Katawaguruma tebako also shows cherry blossoms, a motif which does not occur at all in the Nara period and is rare in the Heian period.

14 Though neither Katawaguruma box permits precise dating, they can in all certainty be assigned to the end of the Heian and the middle of the Kamakura period respectively.

15 A. Soper, 'The Rise of Yamato-e.'

16 Akikusa-mon-tsubo, in the possession of the Keiō University, Tōkyō.

17 Very few landscape representations have survived from the Heian period. The paintings on the door panels of the Byōdō-in and the so-called Sensui-byōbu (screen) of the Tō-ji date from the second half of the eleventh century. The lacquer chest, however, was certainly not made before the twelfth century.

18 Round patterns of this kind, known as 'ban-e' in Japanese, can consist of birds, quadrupeds or flowers. In the Heian period, sources referring to lacquerwork frequently mention such patterns; they also occur in textiles. In this context, it is worth noting that the end of the Heian period saw the origin of those emblematic patterns in court costumes, which, by means of small differences, indicate the rank of the wearer and from which the family crests (mon) later evolved. Cf. T. Yamanobe, Textiles: Design of Japan.

19 The decoration of one of the hyōmon boxes, so rare in the Heian period, provides a further example of patterns which resemble family crests. This box, whose date of origin is close to that of the small chest in the Kongōbu-ji, is illustrated in Nihon Bijutsu Taikei, vol.7, no 48. A priest's seat in the Tō-ji temple, thought to date from the twelfth century, also

has round patterns and segments of round pattern in mother-of-pearl inlay; it is illustrated in Tōji and its Cultural Treasures, no. 100.

20 Cf. H. Arakawa, Makie, p.43.

21 Illustrated, among others, in T. Yoshino, Japanese Lacquer Ware, fig. 26, and in Y. Yashiro, Art Treasures of Japan, vol.1, pl.241.

22 'Hōō-emmon raden-karabitsu,' exhaustively treated by S. Mizoguchi in Museum (no 96). The lid of the chest is extensively restored; its mother-of-pearl inlays all appear to be of more recent date. There are smaller, later copies of this chest such as, for example, the one in the Hakutsuru Museum near Kobe. Similar in technique and form to this round pattern is the double phoenix pattern on a small sword, decorated with raden and heijin, from the Itsukushima-jinja on Miyajima island.

23 In the Ruijūzatsu-yōsho, a manuscript dating from the end of the Heian period.

24 For saddles of the Heian and Kamakura periods see J. Okada, 'Mei-an-fu.'

25 Detailed illustrations of both these representations of waves in the Japanese periodical, Color Design, no 8 (1960).

26 A rather more complex form of this strangely shaped pond is part of a roughly contemporary small silver sculpture in the Kasuga-taisha in Nara. There, a piece of flat silver engraved with wavy lines represents the pond on which are mounted two silver herons in the round, measuring 7cm each. Illustrated in National Treasures of Japan edited by the Commission for the Protection of Cultural Properties, Series v, no 67 (1959).

27 Illustrated in Nihon Bijutsu Taikei, vol.7, pl.59.

28 Cf. Kokuhō-jiten, p.241.

29 For the inscriptions see T. Akiyama, 'Itsukushima-jinja shozō kogata hiōgi-e ni tsuite.' According to Akiyama, the inscriptions read: 'Donated by Saeki Kagehiro, governor of the province of Aki, to the second (on the other chest: the fourth) sanctuary on the 20th day of the 3rd month of the 2nd year of Juei (1183) on the occasion of his official visit as the new governor to the principal shrine of the province.' Akiyama argues that these are not original dedicatory inscriptions but later additions. According to him, the age of the chests is not, however, affected by this problem.

30 M. Nakano, in 'Hōrai-mon-kagami,' traces the development of the Hōraisan motif on the basis of dated mirrors.

31 Fifty inner boxes are said to have survived. There are chests today in the National Museum in Kyōto (dated An-gen gannen, or 1175), in the National Museum in Tōkyō (1175), in the Nanatsudera (1175) and in Osaka; when I was in Japan in 1965, I made vain attempts to discover the location of an alleged fifth chest. One of the chests is said to be dated 'An-gen 7th year' (1182).

32 In addition to line drawings in red lacquer, the representation on the lid of the Kyōto box shows white 'gofun' painting (gofun: pulverized mussel shells) under the gold dust for the face and the unclad parts of the body.

33 Tebako generally have the type of lid, known in Japanese as 'awase-buta,' which sits on the box, and in which, therefore, as in inrō, the lid and sides of the box lie in the same vertical plane. Only in the Heian period were tebako also made with overlapping lids such as, for example, the Katawaguruma box and this sparrow box.

34 See *Kokuhō-jiten*, pp. 183-4.

CHAPTER 4

1 Recent restoration work on the Konjiki-dō haas led one to suspect that, at least in the Chūson-ji lacquers, gold panned from rivers in the neighbourhood may have been used instead of yasuri-fun. Research is still in progress.

2 For the manufacture and description of the different types of dust up to recent times cf. H. Arakawa, *Makie*, p. 22ff.

3 Cf. similar use of heijin on the lotus scroll box, see p. 32.

4 Mirrors of the Heian and Kamakura periods, which often show birds in flight, illustrate this development particularly well.

5 Cf. B. von Ragué, 'A Part of the Western Paradise.'

6 Published in the Boston Museum of Fine Arts *Bulletin* (1926), p. 42.

7 Inscription with date in the interior of the lid.

8 A particular form of wooden gate always to be found near Shintō shrines.

9 Cf. G. Yoshida, 'Waga-makie-monyō ni arawaretaru bungakuteki yōsu ni tsuite.

10 For the same motif, cf. Pl. 43.

11 The *Zōei-ki* of the Ōmi Hioyshi-jinja, which dates from 1136, alone gives the names of twenty-seven lacquermasters; however, no specific works can be linked with them. Cf. H. Arakawa, *Makie*, p. 27, where all the names are listed.

12 My thanks for this information to Mr M. Yoshimura of the National Museum in Kyōto, who also showed me photographs as further proof.

13 The mother-of-pearl is not inlaid in black lacquer but in 'mokume-nuri,' that is, in a lacquer surface which simulates wood grain. Mokume-nuri was very popular in the Kamakura period. A base in the Yakushi hall of the Jomyo-ji (Wakayama-ken),

which also dates from the thirteenth century, shows mother-of-pearl inlays in a similar 'Nara renaissance' style. Illustrated in *Bukkyō Bijutsu*, vol.3 (June 1925), pl.4.

14 An interesting 'copy' of this sutra box, made in about 1900 and with its proportions slightly altered, is now in the collection of Dr Kurt Herberts, Wuppertal.

15 The 'Poem of the East Fence' by the poet T'ao Yüan-ming (or Ch'ien) (365-427), translated by J.R. Hightower in *The Poetry of T'ao Ch'ien* (Oxford 1972), p.130. The motif of the chrysanthemums by the fence occurred frequently in the Chinese-influenced naga-uta of early Japanese poetry; beginning with the end of the twelfth century it is occasionally also used in the purely Japanese 'waka' (poems).

16 'Ikakeji-gyōyō-raden-tachi,' Tsurugaoka Hachiman-gū, Kamakura. Cf. *Kokuhō-jiten*, p.242.

17 'Karakusa-raden suebako,' Daigo-ji, Kyōto. Illustrated in *Nihon Bijutsu Taikei*, vol.7, no 69.

18 A few Japanese experts like Arakawa, for example, also describe this ground as 'hirame-ji.' The dust must therefore be regarded either as coarse nashiji-fun or as fine hirame-fun.

19 The butterfly box is one of the earliest instances of the combination of makie with silver hyōmon.

20 The armour belongs to the Kasuga-taisha in Nara.

21 Cf. *Nihon Bijutsu Taikei*, vol.9, p.194.

22 Okada in *Sekai Bijutsu Zenshū* (Kadokawa), vol.6, pp.243-4.

23 The use of written characters in a pictorial representation is typically Japanese. In painting, it occurs already in the Heian period (for example in the Heikenō-kyō); in lacquerwork, however, we do not meet it until the end of the Kamakura period. The Japanese employ two terms to describe the pictorial use of written characters: 'ashide-e' (literally: in the style of reed) and 'uta-e' (literally: song picture, poem picture); but no attempt is made at strict differentiation between them. According to G. Yoshida, the word ashide-e occurs for the first time in a manuscript of 960. In ashide-e and uta-e the written characters and the decoration of the object both directly refer to the same theme.

24 Also known as 'Chōseiden-makie-tebako'; a reference to the characters in the interior decoration of the lid.

25 These multi-lobed forms are called 'suhama' in Japanese (approximate translation: sandbank), because of their similarity to certain coastal formations.

26 So, too, in the 'Suhama-chidori makie-tebako,' Nomura collection, Tōkyō, illustrated in *Pageant of Japanese Art*, vol.5, fig.79 and in the 'Kiku-eda makie tebako,' Hatakeyama Museum, Tōkyō.

27 Nevertheless, the box with the painted fans shows five written characters in takamakie in the interior of the lid. The box in the Hatakeyama Museum has mother-of-pearl inlays.

28 The calculation is based on measurments given in the *Kokuhō-jiten*, in the *Shukō meikan* and in *Kokka*, no 303. By itself such an assertion would not carry any conviction, but since it accords with our knowledge of stylistic and technical development, it might be considered conclusive.

29 The earliest surviving comb boxes date from the Kamakura period.

30 It is said that the small square boxes were meant for powder, the rectangular ones for the blacking used to colour the teeth, and the round ones for scent and perfume.

31 Exhaustively treated by J. Okada, 'Sumiyoshi-makie-kushibako,' *Kokka*, no 815 (February 1960).

From written sources, such as the *Ruijūzatsu-yōshō* (end of the Heian period), we know of comb boxes which must have been larger. When the smaller type began to be made is not known.

32 The poem was written by the priest Ji-en, 1155-1225.

33 S. Mizoguchi, *Negoro-nuri no kanshō*.

34 H. Arakawa gives a list of fifty-one dated Negoro lacquers made between 1164 and 1770 in *Kinen-mei Negoro-nuri ni tsuite*.

35 Mizoguchi considers as typical of the 'Japanese style' (traditional since the Heian period) the thin wooden core of the Negoro implements, their simple elegant shapes, the careful lacquering; of the mixed style (beginning with the Kamakura period) the strong robust wooden core, regular, symmetrical, uncluttered shapes, sturdy and expressive, unusually thick lacquer coating. For the 'Chinese style' (mostly of the Muromachi period) he considers as typical, outright imitation of Chinese implements (Yüan and Ming influences), exaggerated curved edges, flared legs with curved outlines, blossom-shaped foliated plates and bowls.

36 Colour plate on the cover of *Nihon Bijutsu Taikei*, vol.7.

37 In a private collection. Referred to by Arakawa in *Museum*, no 92.

38 Cf. S. Nakagawa, 'Ko-Seto no monyō.'

39 Korean mother-of-pearl lacquer wares, which evolved during the twelfth and thirteenth centuries and were both technically and stylistically unlike their Japanese counterparts, were apparently unknown in Japan during the Kamakura period. The chaotic political situation in Korea may be one reason. Neither these Korean lacquerwares, nor the Chinese Yüan dynasty lacquerwares with mother-of-pearl inlays (which,

so far are known virtually by written sources only) combined gold lacquer with mother-of-pearl in the Japanese manner.

CHAPTER 5

1 The Nambokuchō lacquers are dealt with here together with the early Muromachi wares, because in the history of lacquerwork, the end of the Kamakura period marks the end of an era.

2 1338 two Negoro ritual hand-basins in the Hōryū-ji; one illustrated as no 62 in the *Fine Arts of the Kamakura Period* (catalogue, Kyōto, 1961)

   1338 black-lacquer food stand (taka-tsuki); Ōgami-jinja, Nara-ken

   1346 round Negoro tray, Tōkyō Geijutsu Daigaku

   1370 black-lacquer sacrificial table (kumotsu-dai) in the Sata-jinja

   1373 seven food stands (takatsuki), Kisui-in, Nara-ken

   1391 bowl in the form of a temmoku tea bowl, Tōkyō National Museum

3 Kongōbu-ji, Wakayama-ken.

4 Cf. J. Murdoch, *A History of Japan*, vol. 1, p.547.

5 The 'Karabana makie-kutsubako' in the National Museum Kyōto, probably made around 1400 and formerly owned by the Asuka-jinja, provides a further good example of the 'Heian renaissance' in the lacquerwork of the early Muromachi period. Its round pattern and scrolls show unmistakable links with the late Heian period.

6 The back of the chest bears a dedicatory inscription in hyōmon with the date 1357; on the underside are the signature of the lacquermaster Shami Kūgaku, two mother-of-pearl artists and the cabinetmaker. Exhaustively treated by S. Mizoguchi in *Museum*, no 111.

7 The tight, precise shape of the box points to a relatively early date. For the frequent occurrence of the plum branch and crescent moon motif in Chinese art of the fourteenth century, cf. J. Wirgin, 'Some Ceramic Wares from Chi-chou.'

8 Ceramics too show the decline of the austere clarity of Kamakura forms during the Muromachi period.

9 *Butsu-nichi-an kōmotsu-mokuroku*.

10 Letter translated and published by J. Figgess, 'A Letter from the Court of Yung-lo.'

11 The *Kundaikan sayu chōki* was written by Nōami in 1476 and enlarged by his grandson Sōami in 1511. The first section, which deals with painting, was translated into German by O. Kümmel; see *Ostasiatische Zeitschrift*, vol. 1, 1912-13.

12 Cf. *Makieshi-den, nurishi-den*, fourth ed., part 2, pp. 12 and 42.

13 The term 'Kamakurabori' is apparently not used until the Genroku era (1688-1703). Work in the same technique is also known variously as 'Odawara-bori,' 'Echizen-bori,' 'Yoshino-bori,' etc., after other places of manufacture.

14 The Hokke-dō, better known as the Nigatsu-dō, forms part of the Tōdai-ji in Nara.

15 This kōgō is described in Okada's article 'Tsuishu to Kamakurabori'; in *Nihon Bijutsu Zenshi*, vol. 1, p. 434, and in *Nihon Bijutsu Taikei*, vol. 7, p. 171.

16 The Ming manuscript 'Hsiu-shih-lu' describes imitation carved lacquerwork: 'In addition there are certain objects carved in wood (and lacquered over); the skilled worker shuns this technique.'

17 The different theories concerning the origin of Kamakurabori are analysed by J. Okada in his article, 'Tsuishu to Kamakurabori.' Two red-lacquer tables with filigree carving, which cannot, however, be included among the Kamakurabori,

are in the Kenchō-ji, Kamakura (dated 1428) and in the Gan-ō-ji, Kyōto (dated 1432).

18 Formerly in the Hyakusai-ji, Shiga-ken; now in the Biwako Bunkakan. An inscription inside the lid gives the date (O-ei, sixteenth year).

19 Whereas the lacquer on the lid is matt, black with a tinge of brown, on the inside and in those places not exposed to the light it is a deep, glossy black. The lacquer surface has survived astonishingly well; it has no cracks, only a few small marks where it has been accidentally damaged.

20 'San' (chirasu) means scatter; 'mai' (kome) means rice.

21 'Aki no nanakusa': kikyō (*platycodon grandiflorum*) a lilac coloured, star-shaped flower; fujibakama (*eupatorium japonicum Thunb.*), pale lilac umbel; ominaeshi (*patrinia scabioasaefolia*), yellow blossom, slender leaves; hagi (*lespedeza bicolor*), sweet clover; susuki or obana (*miscanthus sinensis*), pampas-grass; kuzu (*pueraria Thunbergiana*), arrowroot; nadeshiko (*diathus superbus L.*), a carnation-like plant.

22 Illustrated in *An Illustrated Catalogue of Famous Masterpieces in the Collection of the Nezu Art Museum*, no 195, fig. 82.

23 This box definitely belongs in the first half of the Muromachi period, but a precise dating is difficult. On the one hand it still retains lively echoes of traditional elements, yet, on the other, technical and stylistic characteristics argue against an early dating. Among the former one might include the use of harigaki and the shading of the patches of earth in the interior of the lid; among the latter, the 'Chinese' rocks, the comb-like wings of the chidori and the complicated way in which the branches change direction. Therefore, a dating of ca 1400 would probably be justified.

24 Nagi being the name of the type of tree depicted; it grows plentifully in the neighbourhood of Kumano. For this box, cf. S. Noma in *Sekai Bijutsu Zenshū* (Kadokawa), vol. 7, p. 217; H. Arakawa, *Makie*, p. 49; and J. Okada in *Nihon Bijutsu Zenshi*, vol. 1, p. 524.

25 *Kumano-shingū go-shimpō-mokuroku*.

26 According to the techniques employed which might, in certain circumstances, facilitate the dating, there are three distinct groups of boxes. The first and largest group has, on a nashiji ground, togidashi, sabiage-takamakie, kirigane and mother-of-pearl inlay; the denser nashiji ground of the second is decorated with makie, kirigane, silver and gilt bronze kanagai (in strong relief in places), as well as with small silver nails representing dew drops; the third group shows, on densely scattered ikake-ji, makie-kirigane and silver kanagai. Cf. also *Kokuhō-jiten*, pp. 245f.

27 *Shionoyama makie-suzuribako*, Tōkyō National Museum.

28 According to temple tradition, the mirror and the case were presented to the Atsuta shrine in 1445 by Chiaki Sakon Shogen Fujiwara no Ason Katsusue. They may well have been made in the same year they were donated. Another round mirror case in the Atsuta-jingū is illustrated in *Nihon Bijutsu Taikei*, vol. 7, no 80. In H. Arakawa's view, it was given at the same time and by the same donor.

29 The Heian period was already familiar with this subject, cf. pp. 54 and 250, n. 22; in the Kamakura period, however, it went completely out of fashion. Since the Hōraisan stories originally derive from China, it is possible that when links with China were close, they occupied a more prominent position in Japanese art than at other times.

30 *Pageant of Japanese Art*, vol. 5, p. 93.

31 An important aesthetic connotation of the Muromachi period denoting concepts of mysterious, unfathomable depth.

32 Quoted in J. Okada, 'Kuchinashi byōkin-raden-bon.' The *Huang Ming wen tse* was written in the Ming period.

33 According to S. Jenyns and W. Watson, *Chinesische Kunst*, p. 286. K. Tomita states that Yang Hsüan received the nickname 'Japanese lacquer' because of his skilful imitations of makie; cf. The Boston Museum of Fine Arts, *Bulletin* (1926).

34 J. Okada, 'Kuchinashi byōkin-raden-bon.'

35 Cf. Wang Yi-t'ung, *Official Relations between China and Japan* 1368-1549, pp. 90ff.

36 Metalwork also shows how strong the formative influence of Ming applied art was on Japan in the fifteenth century. A good example of this is the completely 'Chinese' incense box, dated 1446, in the Daitoku-ji in Kyōto, illustrated in *Sekai Bijutsu Zenshū* (Kadokawa), vol. 7, pl. 93.

37 The literature on the subject sometimes makes incorrect and misleading statements to the effect that the engraved lines were 'filled' with gold. The process is, in fact, carried out as follows: when the engraving is complete, the whole surface is covered with lacquer. This is then wiped off again (lacquer does not harden in dry air). The only place the lacquer remains is in the sunken lines of the engraving. Now, either gold leaf or gold dust is applied to the engraved sections. Both adhere only to the still moist lacquer in the engraved lines and can easily be removed from the rest of the surface.

38 The '*Ko ku yao lun*,' a manuscript of the Ming period, names P'eng Chün-pao as a master of ch'iang-chin in the early Yüan period (1279-1368).

39 The boxes are in the temple of

Dai-sembō in the Fukuoka-ken, in the Jōdi-ji in Ono-michi-shi (Hiroshima-ken) and in the temple of Komyobō (Hiroshima-ken).

40 Quoted in the 'Zenrinkokuhō-ki,' a Japanese manuscript of 1466.

41 In the 'Inryōken-nichiroku' and in the 'Kambun-gyoki,' quoted by Okada in *Bijutsu Kenkyū*, no. 166 (1952), text for pls VII and VIII.

42 A chinkinbori sutra box, probably dating from the Muromachi period, is in the Hosomi collection, Osaka.

43 Accompanying the Kasugayama writing-box is a manuscript 'Jishō-in Yoshimasa-kō go-men suzuri no ki,' in which these three boxes are listed together with two others no longer extant.

44 The landscapes of the Higashiyama lacquer wares may well be compared with Japanese landscape pictures of this period, which are strongly influenced by Chinese painting; for instance with a picture by Minchō, dated 1413, in the Konchi-in in Kyōto, or with a landscape, dated 1447 and attributed to Shūbun, in the National Museum in Tōkyō. The lacquer wares are somewhat conservative by comparison and reflect elements of Yamato-e rather more strongly, yet the style is basically related.

45 See chapter 4, note 23.

46 This poem by Mibu no Tadamine was included in the *Kokin-shū* anthology.

47 Contemporary sources mention that Yoshimasa owned this writing-box. Later, as revealed by the inventory of his collection, it belonged to the calligrapher and painter Shōkadō (1584-1639).

48 No place or river of this name is known today.

49 The National Museum in Tōkyō also has a writing-box decorated with the Shionoyama motif. This piece, however, is by no means as 'heroic' and vigorous as the one in Kyōto.

50 Such as, for example, the Hatsune brazier in the Tōkei-ji (Shinagawa-ken) and the Kaede-tachibana writing-box in the Fujita Museum in Osaka; illustrated in *Nihon Bijutsu Taikei*, vol.7, figs 80 and 90.

51 For his lacquer works Kōami Michinaga is said to have used designs by Tosa Mitsunobu (1434-1525), Nōami (1397-1471) and Sōami (?-1525); of Michikiyo, on the other hand, it is alleged that, since he was a very able painter, he made the designs for his lacquers himself. Yoshimasa commissioned him to decorate with makie furniture and other objects used at the enthronement of the Emperor Go-Tsuchimikado.

52 Cf. H. Arakawa, *Makie*, p.55.

53 After the Nambokuchō period the following dated undecorated lacquer objects were made (see also p.259, n.8):

1395 three vegetable buckets; Tōdai-ji and private collection

1395 three oil jars; Tōdai-ji and private collection

1424 two takatsuki (food stands); private collection

1427 two ritual hand basins; Tōdai-ji

1428 rectangular tray (Tachikara-bon); private collection

1447 small Negoronuri table; private collection

1452 black-lacquer lamp-stand; Tōkyō National Museum

1455 two lobed red-lacquer plates; Saidai-ji (Nara) and Tokiwa-yama-Bunko

1457 five small red-lacquer plates; eight square trays with bevelled corners; seven square trays with inverted corners; all in the Musumida-jinja, Ichinomiya-shi (Achi-ken)

1465 black-lacquer writing-table and writing-box; Kumano-hongū (Wakayama-ken)

1478 round red-lacquer tray; private collection

1478 tray on four legs; private collection

1480 black-lacquer shrine; Fuku-shōju-ji (now National Museum in Nara)

1482 red-lacquer takatsuki; private collection

CHAPTER 6

1 To what extent these places distinguished themselves by making specific types of lacquerwork in the Muromachi period is a moot point; it is not until the Edo period that any written sources substantiate this tradition. It is unknown what form of lacquerwork was made in Yamaguchi; Odawara, where much woodwork originated, produced a variant of Kamakurabori (but no longer does). In Sakai, at least from the end of the Momoyama period, lacquer articles were made for the wealthy merchants, but these were more in the nature of practical items than anything of artistic significance.

2 Cf. J. Okada, 'Mei-an-fu.'

3 R.T. Paine and A. Soper, *The Art and Architecture of Japan*, p.88.

4 For example in J. Okada, 'Igarashi-makie ni tsuite.'

5 Apart from this writing-box by Kōami Sōhaku, there are only the Kōdai-ji doors by Kōami Matazaemon (1596), the Hatsune bookshelves with their accompanying boxes by Kōami Nagashige (1639) and, finally, a picnic box by the same master (cf. Pls 121, 156 and 157).

6 Pictorial representations (for example a hanging scroll, attributed to Tosa Tsunekata, with scenes from the life of Shōtoku Taishi, in the Metropolitan Museum in New York) are proof that this subdivision of writing-boxes existed at least as early as the Kamakura period. All surviving early writing-boxes, however,

have the inkstone in the centre. Beginning only with writing-boxes attributed to Kōetsu and his school, the inkstone is generally placed on the left-hand side.

7 Shishi is a lion-like animal of fable. An illustration of the shishi box is in *Chūson-ji*, p.72.

8 Dated Negoro lacquers of the sixteenth to eighteenth centuries:

1528 round tray on three legs; private collection

1534 red-lacquer hibachi (brazier); private collecton

1568 set of four bowls of different sizes (yotsuwan); private collection

1569 food stand (takatsuki); private collection

1630 food stand (takatsuki)

1646 food stand; Kyōto Bijutsu Daigaku

1654 food stand; Yoshimizu-in

1663 black-lacquer writing-box; Tōdai-ji

1664 food stand; private collection

1666 black-lacquer food stand; private collection

1770 small flat plate; private collection

Bearing the date of 1548 is another small undecorated bowl the dark lacquerground of which was once completely covered by gold foil, now worn off in places. It is now in the S.Y. Lee collection in Tōkyō.

9 All surviving 'rucksacks' appear to have been made in the Tōhoku district, that is, in northern Japan.

10 Kōgō of this size are said to have been used in Buddhist temples to store powdered incense.

CHAPTER 7

1 The dates 1568 and 1615 correspond to the classification generally adopted by Japanese art historians. From the purely historical point of view, however, the Momoyama period is considered to begin with

the deposition of the last Ashikaga shōgun in 1573 and to end with the establishment of the Tokugawa shōgunate in 1603.

2 For the origin of Japanese *cloisonné* cf. p.264, n.19.

3 A preliminary drawing for the decoration of the saddle, attributed to Eitoku, is illustrated in *Sekai Bijutsu Zenshū*, vol.8, p.245.

4 Colour pl.97 in the illustrated catalogue *Tokugawa Bijutsukan*.

5 This motif, so popular in Japan, is based on the following Chinese tale: A monk was determined never again to leave the confines of his monastery. One day he was visited by two friends with whom he engaged in such lively conversation that, without noticing it, he crossed the bridge that marked the bounds of the monastery. When he and his friends realized what had happened, they burst out laughing.

6 Bishū is another name for Owari.

7 The bulk of it was brought to the Nishi-Hongan-ji in Kyōto, where to this day the mighty reception hall and the Hiunkaku pavillion bear witness to the one-time magnificence of the Fushimi Castle.

8 The results of the latest research were published in detail in 1971 by Yoshimura in *Kōdai-ji makie*.

9 According to Yoshimura, this lacquer artist, Kōami Matazaemon, was possibly the son or grandson of a Kōami Matazaemon Sōka, mentioned in the family record, 'Kōami kaden-sho.' No date other than 1596 is known for Matazaemon.

10 Tsukufusuma-jinja on the island of Chikubushima in the northern section of Lake Biwa. The shrine was rebuilt in 1602 by Hideyoshi's son, incorporating parts from the Fushimi Castle.

11 Both illustrated in *Nihon Bijutsu Taikei*, vol.7, figs 98 and 99.

12 The two best-known examples of this style are illustrated in *Nihon Bi-*

jutsu Taikei, vol.7, figs 131 and 151.

13 The earliest dated lacquer work in which harigaki is used is the sutra box of 1409, Pl.79.

14 Cf. T. Volker, 'Japanese Export Lacquer.'

15 The collection of the Electors of Brandenburg in Berlin, for example, contained two shields lacquered in Japan. They were commissioned either by the Great Elector or by Frederick III and their takamakie decoration showed the coat of arms of the Electors of Brandenburg.

16 Cf. S. Nakagawa, 'Iwayuru namban-karakusa no isshu ni tsuite.'

17 A series of lacquer objects depicting Portuguese are illustrated in T. Nishimura, *Namban-bijutsu*.

18 1 Tōkei-ji, Kanazawa-ken
2 Itsuō Bijutsukan, Ikeda-shi near Osaka
3 Private collection K. Tokugawa, Tōkyō
4 Private collection I. Kobayashi
5 Private collection T. Yoshino, Tōkyō (with the letters IHS scraped off)

19 Korean lacquerwork since the end of the Koryo period is a subject worthy of special study, despite the fact that the shortage of precisely datable items presents considerable difficulties. There is a marked contrast with the Ming lacquers carefully and delicately inlaid with mother-of-pearl. So far, however, no one has yet made any attempt to systematically list and study Korean works, although Okada's article 'Kinsei shōki shitsugei ni okeru Ri-chō-raden no eikyō' (The influence of Li mother-of-pearl lacquers on more recent lacquerwork) provides some material.

20 Archduke Ferdinand was a cousin of Philip II of Spain, and it was doubtless either through him, or through Spanish and Portuguese trade links, that the small chest came into his possession.

21 This information comes from a letter written by William Adams, Tokugawa Ieyasu's English adviser. Cf. J. Okada, 'Namban-yō makie-hin ni tsuite' where several such sources are quoted.

22 The National Museum in Tōkyō and the British Museum in London each own a further matching piece. It is significant that a smaller, but equally closely related chest in the Mat-sunaga Kinen-kan in Itabashi near Odawara was purchased in Europe. The inside is lined with velvet and it was probably used as a jewel box.

23 Similar stylized plum scrolls – a comparatively rare motif – occur on a writing-table, dating from around the end of the sixteenth century, now in the Itsukuushima-jinja (Miyajima). The top of the table is divided into zig-zag fields such as can be seen in the Kōdai-ji lacquers. The plum blossoms are worked partly in gold and partly in silver togidashi on nashiji: a colour scheme which is known from contemporary Namban lacquers.

24 In Okada's opinion (in T. Hayashiya, Kōetsu, p.135) the design of the chest should be attributed not to Sōtatsu but to the school of Kōetsu. Since, however, at this early stage one can hardly speak of a Kōetsu style of lacquerwork, it seems not possible to have a work by the Kōetsu school.

25 J. Okada, 'Momoyama-jidai no kōgei, sono dokusōsei ni tsuite'

26 It is not possible to discuss the individual forms in this space. However, at least the following types should be mentioned: 'natsume' (as an individual shape, not in the meaning of the collective term); 'kirinji'; 'kawataro'; 'fubuki'; 'chaoke'; 'shirifukurami', 'yakki', 'nakatsugi'; 'kōaka'; 'dōjime' or 'dōjimari'; 'oshiroitoki.' Some of these forms date from the Momoyama period,

the majority from the Edo period.

27 Cf. U.A. Casal, 'Some Notes on the Sakazuki and on the Role of Sake Drinking in Japan.'

28 Inrō already existed in the late Muromachi period, but apparently they were not worn as fashion accessories, but were hung up in the to-konoma (picture alcove) instead.

29 The first eight masters in this list are taken from the *Nihon bijutsu jiten*, ninth ed., pp.430f.; for the ninth to twentieth masters the list follows Rokkaku Shisui, *Tōyō shikkō-shi*, second ed., pp.226f.:
1 Chōjū (Nagamichi), ca.1360
2 Chōshin (Nagatatsu)
3 Chōtei (Nagasada), active 1487-1488
4 Chōshi (Nagatsugu), 1492-1500
5 Chōhan (Nagashige), 1501-1520
6 Chōshū (Nagahide), 1521-1545
7 Chōshin (Nagachika), lived in Kamakura 1615-1624 and made tea utensils
8 Chōshū (Nagamune) = Tsuishu Heijirō known as Yōsei, died 1654
9 Chōzen (Nagayoshi), died 1680
10 Chōze, died 1719
11 Chōsei (Nagamori), died 1735
12 Chōin, died 1765
13 Chōri (Nagatoshi), died 1779
14 Chōkin, died 1791
15 Chōryū (Nagataka), died 1826
16 Chōei (Nagahide), died 1848
17 Chōhō (Nagakuni), died 1858
18 Kunihei, died 1890
19 ?, said to have died young
20 Tsuishu Yōsei (personal name unknown), 1880-1952
In part the above dates have been revised according to W. Speiser's list of lacquermasters in K. Herberts, *Das Buch der ostasiatischen Lackkunst*. Masters one to seven are all said to have used the name Tsuishu, masters eight to twenty the name Tsuishu Yōsei. Further Tsuishu masters (without the artist name Yōsei) are the following: Yajirozaemon in Kyōto, who was active

around 1688-1703 and is alleged to have been 'better than Monnyū' and his contemporary Jūzaemon, who is said to have specialized in the making of inrō and kōgō for the shōgunate. Allegedly, he not only carried out very delicate work in the exact style of Chinese Wan-li lacquers, but also depicted plants and figures 'in the Japanese style' on his inrō. Then around 1716-1735 there was a certain Tsuishu Yonzei in Edo. In order to avoid the annoying confusion with Tsuishu Yōsei, who also worked for the shōgun, he had changed his original name Yōsei to Yonzei. He chiefly made inrō for the shōgun. Finally in 1854-1860 there are Tsuishu Dewa and his contemporary, Tsuishu Kanshichi, who is thought to have worked in Nagasaki.
This information has been assembled from the cited work by Rokkaku Shisui, Kōgei-shiryō, fifth ed., 1905, p.245 f.; and Makieshi-den nurishi-den, vol.2, 1927, p.12ff.

30 Quoted in Makieshi-den nurishi-den, vol.2, p.13, as being in the possession of Maeda Toshitsugi.

31 Kōgō in the kōka-ryokuyō technique, that is, with red blossoms and green leaves; quoted in Makieshi-den nurishi-den, vol.2, p.13 as being in the possession of Tanaka Kōden.

CHAPTER 8

1 In Far Eastern sagas the hare is often linked with the moon and is frequently represented in the disc of the moon. In Japan hares skimming over wavetops symbolize the light of the full moon playing on the surface of the sea.

2 Pl.139 Mikasayama makie-kakesuzuri.

3 Pl.140 Ishi-hiki makie-bon.

4 Pl.141 Budō urushi-e-bon.

5 Pl.142 Kiku-kiri-mon makie-sumiaka.

6 A further set of Meigetsu-wan is in the collection of the Geijutsu

Daigaku University of Art in Tōkyō.

7 A flute case with hagi decoration, dated 1619, formerly in the possession of the Berlin State Museum but missing since 1945, proves that not only the 'Korean' mother-of-pearl technique but also the 'rediscovered' old raden technique could be linked with the Kōdai-ji style. Illustrated in Kümmel, Ostasiatisches Gerät, pl.140. However, in this case, there are also traces of Korean influence.

8 The only source which mentions that Kōetsu actually made lacquer works is the 'Kōami gyōjō-ki furoku.' Even so it merely says that he 'also made makie.' (quoted from Okada in T. Hayashiya, Kōetsu, p.132).

9 For the exposition of the Kōetsu problem that follows, I have drawn heavily on the chapter on Kōetsu lacquers by Okada in T. Hayashiya, Kōetsu.

10 It is conceivable that the typical Kōetsu lacquers were not made until he settled in Takagamine, in other words, after 1615.

11 Cf. Sh.F. Moran, 'Lacquer Writing-Box by Kōetsu.'

12 According to Y. Yashiro, Art Treasures of Japan, vol.2, p.508, the text reads:
   Azuma-ji no Sano no funabashi kakete nomi
   omoi wataru o shiru hito zo naki,
freely translated as: The boat bridge of Sano in the Eastern provinces reminds me of the love which bridges the gulf between us; but she does not know how very much I love her.

13 In the Yamato Bunkakan, Nara. Illustrated in Nihon Bijutsu Taikei, vol.7, p.136.

14 This writing-box has been much copied; in the Metropolitan Museum in New York alone, there are several copies. But no copy shows the same complete balance and mastery of composition based on the calculated relationship of the various axes and diagonals. Motif, technique and occ-

asionally even the heavily domed shape of the box were imitated but apparently the inherent invisible laws of composition were not grasped. In the author's opinion, the study of composition can sometimes result in deciding whether a given lacquer work should be ascribed to Kōetsu or Kōrin. Accordingly, the well-known writing-box with herons in the Seattle Art Museum, for example, attributed at one time or another to both Kōetsu and Kōrin, should very definitely be attributed to Kōetsu (illustrated in the catalogue: *Japanese Art in the Seattle Art Museum*, no.139, and in Sh.E. Lee, *Japanese Decorative Style*, fig.127.)

15 In the case of the so-called Kōetsu lacquers it has sometimes been suggested that while the written characters are by Kōetsu, the pictorial decoration might have been designed by Sōtatsu. Because of the close collaboration between Kōetsu and Sōtatsu this hypothesis can be neither proved nor refuted. But in shape, decoration and script employed, the lacquers give the impression of being cast in a single mould, and it would seem more appropriate to attribute the new form to a man like Kōetsu, who was also active in the field of applied art (ceramics), than to someone like Sōtatsu, who was a painter pure and simple.

16 *Shinobu makie-suzuribako*, private collection, Tōkyō. The box is illustrated in *Nihon Bijutsu Taikei*, vol.7, figs 131 and 132.

17 Front view illustrated in *Nihon Bijutsu Taikei*, vol.7, fig. 133.

18 Inside the lid, next to the kakihan of Kyūhaku, there is the following inscription: 'Koma Kyūi saku, dō Kyūhaku Yasuaki kore o kiwamu' (made by Koma Kyūi. Kyūhaku Yasuaki, a member of the same family, bears witness to this).

19 They are in the possession of the Reimeikai Foundation, Tōkyō, and the Tokugawa Museum in Nagoya.

20 There is a writing-table (dated 1667) with a writing-box, both by Tatsuke Chōbei, in the Izumo-taisha, Shimane-ken.

21 In the first half of the seventeenth century there were two lines of Igarashi masters in Kyōto. One ('the Dōho line') later went to Kanazawa, the other ('the Tarōbei line') to Edo. For the genealogy of the Igarashi, see Okada in T. Hayashiya, *Kōetsu*, p.133 and figs 86 and 87.

22 Illustrated in Okada, 'Igarashi-makie ni tsuite,' p.4. In this article Okada gives a list of the written sources for and surviving lacquer works by Igarashi Dōho I. Shōbei was given permission to use the name Igarashi. The second line was established by Sōbei, a pupil of Dōho II who had no children.

23 Pl.33 in *Meihōten zuroku*.

24 The saddle and stirrups are part of the collection in the Seisonkaku, a former dowager seat of the Maeda family at Kanazawa.

25 The catalogue of the exhibition 'Kaga-makie-ten' put on by the Museum in Kanazawa (Ishikawa-ken Bijutsukan) in 1961 names the following as more recent masters of Kaga-makie: Yoneda Magoroku, Sawada Sōtaku, Ogaki Masakuni, Sasada Getsugyō and Niki Seihō.

26 The surviving Jogahana-nuri works could hardly have been made before 1800, but anything in this folk-art idiom is extremely difficult to date.

27 This information comes from H.B. Minnich, *Japanese Costume*, p.258.

28 S. Shimura and T. Goke, 'Hyakkō-hishō ni tsuite.'

29 Occasionally, Somada lacquers were also made in Edo. In Okinawa, under Japanese rule since 1608, lacquerwares of this kind had possibly been made for some time under Chinese influence.

30 Approximate translation: 'Custodian of an invisible cultural property,' that is, of the old technique.

CHAPTER 9

1 After T. Yoshino, *Japanese Lacquer
Ware*, p.131; I have been unable,
however, to find out the present
whereabouts of the Sakuragi and
Minowa writing-boxes or where
they are illustrated.

2 *Kōrin hyakka-zu*, vol.1, part 2.

3 Arakawa points out that, according
to a passage in the *Makura no sōshi*,
two-tiered writing-boxes had probably existed already in the Heian
period (H. Arakawa, *Makie*, p.68),
but they were not developed into the
'classic' shape. In the early Edo
period there are two- or three-tiered
boxes shaped like a portable
'kakebako' with a handle mounted
on top; the comb case for travel in
Pl.138 is also a composite. The form
adopted by Kōrin for his Yatsuhashi-
suzuribako, however, seems to be
unique.

4 *Semmen-Narihira makie-suzuribako*;
Nezu Museum, Tōkyō.

5 Sōtatsu had a marked preference for
using fan motifs on his large screens.

6 The drawing is reproduced in *Kōrin
shin-sen hyaku-ga*.

7 The motif of the fan with the portrait
of Narihira was later used on a nar-
rower lacquer box. This box, which
has a red ground, is now in the
Musée Guimet in Paris; illustrated
in the auction sales catalogue of the
Jacques Doucet collection, Paris
1930, pl.XIII, no.33.

8 Cf. Rokkaku Shisui, *Tōyō shikkō-shi*,
p.215. Tsuchida Sōetsu later went to
Edo.

9 H. Arakawa, *Makie*, and *Sekai Bijutsu Zenshū* (Kadokawa), vol.10,
p.189.

10 Rokkaku also states the later period,
see *Tōyō shikkō-shi*, p.229.

11 *Kōrin hyakka-zu*.

12 His dates are not known; his main

period of activity seems to have been
the second and third decades of the
eighteenth century.

13 Also described as 'Biwa-ko makie-
suzuribako.'

14 Illustrated in O. Kümmel, *Ostasiatisches Gerät*, p.125 and O. Kümmel,
Das Kunstgewerbe in Japan, p.48.

15 Kyuhaku II died in 1732, cf.
Makieshi-den nurishi-den, vol.1, p.64.

16 Cf. the article on Ogawa Haritsu in
Sekai dai-hyakka-jiten (Heibonsha),
vol.4 (1963), p.168.

17 Two more writing-boxes by Ritsuō,
dated 1736 and 1746 respectively,
are in the Victoria and Albert
Museum in London; the one dated
1746 is illustrated in E.F. Strange,
Catalogue of Japanese Lacquer, p.1,
pl.x.

18 O. Kümmel, *Das Kunstgewerbe in
Japan*, p.48.

19 The time of origin of Japanese
cloisonné is a matter of controversy
(cf. Sir Harry Garner, *Chinese and
Japanese Cloisonné Enamels*; Garner
pleads for an extremely late dating).
Hirata Dōmin (1595-1646) was allegedly the first Japanese *cloisonné*
master of modern times; he is said to
have learnt the technique in Korea
and, later, to have worked for
Tokugawa Ieyasu. *Cloisonné*, however, had already made a modest
start in the Nara and Heian periods:
for example, in the Byōdō-in near
Kyōto.

20 Active ca 1751-1771.

21 Cf. B. von Ragué, 'Iizuka Tōyō, sein
Werk und seine Schule.'

22 The names Kyūhaku, Kyūzō, Kyūi
and Yasutada occur over a number of
generations, so the signatures alone
cannot be relied upon for the dating.

23 The bottommost of the compart-
ments is designed to hold sake,
therefore this box is a so-called
'hanami-jūbako,' which was designed to carry both food and rice
wine when the owner went cherry-
blossom viewing. The signature and
date are given on its old container

box.

24 Kimma is an engraving technique in which the black-lacquer ground is first painted over with a rubber-like solution. The decoration is engraved through this and, finally, the whole surface is covered with red lacquer. After it has dried, the object is washed down, thereby removing the layer of rubber together with the superimposed red lacquer. Accordingly, red lacquer is left only in the lines engraved through the rubber layer. Today the term 'zonsei-nuri' is used to describe a form of lacquer painting on a lacquer ground, the final stage of which involves engraving the outlines of the design and, usually, giving them additional emphasis by sprinkling in gold dust. Cf. B. von Ragué, 'Zur Technik ostasiatischer Lackarbeiten.'

25 Cf. B. von Ragué, 'Ein Schnitzlack-kōgō von Zōkoku,' which also has a picture of a dated kōgō by Zōkoku.

26 An inrō by Morimasa, decorated with a guri pattern and dated 1839, is in the Museum für Ostasiatische Kunst in Cologne.

27 This information, in addition to almost all the dates significant for lacquerwork of the laterr period, has been assembled by Rokkaku Shisui in the list of lacquermasters at the end of his book, *Tōyō shikkō-shi*.

CHAPTER 10

1 Cf. T. Maeda, 'Meiji Crafts.'

2 The Metropolitan Museum of Art in New York (Metrop. Mus. 36. 100. 165 a, b), for instance, has a tebako dated 1876 by Shōmin, which an inscription on the bottom of the box expressly describes as a copy of a tebako of the Kamakura period (in the possession of the Hachiman-gū in Kamakura).

3 Fenollosa came to Japan in 1878.

4 Wagner came to Japan in 1868. His

1875 report on the World Exhibition of 1873 in Vienna is the first foreign document to come out expressly in favour of the revival of traditional Japanese art.

5 Cf., for instance, a tebako in the Tōkyō National Museum, illustrated in *Nihon Bijutsu Zenshi*, vol. 27, fig. 1274.

6 In the Tōkyō National Museum.

7 For the paintings on paper, the Tōkyō Geijutsu Daigaku catalogue (*Zoshen-zuroku, kindai chōkoku kōgei*) gives the date 1872; cf. also *Makieshi-den nurishi-den*, vol. II, fig. 1274.

8 In more recent Japanese publications Taishin's date of birth is always given as 1825, in older sources sometimes as 1829 or 1837.

9 Besides Zeshin, the first members of the Academy included five painters, two sculptors, a metal and a textile artist.

10 The decision to found the Tōkyō National Museum (known at the time as the Imperial Museum) was taken in 1871; the building was completed in 1882. Like the National Museums in Kyōto and Nara (both founded in 1889) the National Museum in Tōkyō is supervised today by the National Committe for the Preservation of Cultural Properties, a division of the Ministry of Education.

11 A colour plate of a small container by Ikkokusai, shaped like a small, three-tiered basket and dated 1889, appears in K. Herberts, *Das Buch der ostasiatischen Lackkunst*, p. 143.

12 *Kusabana-chōjū-mon ko-tebako.*

13 For the modern masters named here and on the following pages, reference should be made to the generously illustrated catalogues of the annual exhibition, *Nihon dentō-kōgei-ten*, in particular to the jubilee edition of 1964, *Nihon dentō-kōgei-ten, jūshūnen kinen-zuroku*, which contains short biographies.

Bibliography

Akiyama Terukazu. 'Itsukushima-jinja shozō kogata hiōgi-e ni tsuite'
(Three painted small fans in the possession of the Itsukushima shrine),
Bijutsu Kenkyū (no 172, 1953)
– *Japanische Malerei*. Geneva 1961.
Arakawa Hirokazu. 'Kinen-mei Negoro-nuri ni tsuite' (On dated Negoro
lacquers), *Museum* (no 92, November 1958)
– 'Raden' (Lacquers with mother-of-pearl inlay), *Museum (no* 96, March
1959, and no 105, December 1959)
– 'Shoki makie-hin ni tsuite' (On early makie works), *Museum* (no 119,
February 1961)
– *Makie*. Atami 1962
Art, Japanese, in the Seattle Art Museum. Seattle 1960
Arts, Fine, of the Kamakura Period (catalogue). Kyōto National Museum 1961
Arts, Japanese, and Crafts in the Meiji era. Ueno Naoteru, ed. English adapta-
tion by Richard Lane. Tōkyō 1958
Bijutsu Kenkyū. The Journal of Art Studies. Tōkyō, 1932ff.
Boston Museum of Fine Arts. *Bulletin*. 1926
Boyer, M. *Japanese Export Lacquers from the* 17th Century in the National
Museum of Denmark. Copenhagen 1959
Bukkyō Bijutsu (periodical). Nara 1924ff.
Casal, U.A. 'Some Notes on the Sakazuki and on the Role of Sake Drinking
in Japan,' *The Transactions of the Asiatic Society of Japan*, second series
(vol.19, 1940)
– *Japanese Art Lacquers*. Monumenta Nipponica Monographs no 18. Tōkyō
1961
*Catalogue, An Illustrated, of Famous Masterpieces in the Collection of the Nezu Art
Museum* (Japanese). Tōkyō 1955
Chizawa Teiji. 'Kōrin and His Art,' *Oriental Art* (vol.VI, 1960)
Chūson-ji (Japanese with English summary). Tōkyō 1959
Color Design (Japanese periodical) (vol.6, nos 8 and 9, 1960)
'Exhibition of Japanese Old Art Treasures' in *Tōkyō Olympic Games*
(catalogue). Tōkyō National Museum 1964
Exhibition of National Treasures of Japan (catalogue). Tōkyō National Museum
1960
Feddersen, M. *Japanisches Kunstgewerbe*. Braunschweig 1960
Figgess, J. 'A Letter from theCourt of Yung-lo,' *Transactions of the Oriental
Ceramic Society* (1962-3)
Garner, Sir Harry. *Chinese and Japanese Cloisonné Enamels*. London 1962
– *Chinese and Associated Lacquer*. 1973
Geisteswelt, Chinesische. W. Speiser and G. Debon, eds. Baden-Baden 1957
Hammitzsch, H. 'Geschichte Japans,' *Abriss der Geschichte aussereuropäischer*

Bibliography   *Kulturen* (München-Wien, vol. 2, 1964)

Harada Jiro. *English Catalogue of Treasures in the Imperial Repository Shōsōin*. Tōkyō 1932

Hasumi Toshimitsu. *Japanische Plastik*. München 1961

Hayashiya Tatsusaburō. *Kōetsu* (Japanese). Tōkyō 1964

Herberts, K. *Das Buch der ostasiatischen Lackkunst*. Düsseldorf, 1959. English edition, *Oriental Lacquer: Art and Technique*. London 1962

Ijima Shunkei. See Kyusojin Noboru

Inoue Tadashi. 'Kasuga-taisha hirayanagui ni tsuite' (On a quiver in the possession of the Kasuga shrine), *Kokka* (no 867, June 1964)

Jenyns, S. and W. Watson. *Chinesische Kunst*. Fribourg 1963

Kaga-makie-ten (Catalogue of exhibition of Kaga lacquers). Kanazawa 1961

Kayamato Tojin. 'Tamamushi -zushi no baai. Nihon bijutsu ni oyoboshita Chōsen no eikyō' (The Tamamushi shrine. On Korean influences on Japanese art), *Museum* (no 23, February 1953)

Kobayashi Gō and Tsuneo Fujita. *Nihon bijutsu-shi-nempyō* (*Chronological table of Japanese art*). Tōkyō 1952

Kōgei-shiryō (Materials in applied art). Tōkyō Teishitsu Hakubutsukan. Fifth ed. Tōkyō 1905

Kokka. Tōkyō 1889ff.

Kokuhō-jiten (Encyclopedia of Japanese national treasures). Tōkyō 1961

Kokuhō tsurezure-ori Taima-mandara. Tōkyō 1963

Kōrin hyakka-zu (100 selected drawings by Kōrin). Kyōto; first ed. 1815; second ed. 1890

Kōrin shin-sen hyaku-ga (New selections of 100 drawings by Kōrin). No date or place of publication

Kümmel, O. *Das Kunstgewerbe in Japan*. Berlin 1911

– 'Die Chinesische Malerei im Kundaikwan Sayuchōki,' *Ostasiatische Zeitschrift* (vol. 1, 1912-13)

– *Ostasiatisches Gerät*. Berlin 1925

– 'Beiträge zur Künstlergeschichte,' *Ostasiatsiche Zeitschrift* (vol. 13, 1926)

– *Die Kunst Chinas, Japans und Koreas*. Wildpark-Potsdam 1929

Kusogami Noboru. See Kyusojin Noboru

Kyusojin Noboru and Shunkei Iijima. *Kokuhō Nishihongan-ji-hon sanjūrokunin-shū* (The Sanjūrokunin-shū Collection in the Nishihongan-ji). Tōkyō 1944

Lee, Sh. E. *Japanese Decorative Style*. Cleveland 1961

Lewin, B. *Aya und Hata*. Wiesbaden 1962

Maeda Taiji. *Japanese Decorative Design*. Tourist Library no 23. Tōkyō 1957

– 'Meiji Crafts,' section one, *Japanese Arts and Crafts in the Meiji Era*. Tōkyō 1958

Makieshi-den nurishi-den (Biographies of lacquer and gold-lacquer masters). Fourth ed. Tōkyō 1927

Meihōten zuroku (Catalogue of the exhibition of famous art treasures). Ishikawa-ken Bijutsukan. Kanazawa 1960

Miller, R. A. *Japanese Ceramics*. Tōkyō 1961

Minnich, H. B. *Japanese Costume*. Tōkyō 1963

Mizoguchi Saburō. 'Hiōgi-mon-chirashi makie-tebako' (Toilet case with decoration of irregularly disposed groups of hinoki-wood fans), *Museum* (no 11, February 1952)

– 'Hōō-emmon raden-karabitsu' (Chest with phoenix round pattern),

Museum (no 96, March 1959)
- 'Kingin-dei-e shippibako' (Dry-lacquer box with painted decoration in gold and silver), *Museum* (no 96, March 1959)
- 'Negoro-nuri no kanshō' (Toward appreciation of Negoro lacquers), *Negoronuri meihin-ten* (Catalogue of exhibition of major examples of Negoro lacquerwork). Tōkyō 1960
- 'Sumiyoshi makie-karabitsu' (Lacquer chest with Sumiyoshi decoration), *Museum* (no 111, June 1960)
Moran, Sh.F. 'Lacquer Writing-Box by Kōetsu,' *Oriental Art* (vol. VII, 1961)
Morita Kimiō. *Nihon no monyō* (Japanese patterns). Second ed. Tōkyō 1960
Murdoch, J. *A History of Japan*. Vols 1-3. London 1925-6
Museum (art magazine edited by the Tōkyō National Museum). Tōkyō 1951ff.
Nakagawa Sensaku. 'Iwayuru namban-karakusa no isshu ni tsuite' (On one type of so-called Namban scrolls), *Bijutsu Kenkyū* (no 159, 1950)
- 'Ko-Seto no monyō' (The decoration of Ko-seto ceramics), *Bijutsu Kenkyū* (no 201, 1958)
Nakano Masaki. 'Hōrai-mon-kagami' (Mirror with the Hōrai motif), *Museum* (no 66, September 1956)
National Treasures of Japan. The Commission for the Protection of Cultural Properties, eds. Series V. Tōkyō 1959
Negoronuri meihin-ten (Exhibition of major examples of Negoro lacquerwork. Catalogue). Tōkyō (Isetan department store) 1960
Nihon Bijutsu Taikei. Vols I-II. Tōkyō: Kodansha 1959-61
Nihon Bijutsu Zenshi. Vols 1, 2. Tōkyō: Bijutsu Shuppan-sha 1959, 1960
Nihon Bijutsu Zenshū. Vol. VI. Tōkyō: Kadokawa 1962
Nihon dentō-kōgei-ten, jūshūnen kinen-zuroku (Exhibition of traditional Japanese arts and crafts; illustrated catalogue to mark the tenth anniversary). Tōkyō 1964
Nihon kokuhō-ten (catalogue). See *Exhibition of National Tresaures of Japan*
Nihonshi jiten (Encyclopedia of Japanese history). Kohada Jun, ed. Tōkyō 1961
Nishimura Tei. *Namban-bijutsu* (Namban art). Tōkyō 1958
Okada Jō. 'Namban-yō makie-hin ni tsuite' (On makie works in Namban style), *Yamatoe-e kenkyū* (1942)
- 'Kuchinashi byōkin-raden-bon' (Tray with kuchinashi decoration painted in gold lacquer and inlaid with mother-of-pearl), *Museum* (no 6, September 1951)
- 'Ao-urushi-nuri chinkinbori umpo-mon kyō-hitsu' (Green lacquer sutra box with clouds and phoenixes in chinkinbori), *Bijutsu Kenkyū* (no 166, 1952)
- 'Mei-an-fu' (Report on famous saddles), *Museum* (no 29, August 1953)
- 'Momoyama-jidai no kōgei, sono dokusōsei ni tsuite' (On the originality of the applied art of the Momoyama period), *Museum* (no 34, January 1954)
- 'Bunken-jō yori mita Kōrai-raden' (Mother-of-pearl lacquers of the Kōrai period, considered from the point of view of written sources), *Bijutsu Kenkyū* (no 175, 1954), pp.42ff.
- 'Kinsei shoki shitsugei ni okeru Ri-chō-raden no eikyō' (The influence of Li mother-of-pearl lacquers on more recent [Japanese] lacquerwork), *Museum* (no 53, August 1955)

Bibliography

– 'Igarashi-makie ni tsuite' (On the lacquer works of the Igarashi masters), *Museum* (no 71, February 1957)
– 'Tsuishu to Kamakurabori' (Carved lacquer and Kamakurabori), *Museum* (no 80, November 1957)
– 'Shippibako' (Dry-lacquer boxes), *Museum* (no 161, August 1964)
Pageant of Japanese Art, Vol. 5. Tōkyō 1954
Paine, R.T., and A. Soper: *The Art and Architecture of Japan*. London 1955
v. Ragué, B. 'Zur Quellenkunde koreanischer Lacke mit Perlmutt-Einlagen,' *Oriens Extremus* (vol. 8: no 2, 1961)
– 'Zur Technik ostasiatischer Lackarbeiten,' *Nachrichten der Gesellschaft für Natur- und Völkerkunde Ostasiens* (no 92, 1962)
– 'Ein Schnitzlack-kōgō von Zōkoku,' *Nachrichten der Gesellschaft für Natur- und Völkerkunde Ostasiens* (no 93, 1963)
– 'Iizuka Tōyō, sein Werk und seine Schule,' *Oriens Extremus* (vol. 11: no 2, 1964)
– 'A Part of the Western Paradise,' The Cleveland Museum of Art *Bulletin* (vol. 53: no 1, 1966)
Rokkaku Shisui. *Tōyō-shikkō-shi* (History of Far Eastern lacquerwork). Second ed. Tōkyō 1960
Sanjūrokunin-shū, Nishihongan-ji-hon. Kyōto: Seigei-Shuppan 1920
Sekai Bijutsu Zenshū (World history of art). Vols 1-18. Tōkyō: Kadokawa 1961-5
Sekai dai-hyakka-jiten (Large encyclopedia of the world). Vols 1-33. Tōkyō: Heibonsha 1955-63
Shimura Senkichi and Goke Tadaomi. 'Hyakkō-hishō ni tsuite' (On the Hyakkō-hishō), *Museum* (no 158, May 1964)
Shisui. *See* Rokkaku Shisui
Shūko meikan (Catalogue of the Ōkura Shūkokan Museum, Tōkyō). Sh. Okazaki, ed. Tōkyō 1962
Soper, A. 'The rise of Yamato-e,' *The Art Bulletin* (vol. 24, no 4, 1942)
– *See* Paine, R.T.
Speiser, W. *Die Kunst Ostasiens*. Berlin 1946
– *Lackkunst in Ostasien*. Baden-Baden 1965
Strange, E.F. *Catalogue of Japanese Lacquer*. London: Victoria and Albert Museum 1924-5
Sullivan, M. *The Birth of Landscape Painting in China*. London 1962
Swann, P. *Art of China, Korea and Japan*. London 1963
Taima mandara zushi zufu. Tōkyō: Bunkazai Hogo Iinkai 1963
Tanaka Ichimatsu. *Momoyama no bi* (Art of the Momoyama period). Tōkyō 1960
Tanaka Shimbi. *Sanjūrokunin-shū* (The Sanjūrokunin-shū Collection in the Nishihongan-ji). Tōkyō 1960
Toji and Its Cultural Treasures. Tōkyō 1958
Tokugawa Bijutsukan (Illustrated catalogue of the Tokugawa Museum in Nagoya). Tōkyō 1962
Treasures from the Shōsōin. (Catalogue). Tōkyō National Museum 1959
Treasures of the Shōsōin. Vols. 1-3. Tōkyō: Asahi Shimbun-sha 1960-2
Ueno Naoaki and Manshichi Sakamoto. *Nihon chōkoku zuroku* (Japanese sculpture illustrated). Tōkyō 1957
Ueno Naoteru, ed. *Japanese Arts and Crafts in the Meiji Era*. English adaptation by Richard Lane. Tōkyō 1958

Umehara Sueji. 'Nihon ni okeru tasaiyū no yōki' (Polychrome glazed
  ceramics in Japan), *Bijutsu Kenkyū* (no 226, January 1963)
Volker, T. 'Japanese Export Lacquer,' *Oriental Art* (vol. 3, 1957)
Wang Yi-t'ung. *Official Relations between China and Japan 1368-1549*.
  Harvard-Yenching-Institute Studies IX. Cambridge, Mass. 1953
Warner, L. *The Enduring Art of Japan*. New York 1952
Watson, W. *See* Jenyns, S.
Wirgin, J. 'Some Ceramic Wares from Chi-chou,' The Museum of
  Far-Eastern Antiquities *Bulletin* (series 34, 1962), Stockholm
Yamanobe Tomoyuki. *Textiles: Design of Japan*. Vols 1-3. Osaka 1959-61
Yashiro Yukio. *Art Treasures of Japan*. 2 vols. Tōkyō 1960
Yoshida Gyō. 'Waga-makie-monyō ni arawaretaru bungakuteki yōsu ni
  tsuite' (On literary elements in Japanese lacquer decoration), *Hō-un* (no 8,
  1933), Kyōto
Yoshimura Motoo. *Kōdai-ji makie*. Kyōto 1971
– *Momoyama makie*. Kyōto 1971
Yoshino Tomio. *Japanese Lacquer Ware*. Tourist Library no 25. Tōkyō 1959
Yoshioka Michitaka. 'Katawaguruma makie-raden-tebako' (Toilet case with
  a motif of wheels in water), *Museum* (no 23, February 1953)

List of dated lacquer objects

(dates in square brackets indicate that the item is illustrated)

YEAR	OBJECT	PLATE NO.	PAGE
NARA PERIOD			
764	Quiver; Shōsōin		10
HEIAN PERIOD			
[919]	Manuscript box; Ninna-ji	14	27
1053	Hōō-dō, Byōdō-in		40
[1124]	Konjiki-dō, Chūson-ji	21 – 3	38 – 40
[ca 1131]	Quiver; Kasuga-taisha	26	44
1164	Red-lacquer food stand; private collection		255[34]
1165	Black-lacquer food stand; private collection		53
[1175]	Sutra chest; Nanatsu-dera	42	56
[1175]	Sutra boxes; Tōkyō National Museum	43	57
1183	Two red-lacquer sword cases; Itsukushima-jinja		54
[1183]	Two small chests with cranes; Itsukushima-jinja	40	54
KAMAKURA PERIOD			
[1228]	Toilet box; Rinnō-ji	48	66
[1242]	Doors of the Mandara shrine; Taima-dera	49	67
[1243]	Base of the Mandara shrine; Taima-dera	50	68
1261	Negoro bowl; private collection		255[34]
1262	Negoro tray; private collection		255[34]
1263	Red-lacquer portable shrine; Sugimoto-jinja, Kōchi province		
1285	Black-lacquer shrine; Ryōzan-ji, Nara province		
1298	Negoro plates, fourteen items; Tōdai-ji and private collections		255[34]
1305	Two red-lacquer wooden shields; Taishin-jinja		255[34]
[1307]	Three Negoro vegetable buckets; private collection	69	87
1307	Three Negoro trays; private collection		255[34]
1312	Altar base; western pagoda, Koyasan		
[1330]	Two oil jars; Tōdai-ji	68	86
1332	Large red-lacquer basin; private collection		255[34]

YEAR	OBJECT	PLATE NO.	PAGE

NAMBOKUCHŌ PERIOD

1338	Black-lacquer food stand; Ōgami-jinja		255²
1338	Two hand-basins; Hōryū-ji		255²
[1342]	Box with polypodia; Kongōbu-ji	70	92
1346	Negoro tray; Tōkyō Geijutsu Daigaku		255²
[1357]	Sumiyoshi chest; Tōkyō National Museum	73	95
1370	Black-lacquer sacrificial table; Sata-jinja		255²
1373	Seven red-lacquer food stands; Kisui-in		255²
[1382]	Small rosary box; Tō-ji	78	101
1391	Red-lacquer bowl; Tōkyō National Museum		255²

MUROMACHI PERIOD

1395	Three vegetable containers; Tōdai-ji and private collection		258⁵³
1395	Three oil containers; Tōdai-ji and private collection		258⁵³
[1409]	Sutra box; Biwako Bunka-kan	79	101
1424	Two red-lacquer food stands; private collection		258⁵³
1426	Toilet box; Kitano Temman-gū		
1427	Two hand-basins; Tōdai-ji		258⁵³
1428	Negoro tray; private collection		258⁵³
1428	Red-lacquer table with carving; Kenchō-ji		256¹⁷
1432	Red-lacquer table with carving; Gan-ō-ji		256¹⁷
[1445]	Mirror box; Atsuta-jinja	85	106
1447	Small Negoro table; private collection		258⁵³
1452	Black-lacquer lamp stand; Tōkyō National Museum		258⁵³
1455	Two red-lacquer plates; Saidai-ji and Tokiwayama-bunko		258⁵³
1457	Five small red-lacquer plates; Masumida-jinja		258⁵³
1457	Eight Negoro trays; Masumida-jinja		258⁵³
1457	Seven Negoro trays; Masumida-jinja		258⁵³
1465	Black-lacquer writing-table and writing-box; Kumano hongū		258⁵³
[1467]	Sacrificial table; Kasuga-taisha	80	102
1478	Tray on four feet; private collection		258⁵³
1478	Red-lacquer tray; private collection		258⁵³
1480	Black-lacquer shrine; Nara National Museum		258⁵³
[1481]	Kamakurabori-kōgō; Kinren-ji	76	99
1482	Red-lacquer food stand; private collection		258⁵³
[ca 1515]	Small incense box; Tōkyō Geijutsu Daigaku	98	125
[1516]	Saddle; private collection	99	126
1523	Toilet box; Iihiraki-jinja (Kyūshū)		
1528	Negoro tray; private collection		259⁸

YEAR	OBJECT	PLATE NO.	PAGE
1534	Red-lacquer brazier; private collection		259[8]
1548	Small bowl; S.Y. Lee, Tōkyō		259[8]
[1564]	Votive tablet; Chūson-ji	107	133
1564	Small box; Chūson-ji		133
1564	Kamakurabori-kōgō; Chion-in		136
[1565]	Kamakurabori-kōgō; Enkaku-ji	110	137

MOMOYAMA PERIOD

1568	Four bowls of different sizes; private collection		259[8]
1569	Negoro food stand; private collection		259[8]
[1577]	Saddle and stirrups; Tōkyō National Museum	111	143
[1596]	Door panels on the Hideyoshi shrine; Kōdai-ji	121	151
[1602]	Chest with ivy decoration; Itsukushima-jinja	132	164

EDO PERIOD

1619	Flute case; formerly Berlin State Museums		262[7]
[1619]	Sumiaka; Sugau Ishibe-jinja	142	175
1630	Negoro food stand; private collection		259[8]
[1639]	Kōami Nagashige: Hatsune-sandana; Reimeikai and Tokugawa Museum, Nagoya	156	189
1646	Negoro food stand; Kyōto Bijutsu Daigaku		259[8]
1654	Negoro food stand; Yoshimizu-in		259[8]
1656	Saddle and stirrups; Kanazawa, Seisonkaku		195
1663	Black-lacquer writing-box; Tōdai-ji		259[8]
1664	Negoro food stand; private collection		259[8]
1666	Black-lacquer food stand; private collection		259[8]
1667	Tatsuke Chōbei: writing-table and writing-box; Izumo-taisha		263[20]
1710	Shiomi Masanari: inrō; formerly Berlin State Museums		208
[1720]	Ritsuō: writing-box; Tōkyō National Museum	170	212
[1734]	Saddle and stirrups; Tōkyō National Museum	169	211
1736	Ritsuō: writing-box; Victoria and Albert Museum in London		264[17]
1746	Ritsuō: writing-box; Victoria and Albert Museum in London		264[17]
1770	Small flat bowl; private collection		259[8]
[1775]	Iizuka Tōyō; writing-box and paper box; Kyōto, Gosho	172,172a	214,215
[1817]	Tachi Gasui: picnic box; private collection	175	220
1839	Gamō Morimasa: inrō; Museum für Ostasiatische Kunst, Cologne		265[26]
1851	Tamakaji Zōkoku: kōgō; private collection		265[25]

YEAR	OBJECT	PLATE NO.	PAGE

MEIJI AND TAISHŌ PERIODS

YEAR	OBJECT	PLATE NO.	PAGE
1876	Ogawa Shōmin: writing-box; Metropolitan Museum of Art, New York		265^2
1881	Shibata Zeshin: lacquer painting; Tōkyō National Museum		229
[1886]	Shibata Zeshin: writing-box; Metropolitan Museum of Art, New York	182	229,230
1889	Ikkokusai: small basket with lacquer decoration; Dr Kurt Herberts, Wuppertal		265^{11}
[1919]	Matsuda Gonroku: covered box; Tōkyō Geijutsu Daigaku	187	238

PRESENT

YEAR	OBJECT	PLATE NO.	PAGE
[1962]	Namba Jinsai: table	194	243
[1963]	Masumura Mashiki: dry-lacquer bowl; Berlin State Museums, Museum of Far Eastern Art	192	242
[1963]	Fujii Kambun: writing-box	196	244
[1963]	Terai Naoji: screen	197	244
[1964]	Okabe Keishō: small incense box	193	243
[1964]	Ōba Shōgyo: box	195	244

Glossary of more common Japanese descriptive terms

aikuchi-zukuri   flush-fitting lid
awasebuta   flush-fitting lid
bako   *see* hako
bentōbako   breakfast-box
bon   tray, flat bowl
bundai   writing-table
bunko   manuscript box
gōsu   small container
gura   *see* kura
hako   box
hashira   pillar
hirayanagui   (flat) quiver
hōjubako   jewel case
irizumi   inverted corners
inrōbuta   flush-fitting lid
inrō   small container for vermilion
   ink pad or medicine
jikirō   food container
jimbako   box for incense wood
jūbako   food container in several
   sections
kabusebuta   overlapping lid
kagamibako   mirror box
kakego   interior box
kakesuzuri   small portable chest
   with inkstone
karabitsu   chest
kashibako   box for pastries
kesabako   stole box
kobako   small box
kōbako   incense box
kōgō   small incense box
kōisu   folding chair
kura   saddle
kushibako   comb box
kutsubako   shoe box
kyōbako   sutra box
kyōshoku   arm-rest

mikoshi   portable shrine
natsume   specific type of tea caddy
obibako   girdle box
oi   wooden rucksack
okibuta   flat lid in the form of a
   board
raiban   priest's seat
sagedansu   small portable
   cabinet-cupboard
sagejū   food container consisting of
   several parts with carrying frame
sai-oke   vegetable container
sakazuki   sake bowl
sammaibon   small sacrificial table
sasshibako   manuscript box
saya   sword scabbard
seiheibako   pyx
shumidan   base of altar or shrine
suebako   open box for priest's
   robes
sumikiri   bevelled corners
sumimaru   rounded-off corners
suzuribako   writing-box
tabikushige   comb case for travel
takatsuki   food stand in the form of
   a small low table
tana   shelf, cupboard
tansu   small portable chest with
   drawer
tantōbako   sword case
tebako   toilet box
tobira   door panels
tōdai   lamp stand
yakumi-tsubo   spice container
yu-oke   hot water jug
zushi   cupboard, cabinet
zushidana   shelf with sliding doors

Japanese names and
technical terms with their corresponding
written characters

abumi	鐙
aikuchi-zukuri	会い口作り
Aizu-nuri	會津塗
Akaji Yūsai	赤地友哉
Akatsuka Jitoku	赤塚自得
an	案
aogai	青貝
Aogai Chōbei	青貝長兵衛
aokin	青金
Asano Sōsaburō	浅野惣三郎
Asata Shinsui	浅田真水
ashide-e	葦手絵
awabi	鮑
awasebuta	合せ蓋
ban-e	蛮絵
bentōbako	弁当箱
boku-shitsu	墨漆
bon	盆
bunko	文庫
byakurō	白臘
chaoke	茶桶
chinkinbori	沈金彫
chiri-i	塵居
chirimaki	塵蒔
Chōbei see Aogai Chōbei	
Chōsei (Chang Ch'eng)	張成
daitai-bori	大体彫
dana see tana	
dōbari	胴張
Dōho see Igarashi Dōho	
dōjime	胴緯
do-shitsu	土漆
egaki-kimma	描蒟醬
e-nashiji	絵梨子地

Japanese names and technical terms

fubuki	吹雪
fuchaku-hō	付着法
Fujii Kambun	藤井観文
Fujikawa Shunzō	藤川舜造
Fujiwara Sadatsune	藤原貞経
fusenryō-mon	浮線綾紋
Gamō Morimasa	蒲生盛雅
gōsu	合子
gura *see* kura	
guri	曲輪
hana-ikada	花筏
Hara Yōyūsai	原羊遊齋
harigaki	針描
Haritsu-zaiku	破笠細工
harinuki	はりぬき
haritsuke-hō	貼付法
heidatsu	平脱
Hidehira-wan	秀衡椀
Higashiyama-makie	東山蒔絵
hiramakie	平蒔絵
hirame	平目
hirayanagui	平胡籙
hōjubako	宝珠箱
Honami Kōetsu	本阿弥光悦
hōsōge	宝相華
hyōmon	平文
Iemon	井右衛門
Iizuka Tōyō	飯塚桃葉
Igarashi Dōho	五十嵐道甫
Igarashi Shinsai	｜｜｜信齋
Igarashi Shōbei	｜｜｜庄兵衛
Igarashi Sōbei	｜｜｜宗兵衛
Igarashi Tajirō	｜｜｜他次郎
Igarashi Tarōbei	｜｜｜太郎兵衛
ikakeji	沃懸地
Ikeda Gembei	池田源兵衛
Ikeda Gentarō	｜｜源太郎
Ikeda Ikkokusai	｜｜一國齋
Ikeda Taishin	｜｜泰真
Inami Kirokusai	井波喜六斉
inrō	印籠
irizumi	入角
iro-togidashi	色研出
Isoi Joshin	磯井如真

Itchō *see* Kawanobe Itchō	
Jigoemon	治五右衛門
jikirō	食籠
jimbako	沈箱
Jogahana-nuri	城端塗
Jōken-in-jidai-mono	常憲院時代物
jūbako	重箱
jūyō mukei-bunkazai hojisha	重要無形文化財保持者
kabusebuta	被せ蓋
Kafuku-sha	避福社
kagamibako	鏡箱
Kajikawa Hikobei	梶川彦兵衛
Kajikawa Kyūjirō	梶川久次郎
kakego	懸子
kakesuzuri	懸硯
kamaboko-gata	かまぼこ型
Kamakurabori	鎌倉彫
kanagai	金貝
kannyū-hō	嵌入法
kanshitsu	乾漆
karabitsu	唐櫃
kashibako	菓子箱
Kawakubo Kazu	川窪和
Kawanobe Itchō	川之辺一朝
Kawari-nuri	変塗
Kawatarō	川太郎
kesabako	袈裟箱
keshi-makie	消蒔絵
Kimma-nuri	蒟醤塗
Kimura Hyōsai	木村表斎
kingindei-e	金銀泥絵
kingin-e	金銀絵
kinrinji	金輪寺形
kirigane	切金
Kitagawa	喜多川
kōaka	甲赤
Kōami Chōan	幸阿弥長晏
Kōami Chōgen	｜｜｜長玄
Kōami Kyūjirō	｜｜｜久次郎
Kōami Michikiyo	｜｜｜道清
Kōami Michinaga	｜｜｜道長
Kōami Nagafusa	｜｜｜長房
Kōami Nagashige	｜｜｜長重
Kōami Nagasuku	｜｜｜長救

Kōami Nagayasu	幸阿弥長晏
Kōami Sōhaku	｜｜｜宗伯
kobako	小箱
kōbako	香箱
Kōdai-ji-makie	高台寺蒔絵
kodō	鼓胴
Kōetsu *see* Honami Kōetsu	
kōgō	香合
kōisu	交椅
kōka-ryokuyō	紅花綠葉
Koma Kansai	古満寛哉
Koma Kyoryū	｜｜巨柳
Koma Kyūhaku	｜｜休伯
Koma Kyūi	｜｜休意
Koma Yasuaki	｜｜安章
Koma Yasutada	古満安匡
Komin *see* Nakayama Komin	
Kōmo Tōzan	河面冬山
kōmori	甲盤
Kōrin *see* Ogata Kōrin	
Kundaikan sayu chōki	君臺觀左右帳記
kura	鞍
Kuroda Tatsuaki	黒田辰秋
kurome	くろめ
kushibako	櫛箱
kutsubako	靴箱
kuyō	九曜
kyōbako	経箱
kyōshoku	挾軾
Mae Taihō	前大峰
makibokashi	蒔暈
makie	蒔絵
maki-hanashi	蒔放
makkinru	末金鏤
maru-fun	丸粉
Masumura Mashiki	増村益城
Masazane *see* Shiomi Masanari	
Matsuda Gonroku	松田権六
Matsunami Hoshin	松波保真
Meigetsu-wan	明月椀
mikoshi	神輿
Mimi no Sukune	三見宿弥
mitamaya	靈屋
mitsuda-e	密陀絵

mitsudasō	密陀僧
mitsu-wan	三つ椀
Miura Meihō	三浦明峰
Mizoguchi Saburō	溝口三郎
Mochizuki Hanzan	望月半山
mokume-nuri	木目塗
Monnyū	門入
Nagata Yūji	永田友治
nakatsugi	中次
Nakayama Komin	中山胡民
Namba Jinsai	難波仁斉
namban-karakusa	南蛮唐草
namban-makie	南蛮蒔絵
nashiji	梨子地
natsume	棗
negoro-nuri	根来塗
Niki Seihō	二木成抱
nindō-karakusa	忍冬唐草
Ninomiya Tōtei	二宮桃亭
Noda Minoru	野田稔
Oba Shōgyo	太場松魚
Ōgaki Masakuni	大垣昌訓
Ogata Kōrin	尾形光琳
Ogawa Haritsu	小川破笠
Ogawa Shōmin	小川松民
oi	笈
Okabe Keishō	岡部敬象
Ōki Toyosuke	大喜豊助
okibuta	置蓋
Okude Jusen	奥出寿泉
oshiroitoki	白粉解
Ōta Kazuko	太田加津子
Otomaru Hiroshi	音丸寛
Otomaru Jun	｜｜淳
Otomaru Kaoru	｜｜謙
Otomaru Kōdō	｜｜耕堂
raden	螺鈿
raiban	礼盤
rinkagata	輪花形
Ritsuō	笠翁
Rokkaku Shisui	六角紫水
ryōshibako	料紙箱
sabi	錆
sabiage-takamakie	錆上高蒔絵

sagedansu	提箪笥
sagejū	提重
sakazuki	杯
sandana	三棚
Sano Chōkan	佐野長寛
Sasada Getsugyō	笹田月暁
sasshibako	冊子箱
Sawada Jisaku	沢田次作
Sawada Sōtaku	沢田宗沢
saya-nuri	鞘塗
seiheibako	聖餅箱
Shami Kūgaku	沙弥空覚
Shibata Zeshin	柴田是真
Shibayama Yasumasa	芝山易政
shibui	渋い
Shiihara Ichidayu	椎原市太夫
Shimizu Genjirō	清水源四郎
Shimizu Kamon	｜｜嘉門
Shimizu Kyūbei	｜｜九兵衛
Shinjirō	新次郎
Shiomi Masanari	塩見政誠
shippi	漆皮
Shirayama Shōsai	白山松哉
shirifukurami	尻膨
shishiai-makie	肉合蒔絵
Shōmin *see* Ogawa Shōmin	
shumidan	須弥壇
Shunkei-nuri	春慶塗
Shunshō *see* Yamamoto Shunshō	
soku	壌
soku-nuri	壌塗
Somada Kiyosuke	梲田清輔
suebako	居箱
sugorokuban	双六盤
suhama	洲浜
sumi-aka	角赤
sumie-togidashi	墨絵研出
sumikiri	角切
sumimaru	角丸
suzuribako	硯箱
tabi-kushige	旅櫛笥
Tachi Gasui	城雅水
Tadokoro Hōsai	田所芳哉
Taguchi Yoshikuni	田口善国

Taishin *see* Ikeda Taishin	
takamakie	高蒔絵
Takano Shōzan	高野松山
takatsuki	高坏
Tamakaji Zōkoku	玉楮象谷
tana	棚
Tanida Chūbei	谷田忠兵衛
tansu	簞笥
tantōbako	短刀箱
Tate Junsuke	舘順助
Tatsuke Chōbei	田[附]付長兵衛
tebako	手箱
tekitō	笛筒
Terai Naoji	寺井直次
tobira	扉
tōdai	灯台
togidashi	研出
Tōtei *see* Ninomiya Tōtei	
Tōyō *see* Iizuka Tōyō	
Tsuchida Sōetsu	土田宗悦
Tsugaru-nuri	津輕塗
tsuikoku	堆黒
tsuishu	堆朱
Tsuishu Chōei	堆朱長英
Tsuishu Chōhan	｜｜長繁
Tsuishu Chōhō	｜｜長邦
Tsuishu Chōin	｜｜長韻
Tsuishu Chōjū	｜｜長充
Tsuishu Chōkin	｜｜長均
Tsuishu Chōri	｜｜長利
Tsuishu Chōryū	｜｜長隆
Tsuishu Chōsei	｜｜長盛
Tsuishu Chōshi	｜｜長嗣
Tsuishu Chōshin	｜｜長親
Tsuishu Chōshin	｜｜長辰
Tsuishu Chōshū	｜｜長宗
Tsuishu Chōtei	｜｜長貞
Tsuishu Chōze	｜｜長是
Tsuishu Chōzen	｜｜長善
Tsuishu Dewa	｜｜出羽
Tsuishu Heijirō	｜｜平十郎
Tsuishu Jūzaemon	｜｜十左衛門
Tsuishu Kunihei	｜｜國平
Tsuishu Yajirōzaemon	｜｜屋治郎左衛門

Tsuishu Yonzei	堆朱養清
Tsuishu Yōsei	∣∣楊成
Tsuji Hokuyōsai	辻北陽斉
tsukegaki	付描
tsukue	机
tsuyakeshi	艶消
Uematsu Hōbi	植松抱美
urushibe	漆部
urushi-e	漆絵
uta-e	歌絵
wabi	佗
Wakaemon	若右衛門
Wakasa-nuri	若狭塗
warigai	割貝
yakigane	燒金
yakitsubo	薬壺
yakki	薬器
yakugai	夜久貝
yakumi-tsubo	薬味壺
Yamada Jōka	山田常嘉
Yamamoto Shunshō	山本春正
Yamanaga Kōho	山永光甫
Yamazaki Katsutarō	山崎覚太郎
yasuri-fun	鑢粉
Yōmo (Yang Mao)	楊茂
Yoneda Magoroku	米田孫六
Yōsei	楊成
Yoshida Baidō	吉田楳堂
Yoshida Genjūrō	吉田源十郎
yotsu-wan	四つ椀
Yōyūsai *see* Hara Yōyūsai	
yūgen	幽玄
Yūji-age	友治上
yu-oke	湯桶
yushoku	油色
zen	膳
Zeshin *see* Shibata Zeshin	
Zōkoku *see* Tamakaji Zōkoku	
Zonsei-nuri	存星塗
zushi	厨子
zushi-dana	厨子棚

Period table

Jōmon period ca 250 BC
Yayoi period ca 250 BC–250 AD
Kofun (tumulus) period ca 250–552
Asuka and Hakuhō period 552–710
Nara period 710–794
Heian period 794–1185
Kamakura period 1185–1333

Nambokuchō period 1333–1392
Muromachi period 1392–1568
Momoyama period 1568–1615
Edo period 1615–1868
Meiji period 1868–1912
Taishō period 1912–1926
Shōwa period 1926–

Japanese provinces

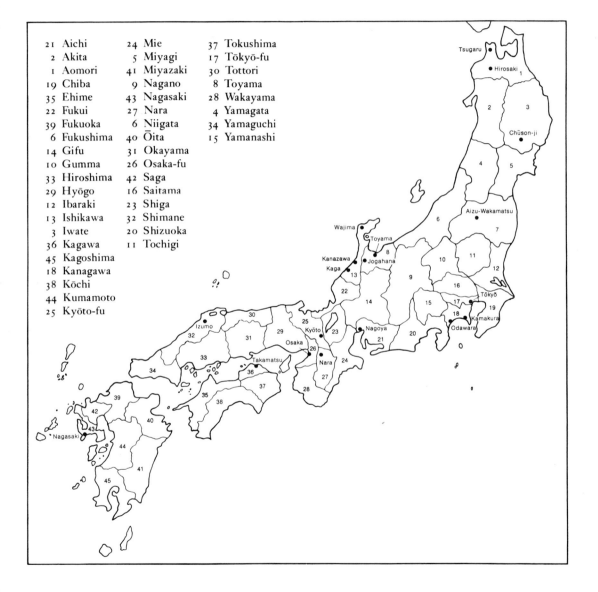

21 Aichi
2 Akita
1 Aomori
19 Chiba
35 Ehime
22 Fukui
39 Fukuoka
6 Fukushima
14 Gifu
10 Gumma
33 Hiroshima
29 Hyōgo
12 Ibaraki
13 Ishikawa
3 Iwate
36 Kagawa
45 Kagoshima
18 Kanagawa
38 Kōchi
44 Kumamoto
25 Kyōto-fu

24 Mie
5 Miyagi
41 Miyazaki
9 Nagano
43 Nagasaki
27 Nara
6 Niigata
40 Ōita
31 Okayama
26 Osaka-fu
42 Saga
16 Saitama
23 Shiga
32 Shimane
20 Shizuoka
11 Tochigi

37 Tokushima
17 Tōkyō-fu
30 Tottori
8 Toyama
28 Wakayama
4 Yamagata
34 Yamaguchi
15 Yamanashi

Index

Regular numerals indicate page numbers, numerals in *italics* the numbers of plates. Names of lacquer masters appear in upper and lower caps, names of objects in *italics*. Only some of the Notes are indexed; 256 (²¹), for instance, directs the reader to Note (²¹) on page 256.

Adams, William 261 (²¹)
aikuchi-zukuri s. awasebuta
Aizu-bon 197
Aizu-nuri 197
Aizu-Wakamatsu 196-197, 199
AKAJI YŪSAI 246, *199*
AKATSUKA JITOKU 236, 237
aki no nanakusa 256 (²¹)
Akikusa makie-bunko 149, 153, *115*
Akikusa makie-kasho-tansu 149, *116*
Akikusa makie-yu-oke 149-150, *117*
Akino makie-tebako 103-104, *81, 82*
Akino ni shika makie-tebako 63-64, 75, 81, *45, 46*
Akishino-dera (Nara) 7
Akita (province) 4
amber 14
Ambras (Coll.) 158
Amida Raigō 65
Ampuku-ji (Ōsaka) 193, *160*
Annam 14
ANSHO s. KOMA KYUHAKU II.
Antoku (Emperor) 54
aogai 112, 125, 133, 138, 197, 204, 233
AOGAI CHŌBEI 197
aogai-nuri 197
aokin 32, 46, 59, 75
Aomori (province) 4, 198
Arakawa Hirokazu 46
arm rest (Fujita Museum, Ōsaka) s. *Kachō makie kyōshoku*
ASANO SŌSABURŌ 234
ASATA SHINSUI 245
Ashi no bo makie-gura 143, *111*
ashide-e 88, 254 (²³) s. also: calligraphy as decoration; uta-e

Ashikaga Takauji 90
Ashikaga Yoshimasa 90, 97, 112, 113, 116, 118, 124, 166, 195
Ashikaga Yoshimitsu 90, 97
Ashikaga Yoshinori 111
Ashimori-shi (place) 243
Atami-Museum 178, *145, 148*
Atsuta-jinja (Nagoya) 105, *85*
autumn field tebako (Izumo-taisha) s. *Akino ni shika makie-tebako* 45, 46
Awabi (island) 66
awabi shells 158, *177*
awasebuta 113, 253 (³³) s. also lid forms

Bälz, Erwin von 232
BAIDO s. YOSHIDA BAIDŌ
Baigetsu makie-bundai 106, 108, 115, 127, 132, *86*
Baigetsu makie-tebako 94-96, 102, *74*
ban-e 35, 252 (¹⁸)
Bashō 202, 213
beaded border line 13, 18, 23, 29, 158
Berlin State Museums 208, *184, 192*
Biwako Bunkakan (Shiga province) 79
Biwako makie-suzuribako s. *Hirasan makie-suzuribako* 167
black lacquer (base) 4, 10, 27, 28, 53, 59, 75, 84, 100, 107, 134, 135, 145, 154, 171, 185, 192, 195, 204, 213, 217
Bodaiju makie-kōgō 193, *160*
boku-shitsu 18
Borneo 154
Boston Museum of Fine Arts 65, 237
Botan Kamakurabori-kōgō 98, 99, *75*

Index

Botan raden-gura 51, 37
Buddhism 5, 7, 56, 107, 247 (⁷)
Budō makie-seiheibako 156, 124, 125
Budō-risu makie jikirō 171, 136
Budō urushi-e-bon 141
Bunkazai Hogo Iin-kai (Tōkyō) 4, 239,
    1, 27, 191
BUNKIDŌ s. FUJIKAWA SHUNZŌ
Burma 222
Butsu-kudoku makie kyōbako 26, 28, 33,
    65, 19
butterfly tebako s. Cho raden-makie
    tebako 54
byakurō (-fun) 49
Byōdō-in 40, 41

calligraphy as decoration 77, 80, 88, 94,
    103, 115, 118, 120, 180, 202.
    s. also: ashide-e; uta-e
carved lacquer 96-97, 135, 138, 166,
    168, 213, 220, 222, 233, 236-237,
    239, 242
carved lacquer, Chinese 96-99,
    109-111, 167-168, 235
ceramics 46, 86, 90, 153, 154, 163, 184,
    185, 191, 213, 222
CHANG CH'ENG 167
charcoal powder 26
ch'iang-chin 110, 111
Chidori makie-jimbako 124, 98
Chikamatsu 202
China, influence on Japanese
    lacquerwork 5, 14, 18, 22, 32, 35,
    58, 85-88, 91, 93, 97, 99, 102-,
    111-112, 114-115, 121, 138-139,
    155, 167, 171, 174, 197, 213-214 s.
    also: China, lacquerwork; carved
    lacquer, Chinese
China, lacquerwork 11-12, 14, 15, 17,
    91, 96, 99, 109-111, 135-137, 197,
    219
chinkinbori 110-, 138, 197, 198, 219,
    234, 238, 239, 245, 257 (³⁷)
Chion-in (Kyōto) 136
chiri-i 24, 28, 113
chirimaki 249 (³¹)
Chō raden-makie tebako 73-74, 78, 81, 54
CHŌBEI s. TATSUKE CHŌBEI and
    AOGAI CHŌBEI
CHŌEI 261 (²⁹)

CHŌHAN 261 (²⁹)
CHŌHŌ 261 (²⁹)
CHŌIN 261 (²⁹)
CHŌJŪ 261 (²⁹)
CHŌKIN 261 (²⁹)
CHŌRI 261 (²⁹)
CHŌRYŪ 261 (²⁹)
CHŌSEI s. CHANG CH'ENG
CHŌSEI 261 (²⁹)
Chōseiden-makie-tebako 254 (²⁴)
CHŌSHI 261 (²⁹)
CHŌSHIN 261 (²⁹)
CHŌSHŪ 261 (²⁹)
CHŌSHŪ (Nagamune)
    s. TSUISHU HEIJIRŌ
CHŌTEI 261 (²⁹)
CHŌZE 261 (²⁹)
CHŌZEN 261 (²⁹)
Chrysanthemum writing-box s.
    Magaki-kiku raden-ikakeji-suzuribako,
    52
CHŪBEI s. TANIDA CHŪBEI
Chūson-ji (Iwate province) 40-41
Chūson-ji (Iwate province)
    Konjiki-dō 40-43, 58, 59, 65, 71,
    21-23
circular patterns 12, 18, 22, 47, 50, 59,
    74, 76, 169
Cleveland Museum of Art 65, 47
Cloisonné 214
colour contrast and gradation 32, 46,
    50, 58, 62, 65, 75, 79, 88, 154, 171,
    174, 178, 188, 190, 191, 195, 213,
    215
coloured lacquers, coloured-lacquer
    painting 5, 173, 174, 197-198, 214,
    219-220, 228, 233, 235, 238, 246,
    247 (⁸)
coloured makie 188
coloured togidashi 208, 216-217
coloured woodcut 217
colours, colour effects 13, 14, 18, 27,
    46, 79, 88, 137, 154, 171
comb box s. kushibako
copies 207, 227, 228, 237, 262 (⁸), 265 (²)
    s. also: forgeries
coral inlays 190, 195, 212
Daigo-ji (Kyōto) 72, 152
Dainichi Nyorai 41
daitai-bori 251 (⁸)

Date Masamune 161
dōbari 59, 64, 95, 114
DŌHO s. IGARASHI DŌHO
domed lids s. kōmori
do-shitsu 18
dry-lacquer s. kanshitsu; shippi
dust ledge, dust place s. chiri-i
Dutch 142, 154, 155

Echizen-bori 256 (¹³)
Edo 165, 186, 187, 190, 193, 194, 197,
    198-199, 202, 209, 211, 212, 213,
    214, 215, 216, 219, 222
egaki-kimma 142, 154, 155
Eisai 86
Eisei Bunko s. Tōkyō, Eisei Bunko
Eitoku s. Kanō Eitoku
emery 26
e-nashiji 64, 154, 155, 171
'Engi-gyoki' 26
English 155
Enkaku-ji (Kamakura) 96, 137, *110, 135*
Enryaku-ji (Shiga province) *17, 20*
export lacquers 154, 155, 159

Fang Shao 249 (²⁷)
Fenollosa, E.F. 228
Ferdinand (Archduke of Tyrol) 158
figurative representations 65, 100,
    116-117
forgeries 228, 262 (⁸)
    s. also: copies
fuchaku-hō 251 (⁷)
Fūdō Myōō 56
Fuji makie-gura-abumi 212, *169*
FUJII KAMBUN 245, *196*
FUJIKAWA SHUNZŌ 235
Fujita-Museum s. Ōsaka,
    Fujita-Museum
Fujiwara Hidehira 251 (²)
Fujiwara Kiyohira 40
Fujiwara Masatsune 116
Fujiwara Motohira 251 (²)
FUJIWARA SADATSUNE 67
Fujiwara no Tadahiro 250 (¹⁴)
Fujiwara Yorinaga 251 (¹¹)
Fujiwara Yoritsune 67
Fukui (province) 198
Fukushima (province) 196
Funabashi makie-suzuribako (Kōetsu)

179-181, *147*
Furuta Oribe 148, 179, 184
Fusenryō-mon makie-tebako 77, 81, 57
Fushimi Castle 142, 150, 152

GAMŌ MORIMASA 222
Gamō Ujisato 196
Gendai Kōgei Bijutsu-ka Kyōkai 239
Genji Yūgao tebako 129-130, *104*
'Genji-monogatari' 26, 35, 129, 183,
    189
GENJŪRŌ s. YOSHIDA GENJŪRŌ
Gifu (province) 241
Gin-heidatsu hakkaku kagamibako 11, 6
Giron 160
gold dust 15, 17, 25, 32, 57, 59, 62, 64,
    75, 107, 173, 211, 250 (¹⁶)
gold dust, various forms of 26, 32, 44,
    46, 62, 78, 88, 197, 208, 209, 228,
    233, 253 (¹)
gold filings s. yasuri-fun
gold inlays s. heidatsu; hyōmon;
    kanagai
gold lacquer 40, 53, 59, 75, 88, 180,
    185, 192, 219
    s. also: ikakeji; nashiji
gold leaf 41, 135, 164
gold painting on lacquer s. kingin-e
GONROKU s. MATSUDA GONROKU
Goshirakawa (Emperor) 72
Gosho (Kyōto) *172*
Gosho-kuruma suzuribako 192, *159*
Gotō-Kenjō 189-190
Gotō Teijō 195
Go-Tsuchimikado (Emperor) 124
gouache painting 15
Goyōzei (Emperor) 145
guri 136, 222

Hachijō-in (Princess) 57
Hachiman-gū (Wakamiya province) 59
Hachinoe (place) 4
Hachisuka 214
Hagi raden-gura 51, *36*
Hakkakukei-kashiki (Shirayama Shosai)
    233, *185*
Hamamatsu makie-bundai 105-106, *84*
Hamburg, Museum für Kunst und
    Gewerbe 191, *157*

Index

Hana no Shirakawa-suzuribako 116, 139, *94*

Hanabusa Itchō 213

hana-ikada 151

hanami-jūbako 264 ([23])

Hannya Bosatsu 57

HANZAN s. MOCHIZUKI HANZAN

HARA YŌYŪSAI 208, 222, 227, *179*

harigaki 100, 120, 154

harinuki 241

haritsuke-hō 251 ([7])

Haritsu-zaiku 213

Hasu-karakusa makie-kyōbako 26, 28, 31, 32, *18*

Hatsune makie-sandana (Kōami Nagashige) 190, 193, 195, *156*

Hatsune makie-hibachi 258 ([50])

heidatsu 11, 13, 17

heijin 27, 28, 32, 41, 44, 50, 59, 69, 75

HEIJIRŌ s. TSUISHU HEIJIRŌ

'Heikenō-kyō' 51

hempen cloth 8, 10

Herberts, Kurt (coll) 77, *127*, *188*

Hidehira-wan 164, 196, *133*

HIDETSUGI 165

Hideyoshi s. Toyotomi Hideyoshi

Higashiyama lacquers 112-121, 124, 126, 127, 130, 131, 138, 139, 142, 193, 198, 211

Hiōgi-mon chirashi makie-tebako 79, 80, *61*

Hiraizumi (Iwate province) 40

hiramakie 25, 57, 59, 62, 100, 107, 114, 154, 155, 184, 190, 208

hirame-fun 62, 78, 79

hirame-ji 62

Hirasan makie-suzuribako (Shiomi Masanari) 208, *167*

Hirata Domin 264 ([19])

Hirosaki 198

HIROSHI s. OTOMARU HIROSHI

Hiroshima (province) 235, 237

historical sources s. sources

HŌBI s. UEMATSU HŌBI

Hōitsu s. Sakai Hōitsu

Hōjō 124

Hokke-dō (Tōdai-ji) 98

HOKUYŌSAI s. TSUJI HOKUYŌSAI

Hompō-ji (Kyōto) 178, 179, *146*

HONAMI KŌETSU 170, 178-185, 199, 202, 203, 205, 207, 213, 214, 216, *147*, *148*, *149*

Hōō-dō s. Byōdō-in

Hōō-emmon raden-karabitsu 50, 252 ([22]), *34*

Hōrai makie-kagamibako 105, *85*

Hōraisan chinkinbori-tebako 111, *90*

Hōryū-ji (Nara) 5, 10, *2*, *4*

HŌSAI s. TADOKORO HŌSAI

HOSHIN s. MATSUNAMI HOSHIN

Hōsōge gin-hyōmon kesabako 23-25, *13*

Hōsōge karyobinga makie-soku sasshibako 26-28, 29, 31, 32, 34, *179*, *14*

Hōsōge makie bōjubako 26, *16*

Hōsōge makie kyobako 26, *17*

Hsüan-te (Chinese Emperor) 111

'Huang Ming wen tse' 109

'Hyakkō-hishō' 197

hyōmon 11, 23, 25, 62, 73, 77, 245

HYŌSAI s. KIMURA HYŌSAI

IEMON 151

Ieyasu s. Tokugawa Ieyasu

IGARASHI (-master; -school) 130, 145, 179, 195, 263 ([21])

IGARASHI DŌHO I. 195, *162*

IGARASHI DŌHO II. 195

IGARASHI SHINSAI 119, 195

IGARASHI SHŌBEI 263 ([22])

IGARASHI SŌBEI 263 ([22])

IGARASHI TAJIRŌ 234

IGARASHI TARŌBEI 179

Igarashi lacquers 195

Ihara Saikaku 202

IIZUKA TŌYŌ 215, *172*, *172a*

ikakeji 41, 50, 59, 71, 78

Ikakeji gyōyō raden-hirayanagui 71, *53*

Ikakeji gyōyō raden-tachi 71-72, 254 ([16])

IKEDA GEMBEI 198

IKEDA GENTARŌ 198

IKEDA IKKOKUSAI 235

IKEDA TAISHIN 230, 232

Ikeda-shi (place) 160

IKKOKUSAI s. IKEDA IKKOKUSAI

Imari porcelain 202

INAMI KIROKUSAI 245

inlay techniques s. heidatsu, hyōmon, kanagai, kirigane, raden, amber, ivory, coral, tortoise-shell

inrō 165, 195, 207, 211, 215, 217, 223
inrōbuta s. awasebuta
Iris chest (Kongōbu-ji) s. *Sawa-chidori
raden-makie ko-karabitsu 29, 31, 32*
irizumi 114
Ise (place) 213
'Ise-monogatari' 46, 118, 204, 205
Ishi-hiki makie-bon 172, *140*
Ishikawa (province) 194, 198, 241
ISOI JOSHIN 238, 241, 243, 245
Itchō s. Hanabusa Itchō
ITCHŌ s. KAWANOBE ITCHŌ
Itsukushima-jinja (Miyajima) 52, 54,
162, *40, 132*
Itsuō-Museum (Ikeda-shi) 160
ivory 18, 25, 211, 213, 220
ivy decoration, chest with s. *Tsuta
makie-karabitsu 132*
Iwasa-Matabei 189
Iwate (province) 40, 164
Izumo-taisha (Shimane province) 63,
75, *45, 46*

Japanization of Chinese patterns 34, 35,
126, 127, 138, 139, 167, 222, 237,
242
Java 154
Jewel box (Ninna-ji) s. *Hōsōge
makie-hōjubako 16*
Jigen-ji 135
JIGOEMON 197
JINSAI s. NAMBA JINSAI
JISAKU s. SAWADA JISAKU
JITOKU s. AKATSUKA JITOKU
Jogahana-nuri 197, 199
JŌKA s. YAMADA JŌKA
Jōken-in-jidai-mono 209
Jōmon period 4
JOSHIN s. ISOI JOSHIN
JUSEN s. OKUDE JUSEN
JŪZAEMON 261 (²⁹)

kabusebuta (overlapping lid) 113, 137,
204
Kachō makie kyōshoku 26, 28, 29
*Kaede-kiri-kiku-mon
makie-yakumi-tsubo* 150, *118*
Kaede-tachibana makie-bundai 258·(⁵⁰)
Kafuku-sha 234
Kaga 194, 197, 199
Kaga-makie 195, 234

Kai to kaisō makie-kobako 145, 171, *137*
Kaibu makie-kesabako 26, 28, 29, *15*
Ka-in 35
KAJIKAWA (-master; -school) 187, 194,
210, 217
KAJIKAWA HIKOBEI 187
KAJIKAWA KYŪJIRŌ 211
Kajū-ji (Kyōto) 69, *51*
Kakiemon porcelain 202
kakiwari 251 (⁵)
kamabokogata 159
Kamakura:
Enkaku-ji 94-95, 137, *110, 135*
Meigetsu-in 177, *143*
Tōkei-ji 156, *124, 125*
Tsurugaoka Hachiman-gū 65, 66,
71, *52, 52a, 53*
Kamakurabori 84, 91, 96, 97-99, 135-,
138, 167, 235, 256 (¹³)
Kamakurabori guri-kōgō 137, *110*
KAMBUN s. FUJII KAMBUN
KAMON s. SHIMIZU KAMON
kanagai 23, 95, 109, 114, 125, 126, 129,
139, 148, 190, 195, 211
Kanazawa 194, 195, 196, 234, 245
kannyū-hō 251 (⁸)
Kanō (-master; -school) 211, 217
Kanō Eitoku 129, 144
Kanō Masanobu 129
Kanō Motonobu 129
Kanō Sanraku 191
KANSAI s. KOMA KANSAI
kanshitsu 8, 10, 11, 28, 240, 241,
248 (¹⁵)
KAORU s. OTOMARU KAORU
Karabana makie-kutsubako 255 (⁵)
Karakusa raden-ryōshibako 178, *145*
Karakusa raden-suebako 72, 254 (¹⁷)
Karasu-sagi makiebako (Zeshin) 229, *183*
Kashiwa ni mimizuki raden-gura 51, *35*
Kasuga-taisha (Nara) 43, 101, *26, 55, 80*
Kasuga-taisha hirayanagui 43, *26*
Kasugayama-suzuribako 113-116, 120,
139, *92, 93*
Katawaguruma makie-tebako
Heian period 44-46, 53, 58, 75, 81,
251 (¹²), *27, 28*
Kamakura period 75, 77, 81, *56*
Katō Shirozaemon 86
KATSUTARŌ s. YAMAZAKI KATSUTARŌ
KAWAKUBO KAZU 245

Index

KAWANOBE ITCHŌ 226, 228, 231, 232, 233, *181*

kawari-nuri 176, 219

KAZU s. KAWAKUBO KAZU

KAZUKO s. ŌTA KAZUKO

KEISHŌ s. OKABE KEISHŌ

keisodō 198

Kenjō s. Gotō Kenjō

keshi-makie 197

Kikori makie-suzuribako (Kōetsu) 181, *148*

Kiku makie-tebako 129, *103*

Kikuchi 124

Kiku-eda makie-tebako 254 ([26])

Kiku-kiri-mon makie-sumiaka 174, *142*

kimma-nuri 222, 238, 242, 243, 245, 265 ([24])

KIMURA HYŌSAI 234

Kimura Yūbei 133

kingindei-e s. kingin-e

Kingin densō karatachi no saya 17, *10*

kingin-e 14, 15, 16, 22, 27

Kingin-heidatsu shippibako 13, *7*

Kinren-ji (Kyōto) 98, *76*

Kiri makie-tebako 127-129, 132, *101*

kirigane 80, 94, 95, 104, 120, 130, 139, 146, 185, 190, 195, 210

Kiritsu Kōshō Kaisha 226

KIROKUSAI s. INAMI KIROKUSAI

KISAN 165

KITAGAWA 195

Kitano Mandokoro 150, 151

Kitano tea festival 165

Kiyomizu-Sumiyoshi makie-raden-sugorokuban 161, *128*

KŌAMI (-master; -school) 121, 151, 188, 192, 194, 195, 210, 228

KŌAMI CHŌGEN 148

KŌAMI KYŪJIRŌ 151, 188, *121*

KŌAMI MICHIKIYŌ 119, 124

KŌAMI MICHINAGA 119, 132

KŌAMI NAGAFUSA 212

KŌAMI NAGASHIGE 149, 188-189, 192, 195, *156, 157*

KŌAMI NAGASUKU 212

KŌAMI SŌHAKU 132, 188, *106*

Kōami lacquers 118, 120

Kōan (Emperor) 5

Kōbō Daishi 27

Koboku makie-suzuribako (Zeshin) 213, *170*

Kōdai-ji (Kyōto) 131, 149, 150, 151, 152, *115-118, 121*

Kōdai-ji lacquers 127, 143, 149-154, 155, 159, 162, 170, 171, 173, 177, 186, 187, 193, *115-121*

Kōdai-ji makie s. Kōdai-ji lacquers

KŌDŌ s. OTOMARU KŌDŌ

KŌETSU s. HONAMI KŌETSU

Kōetsu lacquers 179, 184, 186, 192, 205, 207, 208, 262 ([8]), *147-149*

Kōfuku-ji (Nara) 7, *3*

Kofun period 5

kōgō 254 ([30])

KŌHO s. YAMANAGA KŌHO

kōka-ryokuyō 135

Kokei-sanshō makie-dana 146, *114*

'Kokin-shū' 182

Kokuryō kingdom 6

kokuso 248 ([16])

KOMA (-master; -school) 188, 194, 210, 217

KOMA KANSAI 220, 222, 223, 224, *178*

KOMA KANSAI II. 207, 223, 224, 228

KOMA KYORYŪ 216, 223, *173*

KOMA KYŪHAKU I. 212, 216, 264 ([22])

KOMA KYŪHAKU II. 212

KOMA KYŪI 187, 264 ([22]), *155*

KOMA KYŪZŌ 264 ([22])

KOMA YASUTADA 216, 264 ([22])

KOMIN s. NAKAYAMA KOMIN

KŌMO TŌZAN 238

kōmori 58, 64, 95, 114, 179, 180, 181

Kōmyō (Empress) 10

Kongōbu-ji (Kōyasan, Wakayama province) 46, 91, *29, 31, 32, 70*

Kongō-ji (Ōsaka) *44*

Konishi 202

Konjiki-dō s. Chūson-ji, Konjiki-dō

Korea, influence on Japanese lacquerwork 5, 6, 18, 142, 155, 156, 157, 176, 177, 178, 179

Korekawa (place) 1

Kōrin s. Ogata Kōrin

Kōrin lacquers 202, 207, 208, *163-165*

Ko-un 98

Kōyasan (Wakayama province) 46

Kümmel, O. 40, 213

Kumano Hayatama-jinja (Wakayama province) 104, 128, *83, 100, 101*

Kundaikan sayu chōki 97

KUNIHEI 261 ([29])

Kurikara-ryū makie kyōbako 56, 65, *41*
KURODA TATSUAKI 246, *198*
kurome 10
Kurume (place) 238
Kusabana-chōjū-mon ko-tebako (Matsuda
Gonroku) 265 ([12]), *187*
kushibako 82, 254 ([31])
Kusumi Morikage 165
kuyō 74
Kyôngju, Korea 6
Kyōōgokoku-ji s. Tō-ji (Kyōto)
KYORYŪ s. KOMA KYORYŪ
Kyōto 22, 38, 40, 76, 90, 97, 112,
124, 159, 170, 179, 185, 186, 187,
193, 194, 198, 202, 203, 207, 208,
211, 214, 222, 234, 246
Kyōto
Chion-in 136
Daigo-ji 72, 152
Gosho *172*
Hompō-ji 178, 179, *146*
Kajū-ji 69, *51*
Kinren-ji 98, *76*
Kōdai-ji 149, 150, 151, 152, *115-118,
121*
Kyōōgokoku-ji s. Kyōto, Tō-ji
Nanzen-ji 98, *75*
National Museum 233, *95*
Ninna-ji 26, 145, 179, *14, 16, 113*
Nishihongan-ji *150*
Tō-ji 26, *15, 78*
Zuikō-ji 155, *123*
KYŪBEI s. SHIMIZU KYŪBEI
KYŪHAKU s. KOMA KYŪHAKU
Kyūhaku Yasuaki 263 ([18])
KYŪI s. KOMA KYŪI
'Kyūji hongi' 5
KYŪJIRŌ s. KŌAMI KYŪJIRŌ
Kyūshū 197, 238

Lacquer, Department of 7
lacquer as tax 7
lacquer inlays 43
lacquer painting s. coloured lacquers;
kingin-e
lacquer painting on paper 229
lacquer technique s. techniques of
lacquer
lacquer tree 4, 5, 7
laque burgautée 197

lead, lead inlays 49, 180, 183, 184, 203,
204, 205, 207, 213
leather 10
Lee, S.Y. 249 ([28]), 259 ([8])
lid forms s. awasebuta, kabusebuta,
okibuta
Lolang (Korea) 17, 237
lotus scroll box s. *Hasu-karakusa
makie-kyōbako, 18*

MAE TAIHŌ 198, 238, 239, 245, *190*
Maeda Toshitsune 194
Maeda Tsunanori 197
Magaki-kiku raden-ikakeji-suzuribako 70,
87, *52*
Magaki-kiku-tebako 126, *100*
maki-bokashi 47, 57, 59, 62, 79, 120,
130, 192
makie 18, 23, 25-, 32, 40, 55, 59, 65, 82,
109, 126, 138, 151, 159, 171, 176,
182, 197, 222, 233, 234, 237, 239,
245
s. also hiramakie, takamakie,
togidashi
Makie ni-shū tantōbako 161, *130*
maki-hanashi 154
makkinru 17, 26
'Makura no sōshi' s. Sei Shōnagon:
Makura no sōshi
Mandara-dō-zushi kingin-dei-e bashira 22,
11
manuscript box (a.d. 919; Ninna-ji) s.
*Hōsōge karyobinga makie-soku
sasshi-bako 14*
marufun 78, 79
MASANARI s. SHIOMI MASANARI
MASAZANE s. SHIOMI MASANARI
MASHIKI s. MASUMURA MASHIKI
MASUMURA MASHIKI 241, *192*
Matsu ni tomoe-mon raden-gura 112, 129,
91
MATSUDA GONROKU 237, 238, 239,
245, *187*
Matsudaira Sadanobu 219
matsugui-tsuru 54, 102
Matsugui-tsuru ko-karabitsu 54, *40*
Matsugui-tsuru makie-sammaibon 101, *80*
Matsumine (Yamagata province) 4
MATSUNAMI HOSHIN 241
Meigetsu-in (Kamakura) 177, *143*
Meigetsu-wan 176, 177, *143*

Index

Meigetsu-zen 177, *144*
MEIHŌ s. MIURA MEIHŌ
Meiji (Emperor) 232
metalwork 34, 46, 87, 90, 99, 126, 184,
    191, 212, 213
Mikasayama makie-kakesuzuri 172, *139*
MIMI NO SUKUNE 5
Minamoto 55
Minamoto Yoritomo 72
Minamoto Yoriyoshi 72
Minamoto Yoshimasa 66
MINORU s. NODA MINORU
Mishima-taisha (Shizuoka
    province) 77, 87, 93, 139, *59, 60*
Misu-matsu makie-suzuribako 150, 153,
    120
Mitamaya (Kōdai-ji) 150, *121*
mitsuda-e 14, 17, 112, 174, 197, 214,
    233
mitsudasō 15
mitsu-wan 164
MIURA MEIHŌ 245
Miyagi (province) 4, 164
Miyajima, Itsukushima-jinja 52, 54,
    162, *40, 132*
Miyazaki Yūzensai 202
Mizoguchi Saburō 50, 237
MOCHIZUKI HANZAN 213
mokume-nuri 253 (*13*)
Momo raden-makie rinkagata-bon 110, *89*
MONNYŪ 97, 166
Morikage s. Kusumi Morikage
MORIMASA s. GAMŌ MORIMASA
mother-of-pearl, mother-of-pearl
    inlays s. raden
mother-of-pearl dust 213
Munich, Staal. Museum für
    Völkerkunde 161, *129*
Murasaki Shikibu 35
Mushikago makie-kashibako (Nakayama
    Komin) 227, *180*

NAGAFUSA s. KŌAMI NAGAFUSA
Nagasaki 197
NAGASUKU s. KŌAMI NAGASUKU
NAGATA YŪJI 207, 208
NAGAYASU s. KŌAMI KYŪJIRŌ
Nagi makie-tebako 104-105, 128, 162, *83*
Nagoya:
    Atsuta-jinja 105, *85*
    Nanatsu-dera 57, *42*

Tokugawa-Museum 129, 145,
    263 (*19*), *102, 131, 156*
Nakamura Kuranosuke 202
NAKAYAMA KOMIN 226, 230, 233, *180*
NAMBA JINSAI 243, *194*
Nambanjin makie-kōisu 155, *123*
Namban lacquers 143, 154-162, 176,
    178
Namban scrolls 155, 156, 161
Nami ni usagi makie-tabikushige 171, *138*
Namioka (Aomori province) 4
Nanatsu-dera (Nagoya) 57, *42*
Nanzen-ji (Kyōto) 98, *75*
Nanzen-ji-kōgō s. *Botan
    Kamakurabori-kōgō*, *75*
NAOJI s. TERAI NAOJI
Nara:
    Akishino-dera 7
    Hōryū-ji 5, *2, 4*
    Kasuga-taisha 43, 101, *26, 80*
    Kōfuku-ji 7, *3*
    National-Museum 26, 233, *18*
    Oku-in *41*
    Shōsōin 9, *5-10*
    Tamukeyama Hachiman-gū 53
    Tōdai-ji 7, 53, *68*
    Tōshōdai-ji 7
Nara renaissance 69
Narihira writing-box s. *Semmen-Nari-
    hira makie-suzuribako*, *165*
nashiji (-fun) 62, 64, 73, 79, 92, 104,
    107, 109, 130, 146, 153, 193, 195
Nashiji makie-tansu 161, *131*
Nashiji matsu-ume makie-tebako 129, *102*
natural-wood base 16, 84, 208
Negoro-ji 84, 133-134
Negoro lacquers s. Negoro-nuri
Negoro-nuri 54, 84, 85, 87, 88, 134,
    135, 138, 139, 235, 255 (*34*), 259 (*8*)
Negoro-nuri sai-oke 85, *69*
Nenohi-dana 183, *151*
New York, The Metropolitan Museum
    of Art *182*
Nezu-Museum s. Tōkyō,
    Nezu-Museum
'Nihon Dentō-Kōgei-ten' 239, 265 (*13*)
Nihon Kōgei-kai 239
Nihon Shikkō-kai 231
NIKI SEIHO 263 (*25*)
Nikkō:
    Rinnō-ji 66, *48*

Tōshōgū 167, 192, 212, *158*
Ninna-ji (Kyōto) 26, 91, 145, 179, *14, 16, 113*
NINOMIYA TŌTEI 219
Ninsei s. Nonomura Ninsei
Nishihongan-ji (Kyōto) 43, *150*
Nōami 97
Nobe ni suzume makie-tebako 57, 63, 64, 81, *44*
Nobunaga s. Oda Nobunaga
NODA MINORU 245
Nonomura Ninsei 185, *153*
Nonomura Sōtatsu 162, 180, 184, 205
Noto (peninsula) 219
Numazu (Miyagi province) 4

ŌBA SHŌGYO 245, *195*
Oda Nobunaga 142, 176
Oda Urakusai 176, 179
Odawara 124, 259 (¹)
Odawara-bori 256 (¹³)
OGAKI MASAKUNI 263 (²⁵)
OGATA KŌRIN 46, 202-208, 212, 213, 216, 224, *163-166*
Ogata Sōhaku 202
Ogata Sōken 202
OGAWA HARITSU 212, 213, 216, 220, *170*
OGAWA SHŌMIN 227, 231, 233, 237
Ōgi-chirashi makie-tebako 79, 81, 92, *62*
Ogurayama-suzuribako 130, 145, *105*
oil coating 15
oil painting on lacquer 15
OKABE KEISHŌ 242, *193*
Okada Jō 29, 31, 77, 107, 163, 179, 183
Okakura Kakuzo 237
Okayama (province) 243
ŌKI TOYOSUKE 220
okibuta 114, 205
OKUDE JUSEN 241
Oku-in (Nara province) 41
Oribe s. Furuta Oribe
Oribe ceramics 154, *122*
Ōsaka:
    Ampuku-ji 193, *160*
    Fujita-Museum 26, *19*
    Kongō-ji *44*
    Shitennō-ji 10, *44*
ŌTA KAZUKO 245
Otokoyama-suzuribako 119, 130, *96*
OTOMARU HIROSHI 242

OTOMARU JUN 242
OTOMARU KAORU 242
OTOMARU KŌDŌ 239, 241, 242, *189*
Ōuchi 124

Paine, Robert T. 129
painting techniques s. kingin-e, mitsuda-e, yushoku, coloured lacquers
Paris, Musée Guimet 209
Paris, World Exhibition 1900 235
P'ENG CHÜN-PAO 110
Persia 12, 13
plum blossoms motif s. *Baigetsu makie-tebako 74*
plum tree motif s. *Baigetsu makie-bundai 86, Ume makie-tebako 59, 60*
Philippines 154
Phoenix Hall (Hōō-dō) s. Byōdō-in
Phoenix motif s. *Hōō-emmon raden-kara-bitsu, 34*
picture-nashiji s. e-nashiji
'pillow book' s. Sei Shōnagon: Makura no sōshi
'pine-chewing crane' s. matsugui-tsuru
'Po-chê-pien' 14
Po Chü-i 77
polish 25, 26, 57
Portuguese 142, 154, 155
proportions s. shapes, development of

raden 14, 17, 18, 25, 32, 35, 38, 40, 41, 46, 50, 51, 59, 62, 63, 68, 69, 71, 72, 73, 75, 76, 83, 84, 103, 104, 105, 112, 155, 156, 158, 159, 173, 176, 177, 183, 184, 195, 197, 207, 211, 233, 245
Raden-gyoku no obi-bako 14, *8*
Raden hakkaku shumidan 41, *24*
Raden-heijin-an 41, *25*
Raden heijin-tōdai 41
Raiyu Sōjō 84
raw lacquer 7
red lacquer (base) 4, 10, 25, 53, 57, 66, 84, 85, 111, 134, 135, 137, 177, 214
Reimeikai Foundation (Tōkyō) 263 (¹⁹)
Renchi makie-kyōbako 69, 70, *51*
Renchi makie-tobira (Fujiwara Sadatsune) 67-68, 70, *49*
rhus vernicifera 4
Rikyū s. Sen no Rikyū

Index *Rimpō makie-kyōbako* 100-101, *79*
Rindō byakurō-makie raiban 49, *33*
Rinnō-ji (Nikkō) 66, *48*
RITSUŌ s. OGAWA HARITSU
rock crystal 14
rōiro-nuri 217
Rokkaku-Shisui 224, 233, 237
rosary box s. *Tokko-mon makie-gōsu*, *78*
Roshū makie-suzuribako (Kōetsu) 182,
149

Saeki Kagehiro 54
Sagayama makie-suzuribako 119-121,
130, *97*
Saikaku s. Ihara Saikaku
Saitama (province) 4
Sakai (place) 124, 259 (¹)
Sakai Hōitsu 208, 224
Sakura makie-suzuribako 107, 108, 109,
87, 88
Sakura raden-gura 83, *67*
Sakura-sanjaku makie-suzuribako (Kōami
Sōhaku) 132-133, 188, *106*
Sambō-in (Daigo-ji, Kyōto) 152
Sangyō Kōgei Shiken-jo 237, 238
'Sanjūroko-nin kashū' 43, 44, 51, 182
SANO CHŌKAN 222
Sansui makie-dana 209-211, *168*
SASADA GETSUGYŌ 263 (²⁵)
Sawa-chidori raden-makie
ko-karabitsu 46-47, 55, 58, 63, 77,
29, 31, 32
SAWADA JISAKU 234
SAWADA SŌTAKU 263 (²⁵)
sawtooth patterns 156, 158, 159
saya-nuri 219
scrolls, scroll patterns 27, 30, 31, 34,
41, 47, 50, 120, 152, 155, 158, 177,
179
Seattle Art Museum 262 (¹⁴)
Sei Shōnagon: Makura no sōshi 26,
249 (⁷)
SEIAMI 165
Seikaiha raden-gura 51, *38*
SEISEI s. SHIOMI MASANARI
Seki-shitsu bunkanboku no zushi 10, 11, *5*
Semboku (Akita province) 4
Semmen-chirashi makie-tebako 92, *71*
Semmen-Narihira makie-suzuribako
(Kōrin) 205-206, *165*
Semmen-suzuki makie-bon 150, *119*

Sen no Rikyū 143, 176
Sendai 161, 238
SHAMI KŪGAKU 255 (⁶), *73*
shapes, development of 13, 18, 22,
23-24, 28, 30, 32, 33, 34, 35, 46, 56,
58, 59, 88, 91, 92, 95, 113, 114, 137,
138, 152, 159, 162, 163, 164,
165, 172, 183, 235, 240,
s. also: suzuribako, shapes; tebako,
shapes
Shibagaki ni tsuta makie-suzuribako (Koma
Kyūi) 188, *155*
SHIBATA ZESHIN 207, 220, 228-231,
232, *182, 183*
SHIBAYAMA YASUMASA 213
Shibuemon 202
Shiga (province) 101
Shigure raden-gura 83, *66*
SHIIHARA ICHIDAYU 194
Shikoku (island) 214, 222, 235
Shimazu 124
SHIMIZU GENJIRŌ 195
SHIMIZU KAMON 234
SHIMIZU KYŪBEI 194, 195
Shimpuku-ji (Saitama province) 4
SHINJIRŌ 151
Shinobu-kazura makie-raden-bako 91, *70*
Shinobu makie-suzuribako 263 (¹⁶)
SHINSUI s. ASATA SHINSUI
Shiomi-makie 208
SHIOMI MASANARI 208, 209, *167*
Shionoyama makie-suzuribako 117, 118,
120, 121, 124, 133, *95*
shippi 10, 11, 12, 13, 16, 28, 241
Shippi-kingin-e hakkaku no kagamibako
16, *9*
SHIRAYAMA SHŌSAI 226, 231, 233, *185*
shishiai-makie 114, 120, 130, 190
Shisui s. Rokkaku Shisui
Shitennō-ji (Ōsaka) 10, 44
SHŌGYO s. ŌBA SHŌGYO
SHŌMIN s. OGAWA SHŌMIN
Shōmu (Emperor) 9, 29
SHŌSAI s. SHIRAYAMA SHŌSAI
Shōsōin (Nara) 9, 10, 11, 12, 13, 14, 15,
16, 17, 18, 22, 29, *5-10*
Shōtoku Taishi 7
SHŌZAN s. TAKANO SHŌZAN
SHUNKEI 248 (²⁰)
Shunkei-nuri 11, 161, 235, 248 (²⁰)
SHUNSHŌ s. YAMAMOTO SHUNSHŌ

Shunzō s. Fujikawa Shunzō
silver dust 15, 25, 32, 44, 51, 59, 62, 66,
   69, 75, 107, 155, 173
silver inlays 73, 94, 125, 180, 191, 203
   s. also: heidatsu, hyōmon, kanagai
silver painting on lacquer base
   s. kingin-e
simplification 30, 31, 47, 104, 133, 135,
   138
Sōhaku s. Ogata Sōhaku
Sōken s. Ogata Sōken
soku 8
soku-nuri 18
Somada Kiyosuke 197
Sōmin s. Yokoya Sōmin
Soper, Alexander 46
Sōsaburō s. Asano Sōsaburō
Sōtatsu s. Nonomura Sōtatsu
sources 5, 18, 23, 25, 26, 35, 50, 59, 96,
   104, 109, 158, 166
Spanish 142, 154, 155
sparrow tebako s. *Nobe ni suzume
   makie-tebako 44*
'sprinkled picture' s. makie
sprinkling techniques 16, 17, 25, 26,
   27, 28, 32, 64, 78, 87, 109, 138, 197
   s. also hiramakie, makie, makkinru,
   takamakie, togidashi
stole box (Tō-ji) s. *Kaibu makie kesabako
   15*
Sugau-ishibe-jinja (Ishikawa
   province) *142*
Suhama-chidori makie-tebako 254 ([26])
Suhama-u raden-suzuribako 53, 71, *39*
sumi-aka 137, 174, *142*
Sumidagawa makie-suzuribako (Tatsuke
   Chōbei) 193, *161*
sumie-togidashi 217
sumikiri 114
sumimaru 114
Sumino-e suzuribako (Kōrin) 203, *163*
Sumiyoshi 65, 145
Sumiyoshi makie-karabitsu (Shami
   Kūgaku) 92-93, 102, *73*
Sumiyoshi makie-raden-kushibako 82, 83,
   91, 116, *64, 65*
Sumiyohsi makie-suzuribako 145, *112*
Sumiyohsi makie-tebako 66, 74, 81, 93, *48*
Sumiyoshi makie-tsukue 145, *113*
sutra box (Enryaku-ji) s. *Hōsōge makie
   kyōbako 17*

sutra box (Fujita-Museum) s.
   Butsu-kudoku makie kyōbako 19
sutra box with lotus scrolls (Nara
   National Museum) s. *Hasu-karakusa
   makie-kyōbako 18*
Su-tsung (Chinese Emperor) 14
suzuribako, form 52, 72, 113, 117, 179,
suzuribako, oldest surviving 52,
   71-72, *39*
203, 264 ([3])

Tachi Gasui 219, *175*
Tadokoro Hōsai 241, *191*
Taguchi Yoshikuni 245
Taihō s. Mae Taihō
Taihō-ritsuryō 7
Taima-dera (Nara province) 22, 65-70,
   11, 12, 49, 50
Taima-mandara 22
Taima-mandara-zushi no raden-shumidan
   67, 68, *50*
Taima sōge kushi 250 ([11])
Taira 55
Taishin s. Ikeda Taishin
Tajirō s. Igarashi Tajirō
Takagamine (place) 179, 202
takamakie 25, 26, 62, 78, 87, 92, 94,
   104, 107, 114, 115, 130, 138, 139,
   146, 190, 208
Takamatsu 222, 235, 238, 242, 243
Takano Shōzan 238, 239
'Taketori-monogatari' 25
Tamakaji Zōkoku 222, 235, 242, *177*
Tamamushi-zushi (Tamamushi shrine) 5,
   6, 7, 18, 65, 247 ([8]), *2*
Tamukeyama-Hachiman-gū (Nara) 53
Tanida Chūbei 214, *171*
Tanida-nuri 215
Tanpopo ni hisago makie-suzuribako
   (Zeshin) 229, *182*
Tate Junsuke 219
Tatsuaki s. Kuroda Tatsuaki
Tatsuke Chōbei 193, 263 ([20]), *161*
tebako, form 43-46, 57, 63, 64, 66, 73,
   74, 75, 76, 77, 78, 79, 80, 81, 82, 88,
   92, 111, 114, *171*
tebako, oldest surviving 43, *27*
techniques of lacquerwork 5, 10, 18,
   22, 25, 32, 35, 46-47, 49, 57, 59,
   62-63, 73, 77, 83, 87-88, 92, 94, 99,
   100, 112, 114, 120, 130-131, 138,

Index

154, 155, 170-171, 176-177, 183, 190, 211, 233, 237-238, 239
s. also sprinkling techniques, coloured lacquer painting, painting techniques, carved lacquer
TERAI NAOJI 245, *197*
textiles (in relation to lacquerwork) 13, 18, 35, 77, 90, 131, 153, 154, 163, 184, 185, 191
Thailand 14, 222, 243
tin, -inlays, -powder 26, 49, 66, 120, 132, 183, 195, 206
Tōdai-ji (Nara) 7, 9, 18, 53, *68*
'Tōdai-ji kemmotsu-chō' 248 ([17])
togidashi 17, 25, 26, 41, 44, 46, 57, 73, 78, 92, 114, 116, 166, 185, 190, 208, 216, 217, 233, 249 ([5])
s. also: coloured togidashi, sumi-togidashi
toilet box s. tebako
Tō-ji (Kyōto) 26, 249 ([10]) *78*
Tōkei-ji (Kamakura) 156, *124, 125*
Tokko-mon makie-gōsu 100, *78*
Tokugawa Harutomi 219
Tokugawa Iemitsu 186, 187, 189
Tokugawa Ieyasu 142, 150, 161, 167, 179, 186, 213
Tokugawa Mitsumoto 149, 189, 193
Tokugawa Tsunayoshi 167, 209
Tokugawa Yoshimune 213
Tokugawa-Museum, Nagoya 129, 145, 263 ([19]), *102, 131, 156*
Tōkyō 228, 231, 237, 238, 241, 242, 245 (prior to 1869 s. Edo)
Tōkyō:
  Bunkazai Hogo Iinkai *1, 27, 28, 191, 199*
  Eisei Bunko *35, 66*
  Geijutsu Daigaku 231, *98, 181, 187*
  Gotō-Museum *58*
  Hatakeyama-Museum 254 ([26]), *54*
  Keiō University *30*
  National-Museum 17, 50, 56, 75, 79, 106, 107, 148, 182, 233, *33, 34, 36, 37, 41, 43, 56, 61, 63, 71-74, 86-88, 90, 91, 96, 109, 111, 114, 128, 136, 138-141, 144, 147, 149, 154, 155, 159, 161, 164, 167, 169-171, 173, 174, 176, 178-180, 183, 185*
  Nezu-Museum 103, 113, 204, 206, *13, 92-94, 97, 165*

Ōkura Shūkokan 62, *168*
Reimeikai (Foundation) 263 ([19])
Seikadō *152, 153, 163*
Suntory Gallery 57, *105*
Tōkyō Bijutsu Gakkō 231, 237
Tomita, K. 65
tortoise shell 14, 15
Tōshirō s. Katō Shirozaemon
Tōshōdai-ji (Nara) 7
Tōshōgū (Nikkō) 167, 192, 211, *158*
TŌTEI s. NINOMIYA TŌTEI
Toyama (province) 197, 199
Toyama, collection 103, *81, 82*
TŌYŌ s. IIZUKA TŌYŌ
Toyohime 219
Toyotomi Hideyoshi 142, 144, 145, 149, 151, 152, 157, 161, 165, 196
TŌZAN s. KŌMO TŌZAN
transparent lacquer 10, 25, 84
Tsubaki-mon Kamakurabori-oi 135, *109*
TSUCHIDA SŌETSU 207, 208
Tsugaru 198, 199
Tsugaru-nuri 198, 219, 235
Tsuikoku-kōgō 168, *135*
tsuishu 96, 99, 167
TSUISHU (-master, -school) 166, 167, 222, 261, ([29])
TSUISHU DEWA 261 ([29])
TSUISHU HEIJIRŌ 166, 167
TSUISHU KANSHICHI 261 ([29])
TSUISHU YONZEI 261 ([29])
TSUISHU YŌSEI 167, 187
TSUISHU YŌSEI XX. 167, 236, 242, 261 ([29]), *186*
TSUJI HOKUYŌSAI 245
tsukegaki 62, 78, 92, 104, 120
Tsukufusuma-jinja (Chikubushima) 152
Tsunanori Shōunkō s. Maeda Tsunanori
Tsunayoshi s. Tokugawa Tsunayoshi
Tsurugaoka Hachimangū (Kamakura) 70, 72, *52, 52a, 53*
Tsuta makie-karabitsu 162, *132*
tsuyakeshi 205
'Tung hai chi' 109

Uda (Emperor) 29
UEMATSU HŌBI 237
Ujigawa-hotaru makie-ryōshibako-suzuribako (Iizuka Tōyō) 215, *172*

ukiyo-e 217
Ume makie-tebako 77-79, 80, 87, 88, 93,
  139, *59, 60*
urushibe 5
uta-e 77, 88, 115, 118, 254 ([23])
  s. also: calligraphy as decoration;
  ashide-e
'Utsubo-monogatari' 26

Vienna: Kunsthistorisches
  Museum 158, *126*
Vienna: World Exhibition 1873 226,
  233

Wagner, G. 228
Wajima 198, 199, 219, 234, 238, 242,
  245
Wajima-nuri 198, 219, 234
WAKAEMON 151
Wakamiya (province) 59
Wakasa 198, 199
Wakasa-nuri 198
Wakayama (province) 45, 92, 104
warigai 158, 176, 177
Warner, Langdon 7
Western Paradise (Fragment) 65, *47*
wood 16
World Exhibition:
  1873 Vienna 226, 233
  1900 Paris 235
writing-box s. suzuribako
Wuppertal, Kurt Herberts
  collection 77, *127, 188*

YAJIRŌZAEMON 261 ([29])
yakigane 46
Yakugai shells 158
Yakushi Nyorai 57
YAMADA JŌKA 194, 211
Yamagata (province) 4
Yamaguchi 124, 259 ([1])
YAMAMOTO SHUNSHŌ 185, 208, *154*

Yamanaga Kōho 241
Yamato-e 34, 35, 58, 65, 87, 92, 103,
  105, 117
YAMAZAKI KATSUTARŌ 238
Yanagi ni tsubame makie-gura 125, *99*
Yanagi Sōetsu 235
Yang Hsüan 109, 257 ([33])
YANG MAO 167
YASUAKI s. KOMA KYŪHAKU II.
YASUMASA s. SHIBAYAMA YASUMASA
yasuri-fun 17, 27, 62-63
YASUTADA s. KOMA YASUTADA
Yatsuhashi suzuribako (Kōrin) 203-205,
  164
Yayoi period 5
Yokohama 246
Yokoya Sōmin 202
Yōmei (Emperor) 5
YŌMO s. YANG MAO
YONEDA MAGOROKU 263 ([25])
YŌSEI
  s. Tsuishu Yōsei;
    Tsuishu Yōsei xx.
YOSHIDA BAIDŌ 242
YOSHIDA GENJURŌ 238
YOSHIKUNI s. TAGUCHI YOSHIKUNI
Yoshimasa s. Ashikaga Yoshimasa
Yoshimitsu s. Ashikaga Yoshimitsu
Yoshino-bori 256 ([13])
yotsuwan 259 ([8])
YŌYŪSAI s. HARA YŌYŪSAI
Yūji-age 208
Yung-lo (Chinese emperor) 97
YŪSAI s. AKAJI YŪSAI
yushoku 14, 15, 17
Yūzenzome 202

ZESHIN s. SHIBATA ZESHIN
ZŌKOKU s. TAMAKAJI ZŌKOKU
Zonsei-nuri 222, 265 ([24])
Zuikō-ji (Kyōto) 155, *123*
zushi-dana 148

This book
was designed by
WILLIAM RUETER
under the direction of
ALLAN FLEMING
University of
Toronto
Press